# Sikh Religion,
# Culture and
# Ethnicity

# Sikh Religion, Culture and Ethnicity

Edited by

## Christopher Shackle, Gurharpal Singh & Arvind-pal Singh Mandair

Routledge
Taylor & Francis Group

LONDON AND NEW YORK

First Published in 2001
by Routledge

Published 2014 by Routledge

2 Park Square, Milton Park, Abingdon, Oxfordshire OX14 4RN
711 Third Avenue, New York, NY 10017

First issued in paperback 2014

*Routledge is an imprint of the Taylor & Francis Group, an informa business*

Editorial Matter © 2001 Christopher Shackle,
Gurharpal Singh & Arvind-pal Singh Mandair

*British Library Cataloguing in Publication Data*
A catalogue record of this book is available from the British Library

*Library of Congress Cataloguing in Publication Data*
A catalogue record for this book has been requested

ISBN 978-0-700-71389-9 (hbk)
ISBN 978-1-138-86252-4 (pbk)

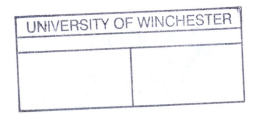

# Contents

# Contributors

**Balbinder Bhogal** is a Lecturer in the Department of Religious Studies at the University of Derby. He is completing his PhD on 'The Word of Guru Nanak: Hermeneutics, Nonduality and Skilful Means' at SOAS, University of London.

**Jeevan Deol** is completing his PhD at St John's College, University of Cambridge. His publications include 'The Minas and their Literature', *Journal of the American Oriental Society* (1998); and 'Surdas: Poet and Text the Sikh Tradition', *Bulletin of SOAS* (2000). He compiled entries in the catalogue of the major international exhibition 'Arts of the Sikh Kingdoms'.

**Arvind-pal Singh Mandair** is a Research Fellow in the Department of the Study of Religions at SOAS, University of London. Besides Sikhism and North Indian religions, his interests include continental philosophy and cross-cultural theory. His publications include *Religion and the Translatability of Cultures* (Manchester: Manchester University Press, forthcoming). He was responsible for constructing and teaching the Sikh and Punjab Studies programme at Coventry University.

**Gurinder Singh Mann** is Kundan Kaur Kapany Professor of Sikh Studies at the University of California, Santa Barbara. His publications include *The Goindval Pothis: the Earliest Extant Source of the Sikh Canon* (Cambridge Mass.: Harvard Oriental Series 51, 1996); and *The Making of Sikh Scripture* (New York: Oxford

University Press, forthcoming). He is Director of the Columbia–UCSB Summer Programme in Punjab Studies at Chandigarh.

**Harjot Oberoi** is Professor of Indian History in the Department of Asian Studies at the University of British Columbia. He is the author of *The Construction of Religious Boundaries: Culture, Identity and Diversity in the Sikh Tradition* (Delhi: Oxford University Press, 1994).

**Christopher Shackle** FBA is Professor of Modern Langages of South Asia at SOAS, University of London. Besides linguistics, his wide academic interests include both comparative literature and comparative religion. He has published extensively on Punjabi and Urdu, and is the compiler of *An Introduction to the Sacred Language of the Sikhs* (London: SOAS, 1983), and *A Guru Nanak Glossary* (2nd ed., New Delhi: Heritage, 1995).

**Gurharpal Singh** is the C.R. Parekh Professor of Indian Politics at the University of Hull. His most recent publication (co-edited with Ian Talbot) is *Region and Partition: Bengal, Punjab and the Partition of the Subcontinent* (Karachi: Oxford University Press, 1999). He was formerly editor of the *International Journal of Punjab Studies*.

**Nikky-Guninder Kaur Singh** is Professor of Religious Studies at Colby College. Her interests focus on poetics and feminist issues. She has published widely in the field of Indian Religions. Her recent books include *The Feminine Principle in the Sikh Vision of the Transcendent* (Cambridge: Cambridge University Press, 1993), and *The Name of My Beloved: Translations of the Verses of the Sikh Gurus* (San Francisco: Harper Collins, 1995).

**Darshan S. Tatla** is a Visiting Fellow in the Department of Sociology and Anthropology at the Punjabi University, Patiala. His recent publications include *Sikhs in North America* (New York: Greenwood, 1991), and *The Sikh Diaspora: the Search for Statehood* (London: UCL Press, 1999).

# Acknowledgements

This book grew out the workshop entitled 'New Perspectives in Sikh Studies' held at the School of Oriental and African Studies on 28–29th May 1998. However not all of the articles published in this volume were presented at the workshop and neither are all the papers read at this event included here. It has been a privilege for the editors of this volume to play their small part towards bringing the contributors' discussions of these issues to publication. The editors gratefully acknowledge the support of those without whose help the original workshop which gave rise to this volume could not have taken place. Generous financial support for the workshop was provided by De Montfort University, by the Research Committee of SOAS, by the Guru Nanak Education Trust and by CRDP (Coventry). The practical organization of the workshop was greatly assisted by Barbara Lazoi of the SOAS Centre of South Asian Studies.

Chapter One

# Introduction:
# New Perspectives in Sikh Studies

*Editors*

Developments in any academic field are too dependent upon complex combinations of clusters of individual and team talent with more general changes in social trends and ideological fashions to make predicting patterns of growth and transformation anything other than a very risky business. It certainly now seems extraordinary that it should have been possible for one of us less than twenty years ago to question the status of Sikh studies as a field that was going to be able to claim genuinely viable academic existence in Western universities (Shackle 1985). That scepticism has for a while now seemed increasingly implausible, and it is certainly strikingly disproved by the variety and vitality displayed in the present volume of essays.

The book has developed from an international workshop held at SOAS on 28–29th May 1998 under the joint auspices of De Montfort University and the SOAS Centre of South Asian Studies. The workshop's title 'New Perspectives in Sikh Studies' was intended to focus the discussion on the many lines of fresh inquiry being pursued by the growing numbers of scholars actively involved in Sikh studies with positions in Western universities, and this purpose was amply fulfilled in the liveliness of the ensuing debates between the participants who were brought together from both sides of the Atlantic, often for their first opportunity to meet face to face.

The opportunity was also provided for reflection upon the development of Sikh studies in the West and how these have typically come to differ from Indian Sikh studies. Whereas Indian scholars, clustered in the universities of Punjab and the surrounding area, are able to rely upon a central institutional position, if at the price of

1

considerable political and ideological constraints, the freedom enjoyed by those in the West is counterbalanced by their lack of institutional density. As tends generally to be the case for any field of study whose practitioners are relatively isolated in their own institutions, international conferences and workshops and the collaborative volumes issuing therefrom have therefore had a particular importance for the development of Western Sikh studies, beginning little more than two decades ago on the West Coast of the United States with the conference organized at Berkeley by two of its leading American pioneers (Juergensmeyer and Barrier 1979).

The Punjab crisis culminating in the events of 1984 radically transformed the face of Sikh studies across the globe. In India these effects were almost entirely negative, including not only the tragic loss of irreplaceable archival resources as the result of army action but also the subsequent stifling of many academic freedoms, especially the freedom to adopt scholarly positions which might be interpreted as impugning the integrity of received but threatened tradition.

In the West a greater variety of effects was experienced. The crisis brought the Sikhs to the centre of world attention and they became for the first time the subject of mainstream political science. At the same time the extreme sensitivities excited by the crisis exacerbated the hostility directed by significant numbers of Sikhs in the West as well as in India against the historicizing critiques of religious traditions associated with Western scholarship, especially with the New Zealand scholar W.H. McLeod ever since the publication of his critical study of the sources for knowledge of Guru Nanak (McLeod 1968). Both these currents were well to the fore of debate at a major international conference held in Canada at Toronto in 1987 which subsequently resulted in a large volume of papers *on Sikh History and Religion in the Twentieth Century* (O'Connell 1988).

As this title itself suggests, Western Sikh studies have been marked in general approach among humanities scholars by a primacy of history over religion, which was hardly displaced by the new found interest of some political scientists in the Sikhs as a case study for the comparative investigation of the threatening workings of religious fundamentalism. More far reaching challenges to the earlier pattern of Western Sikh studies were to come from within Western Sikh society. While a very substantial Sikh population had first been established in Britain as the result of immigration in the 1950s and 1960s, it was the somewhat later settlement in Canada and the United States of Sikhs with a generally higher socio-economic profile which really began to give the diaspora a voice in a field hitherto occupied by a few, mostly non-Sikh Western academics.

Recent years have thus seen the emergence of new demands, both actively expressed and tacitly anticipated, for a Sikh studies agenda capable of addressing the needs of a Sikh diaspora in the English-speaking world which is itself of exceptional size and significance in relation to the parent Indian Sikh community in comparison to most other Asian religious communities now established in the West. First emerging in North America, these demands have been partly articulated through various – not always happy – attempts to boost the position of Sikh studies through the foundation of community funded university posts. They are also starting to be formulated through broader academic agendas for Sikh studies programmes, as broached in the proceedings of a conference held on the East Coast of America at Columbia University in 1989 (Hawley and Mann 1993).

Most of these various lines of development can be seen to underlie the essays contained in the present volume, which itself collectively marks an important step into a future whose unpredictability is happily guaranteed by the volume's intellectual variety and excitement. A glance at the following list of contributors will show that this is the first Sikh studies volume to have both a roughly equal distribution of authors from either side of the Atlantic and an overwhelming majority of Sikh authors with Western academic training. Simultaneous inspection of the bibliography will indicate how their various disciplinary formations have resulted in approaches which draw quite as much upon a wide range of reference to contemporary Western intellectual trends as they do to primary sources in South Asian languages, thus quite successfully avoiding the inward looking cross-references to fellow practitioners which can characterize a small field when it feels itself to be on the defensive.

By contrast, the dominant tone of this volume is a strongly positive one, with individual contributors being quite unafraid to suggest new theoretical approaches in their questionings of many previously unexamined understandings. Although some of the papers originally presented to the workshop had to be excluded during an editorial process guided by the desire to give as wide a range of readers as possible a clear view of leading lines of current inquiry, the scope of those included is still considerable. They are grouped in accordance with the collection's title under the broad categories of religion, culture and ethnicity. The first set of essays explores classic religious formations in Sikhism and ends by relocating the study of religion

3

within Sikh studies, the second broadens the concept of Sikh culture in relation to comparative literature and psychoanalytic theory, and the final set provides searching examinations of the concept of ethnicity in Sikh studies.

The volume opens with Gurinder Singh Mann's essay on 'Canon Formation in the Sikh Tradition' which reconstructs the formation of Sikh scriptural canon based on two elements: the data available in early manuscripts and the way that these manuscripts are located in the context of early Sikh institutional development. The results are both exciting and unnerving, depending on whether the viewpoint is that of received tradition or modern historiography. Mann distinguishes successive stages of a sequential process in which the origins of the Sikh scriptural text are linked to Guru Nanak rather than to the Goindval Pothis, which are a manifestation of the later expansion of scriptural text in the sixteenth century, and examines the formation of the Adi Granth text in the sixteenth century. His analysis provides a comprehensive picture of the text's evolution, one which extends the memory of tradition forwards to the present day and backwards to Guru Nanak as the originator of the scripture. The conviction of traditionalist scholars that Sikh scripture was an ahistorical entity revealed as a totality masks the reality presented by historiographical analysis that Sikh scripture was shaped over time, and in Mann's concluding words, the 'process apparently began in the days of Guru Nanak himself and continues to evolve even as we speak.'

Jeevan Deol's paper then deals with two related processes in the formation of eighteenth century Khalsa identity, namely the discourses and narratives created by the Khalsa in constructing itself as a community of believers and as a body politic. The specific focus of the paper is on the contesting uses and the role of the classical Indian myth of the four ages (*chaturyuga*) in political and religious discourses during the period. Deol argues that the letters of Banda Bahadur initiate a discourse in which the Khalsa and its political ascendency will initiate a new *satyuga*. While several compositions in the Dasam Granth extend this political narrative, other voices within the eighteenth century Panth contest these constructions. A crucial set of texts for understanding the political implications of the *chaturyuga* narrative and the various constructions it enjoyed during the period are the works of the Chhibbar family, particularly the Chaupa Singh Rahitnama and the Bansavalinama. These texts and the history of the Chhibbar family itself are used to flesh out the narrative of political dissent during this period. One of the most intriguing observations made by Deol points to the tension between desire and reality. While the prescriptive texts created by the Khalsa seek to define the community in terms of a corporeal identity and social boundaries that are distinct from a Hindu ritual universe, the realization of these aspirations comes to be linked with a metanarrative derived from the Dasam Granth which places the Khalsa within a framework broadly based on Puranic myth and cosmology.

If the foregoing papers provide new readings of such key historical formations as Sikh scriptural tradition or the Khalsa, the next two papers question the preoccupation of much of Sikh studies with the historical approach particularly in relation to the study of religion. One of the central issues in these papers concerns the way in which scholarship in Sikh studies, despite a rhetorical commitment to multi-disciplinary practice, always already predetermines the nature of the object being studied as an aspect of society. In other words, they ask, why, in accordance with the tenets of social constructivism, questions concerning religion or the religious are automatically reduced to social phenomena. Most religious responses to social constructivism have tended to stick to the belief that religion is *sui generis* – that religion has transcendental or metaphysical foundations.

However, as Arvind-pal Singh Mandair argues, in the case of Oriental religions secular scholarship has managed to dismiss the *sui generis* argument by resort to a paradigm which, insofar as it has come to define the very criteria for academic scholarship in the humanities and social sciences via such notions as 'impartial understanding' 'disinterested inquiry', has come to be regarded as entirely natural, and therefore, insurmountable. This paradigm is centred on the idea that historicism or historical method must be the grounding principle for any inquiry into religion or the religious, steering between the two alternatives of theology and secular historicism. Mandair's argument – written partly as a response to a methodological crisis in Sikh studies – points to a different way of reading the complex relationship between religion and history, one that can be located in Hegel's classic though much ignored text: *Lectures on the Philosophy of Religion*. This alternative genealogy charts the simultaneous emergence of two fields: the philosophy (or theory) of religion and the history of religions, where history defines the criterion for ordering any potential threat from the diversity of religions studied. Given this mutual imbrication of religion and history, many of the problems which faced Hegel and his contemporaries are repeated in the formation of the modern discipline of the history of religions – as exemplified by W.H. McLeod's

5

demarcation of the field of Sikh studies. Mandair demonstrates the far reaching result of deconstructing history's claim to foundational status in the humanities. Critique and critical thinking, long associated solely with the secular domain, can just as easily be associated with approaches to religion and the religious. It serves as a double warning to academic scholarship not to place too much faith in secular reason and to be aware of the ethical and political consequences of translation into a Western context.

Remaining broadly within the space that is opened up for religious thinking in the preceding paper, Balbinder Bhogal explores new ways of resisting what he terms as myths of finality, i.e. the tendency in academic and traditionalist domains towards closed definitive versions of scripture. Despite an apparent conflict between traditional and academic modes of interpretation, both versions valorize and perpetuate forms of timelessness. But as Bhogal argues, this particular tendency which happens to be characteristic of modernist thinking cannot be attributed to the Adi Granth scripture without imposing a certain degree of violence. Taking Guru Nanak's *Japji* as a working example Bhogal shows that it is possible to tease out interpretative strategies from within this text which resist reductionism and absolutization, thereby beginning the task of delineating an internal hermeneutic of the *Japji* itself.

A greater urgency is imparted to this task by the diasporic context within which Bhogal is writing, a context which asks whether the words of Guru Nanak can 'speak again' – more specifically whether they can speak and thereby be heard in English. The main argument of this paper therefore hinges on a close reading of selected passages from the *Japji*, aiming to show that Guru Nanak's *bani* does not make absolute statements about a particular view or *darsana*. This reveals not only the existential relevance of Nanak's *bani* today but just as importantly its resistance to the twin dangers of idolization and classification. By reading Sikh scripture in the context of recent hermeneutic theory, Bhogal calls for a new understanding and recontextualization of Sikh thought, not as a once and for all statement but as an ongoing process of intellectual engagement and political praxis.

Sited in the growing overlap between religious studies and literary studies which is so notable a feature of contemporary Western academic practice, the next two papers focus on two cultural formations which in comparison to the central areas of religion, history and political studies have received relatively little attention in modern Sikh studies, namely comparative literature and psycho-analytic theory in relation to the study of religions. Christopher Shackle's paper on 'The Making of Punjabi Literary History' draws attention to the important though sadly neglected influences on the Sikh and Punjabi literary traditions of its Muslim heritage as primarily articulated by its Sufi poets. Scholars of Punjabi literary history generally agree that the making of twentieth century Punjabi literature owes its primary inspiration to three sources: Sikh scripture and its related texts, the pre-modern works of Sufi poetry and Western literature. Acknowledging this rich background, Shackle's paper explores the original construction and some implications of this tripartite scheme of culture reference through a comparative analysis of the work of two early twentieth century pioneers of Punjabi literary history, the Muslim poet Kushta, and the pioneer Sikh literary historian, Bava Budh Singh. What becomes evident through this comparison are the respective differences and degrees of influence exerted by Sikh and Muslim literary traditions. For example, whereas a striking characteristic of the Muslim materials surveyed by Shackle is the marginality of the Sikh presence to the Punjabi literary enterprise, the importance of parts of the Punjabi Muslim literary and cultural presence to the projects of Sikh religious reform and its associated programme of cultural redefinition can hardly be under-played. Moreover, in view of the drive by Hindu nationalists to reconstruct an overarching Hindu literary and cultural identity by excluding the Muslim heritage especially associated with Urdu, the largely secular Sikh cultural framework in post-independence India has owed much to Budh Singh's pioneering work in continuing to lean heavily upon Sufi poetry as a guarantor of its cultural integrity long after the disappearance of the Muslim presence from Indian Punjab.

An unexpected outcome of the post-1984 representation of Sikhs in the Western media is the increasing attention given to the physical form of the male Khalsa Sikhs, particularly in Western film. Although the Western film and literature have represented Sikhs largely through fragmentary and stereotypical images as terrorists (*Satanic Verses* 1989), taxi drivers or shop keepers (*Coneheads* 1992), Sikhs themselves have seldom appeared as vital characters. As Nikky Guninder Kaur Singh argues in her paper 'The Mirror and the Sikh: Ondaatje's Kip' from this perspective alone Michael Ondaatje's masterpiece *The English Patient* represents something of a breakthrough. For not only is Kirpal Singh a central figure in Ondaatje's novel, he is also the embodiment of Sikh moral and ethical values. Unfortunately, however

Ondaatje's reviewers and admirers have neglected the Sikh elements in the novel, and even the very popular and tantalizing 1996 Miramax film version depicted Kirpal Singh as but a minor figure.

Nikky Singh's paper focuses on the forgotten Sikh character of Kirpal Singh, and explores his transformation from a colonial 'kip' (short for 'kipper grease', perhaps also an inversion of Rudyard Kipling's 'Kim') mechanically diffusing bombs for the British army in Europe during the World War II, to a post-colonial Sikh elder sitting at home in the Punjab. Much happens in between, sometimes slowly, sometimes suddenly. Though Kirpal Singh maintains his Sikh identity throughout Ondaatje's text, his Sikh 'religious' experience radically changes from a formal and rather external lifestyle. Singh follows a Lacanian theory in her interpretation of this as a transformation from a colonial false consciousness to a deeper, more conscious and authentic mode of postcolonial being.

The last three papers in this volume contribute each in their very different ways to new understandings of Sikh ethnicity. In his essay on Sikh ethno-nationalism Gurharpal Singh presents a new departure from conventional theories of Indian ethnic nationalism in India, with special reference to the situation established after Operation Bluestar. He argues for the need to situate Sikh ethno-nationalism in the context of ethno-national movements in India's border states which have been largely misunderstood due to the manner in which ethnicity itself has been defined since 1947. By drawing attention to the ahistorical nature of 'conventional wisdom' and to the interlinked roles of the state and persistence of ethno-nationalist movements in peripheral regions of the traditional readings of political identity in India, his paper suggests the need to reconsider India as an 'ethnic democracy' in which hegemonic control is exercised over ethnic minorities. The Indian state is not therefore a non-national civilizational state but one which has explicitly laid claim to an exclusive ethnicity rooted in an ancient past, which in turn defines the limits of sub-national pluralism. The dynamics of Sikh ethno-nationalism are to be discovered in its dialectical relationship to this meta-ethnicity.

Although also concerned with ethnicity, the next essay by Darshan Tatla, switches our attention towards the Sikh diaspora which is such an important context for the understanding of the volume as a whole, as has been pointed out above. Tatla argues that the Sikh diaspora has contributed to a vigorous debate on the idea of 'Sikhs as a nation' and the need for a Sikh homeland. By exploring the extant literature on the idea of Sikh homeland and Sikh self-perception as an ethnic community, the paper highlights competing visions and asks searching questions about Sikh imagining. Why, for example, has the idea of Punjab as a Sikh homeland come to be naturalized among diaspora Sikhs? How has the incipient Indian nationalism of early Sikh immigrants been replaced by the Punjab as an imagined homeland? Tatla's paper chronicles changes in the meaning of Sikh imagination caused primarily by events on Punjab in the 1980s. By exploring certain nuances of the diasporic imaginings towards different notions of homeland, Tatla situates this construction in terms of the complex set of choices faced by the Sikh elite in the diaspora. The paper draws upon literary writings, individual testimonies and the position of social and political groups in Britain, Canada and the USA.

The last essay in the book represents an innovative departure from the conventional mode of academic writing which takes objectivity and a concomitant censorship of the personal or subjective realm as largely unquestioned norms of academic practice. Harjot Oberoi's concern in his paper is to explore a third space, a location that would encompass the scholar's 'life-world, personal dilemmas and change of heart'. Within the academy, however, such a practice continues to be regarded as suspect. Nevertheless, compelled by repeated reflection on events which have been formative in his career as a social historian and, prior to this, in his personal life, Oberoi presents an autobiographical account of two episodes. The first describes his experience of being terrorized simply for being a Sikh by the mob violence of Hindu nationalism in Delhi in 1984. The second is located in the transnational space of the Sikh diaspora in Canada, and describes the attacks made on him for not being a proper Sikh by self-appointed community spokesmen when he held the Sikh-funded chair of Sikh studies at the University of British Columbia in Vancouver. Implicitly linking these twin experiences to those of the West's archetypal diaspora, Oberoi's 'Tale of Pogroms and Biblical Allegories' raises in painfully personalized form the issues already addressed in more or less direct ways by many contributors to the volume, of somehow finding answers to the double edged question implicit for so many in the Sikh diaspora in facing Gayatri Spivak's paraphrase of Kant: 'It is not possible to become *cultured* in this culture if you are naturally alien to it' (Spivak 1999: 12).

# Chapter Two

# Canon Formation in the Sikh Tradition

*Gurinder Singh Mann*

The compilation of the Adi Granth ('original book'), the Sikh sacred text, took place during the sixteenth and seventeenth centuries. Given the centrality of scripture in the Sikh tradition almost all the subsequent Sikh chroniclers refer to the making of the Adi Granth in some detail. These later authors constructed their accounts primarily around oral traditions, using them with varying degrees of ingenuity. By the middle of the nineteenth century, there emerged a common narrative of the compilation of the Adi Granth, one that continues to hold sway in both popular and scholarly circles.

But there is another source for understanding this process: the scriptural manuscripts themselves, a substantial number of which are still extant (see Appendix to this chapter). These documents, prepared during the sixteenth and seventeenth centuries, were preserved as objects of veneration by their custodian families, who have been generally reluctant to open their treasures for scholarly scrutiny. In my case, however, they very kindly shared with me the family traditions regarding the history of their rare possessions and permitted me to examine these documents and find out details pertaining to their time of compilation and their precise contents.

In this chapter, I present a reconstruction of the formation of Sikh canon based on two elements: data available in early manuscripts, and their firm placement in the context of early Sikh institutional development. The results are quite remarkable – exciting if you see it one way, but unsettling if you see it another. At almost every critical juncture the information available in these manuscripts conflicts with

10

the received wisdom about how the Sikh scripture began, expanded, and became canon.

## The traditional reconstruction

Sikh sources trace the original compilation of the Adi Granth to Guru Arjan (d.1606), the fifth in line of the Sikh Gurus. The date thus proposed is some eighty years after the founding of the Sikh community. During this period, according to the view popularized by Giani Gian Singh, Guru Nanak's hymns and those of his immediate successors survived primarily through oral transmission (Gian Singh 1993: 417). When Guru Arjan decided to compile the Sikh text, we are told, he collected these hymns, scattered in distant Sikh congregations, and had them recorded according to the musical modes in which they were to be sung. The original manuscript compiled in 1604 is still extant and is known as the Kartarpur Pothi (book or volume). Sikh sources proclaim categorically that both the conception and the original compilation are to be seen in that manuscript. And the guiding hand was therefore Guru Arjan's.

Why was this body of hymns organized as a single coherent text by Guru Arjan? Sikh scholars say this happened as a response to external pressure. Guru Arjan acted to keep the hymns of the Sikh Gurus pure and distinct from those of their rivals. During the sixteenth century, there were others who composed hymns and floated them under the name of 'Nanak', the authoritative signature not just of Guru Nanak himself but of all Sikh Gurus. Guru Arjan – so goes the traditional account – was dedicated to separating the authentic from the spurious hymns and ensuring their purity for posterity.

Sikh sources report that following the compilation of the Kartarpur Pothi, two branches of manuscripts proliferated during the seventeenth century. The first consisted of exact copies of the Kartarpur Pothi, and the second was the Khara Mangat version, which included a set of apocryphal hymns not present in the Kartarpur Pothi (Gill 1977: 89–90). Bhai Banno, a follower of Guru Arjan and the compiler of this competing manuscript, added these hymns to obscure the importance of the true Sikh message. Historians who see matters this way are often unaware that in the twentieth century another family of the seventeenth century manuscripts known as the Lahore branch also came to light; no scholar has so far offered a convincing explanation of its origin (Charan Singh 1945: 4).

11

Then comes the stage of canonization, when the scriptural text took the form of the Adi Granth. The Sikh tradition attributes this development to Guru Gobind Singh (d.1708), the tenth and the last Sikh Guru, and the work is believed to have been completed in 1706, at Damdama, Bhatinda. The Adi Granth is claimed to contain the hymns present in the Kartarpur Pothi plus the compositions of Guru Tegh Bahadur, the first Guru to have written hymns after the compilation of the Kartarpur Pothi. Guru Gobind Singh, at the time of his death, elevated the Adi Granth to the position of Guru. It became the Guru Granth Sahib and it replaced the office of the personal Guru. Its newly acquired status allows no scope for further alterations in the text, so from this point onward the Adi Granth is believed to have remained unchanged, and its history during the past three centuries has remained largely unexplored.

This is the traditional account of how Sikh scripture was formed. But if we turn to the extant manuscripts and have a closer look at the times of their creation, a very different picture emerges of its making, its proliferation, its canonization, and its history during the past centuries. Significant alterations have to be made in our understanding of what happened between the time of Guru Arjan and Guru Gobind Singh, and very importantly, the traditional account needs to be extended both ways – back to Guru Nanak and forward almost up to the present day – before we have a truly comprehensive picture of the text's evolution.

## The origin of the Sikh scriptural text

There is impressive evidence to support the view that the compilation of the Sikh scripture began with Guru Nanak (d.1539) himself. All scholars would acknowledge that Guru Nanak was interested in scripture, but most hold that he contested the authority of existing scriptures – Hindu scriptures and those of the Semitic religions (Nabha 1995: 42–50). This is not true. In my view, his criticism of scripture was not directed at the scriptural texts themselves, but at the way these texts were used by the adherents of various traditions associated with them. Most pointedly, Guru Nanak rejects the ritualistic reading of the Veda, a usage that disrupts peace: *pari pari dajhahi santi na ai* (AG 1026), and results in disharmony: *veda parahi te vada vakhanahi* (AG 638).

This distinction between text and its usage offers important background for understanding Guru Nanak's sense of his own

12

mission. Guru Nanak believed that God had assigned him the vocation of singing his praises: *hau dhadhi vekaru karai laia* (AG 150), and that his hymns were the result of direct communications from God: *jaisi mai avai khasama ki bani taisara kari gianu ve Lalo* (AG 722), *ta ma kahia kahanu ja tujhai kahaia* (AG 566). He urged his followers to consider his hymns as the truth and the path to realization: *satigura ki bani sati sati kari manahu* (AG 1028), *gurabani nirabanu sabadi pachhania* (AG 752).

Yet he was not a simply a bard who was satisfied that his divinely inspired hymns be sung. The notable presence in his compositions of metaphors of writing suggests that he was aware of how important it was to preserve them in writing. According to Guru Nanak, inscribing the revelatory message was no ordinary activity but was an act of devotion which demanded the heart and soul of the scribe: *jali mohu ghasi masu kari mati kagadu kari saru. . . . bhau kalama kari chitu likhari gur puchhi likhu bicharu* (AG 16). If successful, in fact, this exercise produces a state of total blessedness: *dhanu su kagadu kalama dhanu dhanu bhanda dhanu masu, dhanu lekhari Nanaka jini namu likhaia sachu* (AG 1291). Passages such as these suggest Guru Nanak must have welcomed and encouraged a process whereby his own hymns were captured on the page.

Against this background, the existence of a very early manuscript known in the tradition as the Guru Harsahai Pothi can be easily understood. No longer an anomaly to be explained away, it now makes perfect sense as a expression of Guru Nanak's own effort to create a written text. The Guru Harsahai Pothi was lost in a train robbery in 1971, but some photographs of it are available. They reveal its early orthography, the absence of any hymns composed by Gurus later than Guru Nanak, and an entirely non-schematic organizational structure – quite unlike the later, more sophisticated Adi Granth. Although the manuscript contains no dated colophon, all these features point to its early origin. This evidence is further supported by a long-standing tradition prevalent in its custodial family that this manuscript was the original pothi of Guru Nanak.

The early recording of Guru Nanak's hymns and the creation of a pothi in a distinct Sikh script (Gurmukhi) seem to relate to the immediate religio-political context in which the new community was founded. Guru Nanak knew the Qur'an and had to be aware of the emphasis it places on the *ahl-i-kitab* ('possessors of a revealed book'). His writings confirm that he was aware that *jizya* – the Muslim tax on unbelievers – was being paid by the Hindus under the category of *mushabih-i-ahl-i-kitab* ('those who resemble the possessors of a revealed book'). So he may well have believed that a Sikh pothi containing hymns manifesting the divine revelation would give his newly founded community a status within the *ahl-i-kitab*, or at least parallel to it. It is likely that Guru Nanak's acceptance of the significance of scripture in the major religious traditions that shaped his world, his awareness of the role of the scripture in the political definition of the community, and above all his belief in the revealed nature of his own hymns would have led him to compile his own hymns to ensure their proper preservation, and simultaneously to provide the new community with a revealed book that would assign it the status and prestige of the *ahl-i-kitab*.

## The expansion of the scriptural text

The doctrine of the unity of guruship evolved quickly after the death of Guru Nanak. His successors were understood to reflect the same divine light that was manifest in Guru Nanak. They used the authoritative signature of 'Nanak' in their hymns, which were then taken as an extension of the spiritual message of the founder of the tradition.

By the time we arrive at the third Guru, Guru Amardas (1552–74), we evidently have a critical mass, for this is the period in which we get the so-called Goindval Pothis (Mann 1996). Compiled during the 1570s, these evidently contained the complete hymns of the first three Gurus. In saying this, I am arguing that the two extant Goindval Pothis were really only half of an original set of four pothis – a number significant for both Muslim and Hindu ideas of canon. In my view, the Goindval Pothis may have been compiled as four books because Sikhs believed that their path was an alternative to that of the Hindus, which enshrined its scripture as four Vedas. It was also an alternative to that of the Semites, who, according to the Muslims, also had four holy books: Toret, Injil, Zabur, and Qur'an (that is, the Torah, the Gospel, the Psalms, and the Qur'an). The four Goindval Pothis established the Sikh community as a rival claimant to scriptural authority.

At this stage, another interesting development occurred. Hymns of fifteen Hindu and Muslim saints called the Bhagats were incorporated into the Goindval Pothis. The inclusion of the hymns of the non-Sikhs in the Sikh sacred text involved a complex process of selection. At the first stage, compositions of the Vaishnava saints that contradicted Sikh theology were discarded. Guru Amardas came right out and called them *kachi bani*, literally 'unbaked', i.e. devoid of any spiritual benefit. The second stage of selection seems to have involved a sifting of the available compositions of those who shared the Sikh theology of a formless personal God, and an effort was made to drop those hymns which did not conform to the Sikh social vision. Thus many hymns attributed to Kabir in other collections that emphasized asceticism are conspicuously missing from Sikh scripture.

Even at this early stage, the Gurus' hymns are deemed quite separate from those of the Bhagats. When the hymns of the Bhagats were introduced into the canon, they served rather to reinforce the distinct theological and social vision of the Sikhs – both because they had been so thoroughly edited and because they were included only at the peripheries of the text. The physical layout of the Goindval Pothis creates a hierarchy of sanctity. Guru Amardas, who may well have been personally responsible for the organization of the Goindval Pothis, placed the hymns of the Gurus at the top and those of others below them. The hymns of the Gurus thus appear as the core revelation. Those of the Bhagats only echoed their message.

Other factors may also have urged the inclusion of the hymns of the Bhagats in Sikh scriptures. Guru Amardas was the first Sikh Guru publicly to invite both Hindu and Muslim religious figures to accept his leadership: *brahamu bindihe te brahamana je chalahe satigura bhae* (AG 849–850 M3), and s*ekha chauchakia chauvaia ehu manu ikatu ghari ani; ehara tehara chhadi tu gura ka sabadu pachhanu. . . . satigura agai dhai pau, . . . ta daragaha pavahi manu* (AG 646 M3). To include the hymns of Sufi and Vaishnava poets may have been a way to show that ordinary Muslims and Hindus also belonged within the Sikh fold.

The inclusion of the hymns of the Bhagats in Sikh scripture may also have been a way to emphasize the social comprehensiveness of the Sikh religious vision. The containment within Sikh scripture of writings of saints from all castes and creeds thus represented the firm Sikh rejection of such distinctions. What better way to manifest Sikh social and spiritual egalitarianism? Many people from other communities responded positively to this Sikh belief, and the Sikh constituency in central Punjab expanded significantly. From the establishment of two towns during the first half century of the community's history (1520–70), we see the emergence of as many as four large Sikh towns in the central Punjab in the last quarter of the sixteenth century.

At the time of Guru Amardas's death in 1574, the Sikh community was considerably larger than it had been under Guru Nanak's patronage, and it possessed much more highly developed social institutions. Scriptural innovations seem to form an integral part of this picture with four volumes of scripture – this was scripture in the full sense, and perhaps it makes sense to introduce the term 'canon' at this stage, although no exactly analogous word emerges at this point in the Sikh community's own history.

Thus the Goindval Pothis offer a complex picture of the expansion of Sikh scripture, and point to an intricate relationship between the evolution of Sikh scripture and that of the community. In these pothis we see the complete corpus of the hymns of the first three Gurus. Whatever we find of them in the Adi Granth is contained here as well, and a number of small discrepancies make it clear that these came first. This leaves no grounds for the view that Guru Nanak's hymns were only available in their oral form until the time of Guru Arjan, the fifth Guru. Not only that, it seems likely too that the complete corpus of the hymns of the Bhagats also entered the canon during this phase. We lack two of the original Goindval Pothis, so we cannot be absolutely sure, but those sections which we do have are exactly as they will appear in the Kartarpur Pothi and the Adi Granth. Furthermore, the general principles of organization, the division of hymns around the musical modes, and the placement of the hymns according to length are all features of the later canon that appear equally in the Goindval Pothis.

From this point onward, all that was involved in expanding the scriptural text was a process of updating – that is, incorporating the hymns of the successor Gurus. As the traditional sources report – and as is corroborated by information found in the extant manuscripts – Guru Arjan succeeded in obtaining access to the Goindval Pothis. He added to their contents his own hymns and those of his father. The Kartarpur Pothi built on the sacred corpus present in the Goindval Pothis and further elaborated the organizational principles it had used. The overall process was thus logical, incremental, and apparently organic. The information available to us really offers no basis for the traditional belief that Guru Arjan compiled Sikh scripture in one great act of creativity for the purpose of keeping the Gurus' writings pure, untainted by the spurious production of a group of conspiratorial others.

# The Sikh text during the seventeenth century

As we know, the Kartarpur Pothi was inscribed in 1604. The earliest extant copy is the Khara Mangat Pothi recorded in 1642, and over twenty-five other manuscripts compiled between 1642 and 1692 are extant. From a textual point of view, this is a radically altered landscape – much more dense and complex – but one fact remains constant. Once again, the information available in the extant manuscripts tends to challenge the traditional view of the evolution of Sikh scripture.

First, these manuscripts force us to regard as inaccurate the traditional perception that the Khara Mangat Pothi was the first copy ever made of the Kartarpur Pothi. We now know that copies of the Kartarpur Pothi began to be made soon after its compilation, and that the early copies to have come to notice were prepared in 1605 and 1610. We also have references to others prepared in the 1630s.

A second belief also stands in need of correction, namely, the idea that the Khara Mangat version included additional compositions not present in the Kartarpur Pothi, and that this occurred as a result of Bhai Banno's deliberate effort to confuse the Sikh message. With the exception of a single hymn, all the so-called apocryphal compositions appear not only in the Khara Mangat family of copies but also in the original inscription of the Kartarpur Pothi itself, and in all the other manuscripts of that immediate period.

Hence the traditional perception that the Kartarpur Pothi and the Khara Mangat Pothi generated two distinct branches of manuscripts during the seventeenth century is not supported by the evidence presented in the extant manuscripts themselves. The idea that there was a true family of manuscripts (Kartarpur) and a false one (Khara Mangat) was evidently the creation of nineteenth century writers who did not know the precise contents of the Kartarpur Pothi and hence could not understand the relationship between it and other manuscripts related to it. The idea of contrasting good and bad recensions seems to have more to do with nineteenth century perceptions of reality – the sacred one, and the threatening other – than anything the seventeenth century produced.

And then there is the matter of the so-called Lahore family of the seventeenth century manuscripts. The first extant manuscript of this line was prepared in 1605, and is known as the Burha Sandhu Pothi (Charan Singh 1945: 4–6). The manuscript was taken to the north-west of Punjab, and it served as a source for generating a set of manuscripts in that region. This line differs from the Kartarpur Pothi line, primarily in its final portions.

How can we explain these variations? Internal evidence in the Kartarpur Pothi confirms that it was compiled in 1604, but a close examination of its layout shows that changes continued to be made in it until the death of Guru Arjan in 1606. The Burha Sandhu Pothi was copied from the Kartarpur Pothi in 1605, at a time when the Kartarpur manuscript had not yet attained its final shape. Once this early manuscript reached the north-west of Punjab, local scribes happily copied it without perceiving any differences between it and the final version of the Kartarpur Pothi. They were too far away to know about the latter.

Finally, there is the universally accepted idea that it was Guru Gobind Singh who added hymns of Guru Tegh Bahadur, the ninth Guru, into the Sikh canon. Yet we have two extant manuscripts compiled in 1674 which contain Guru Tegh Bahadur's hymns. This leaves no space for doubt that the hymns of Guru Tegh Bahadur were introduced into the Sikh text during his own lifetime. But there is one remaining complication. The manuscripts prepared in 1674 were not the same as that of the Adi Granth, and this calls into question a second aspect of the traditional view of how the canon was closed. According to the second aspect of the traditional understanding, the addition of the hymns of Guru Tegh Bahadur to the text of the Kartarpur Pothi automatically created the text of the Adi Granth. But this is not so. The contents of the manuscripts prepared in 1674 are different from the text of the Adi Granth.

## The Adi Granth

Traditional sources claim that the Adi Granth was compiled under the supervision of Guru Gobind Singh in 1706 at Damdama, Bhatinda. According to this view, the crucial fact to note is that Guru Gobind Singh added his father's hymns to the existing text. But as we have seen, there are several basic flaws in this view. First, Guru Tegh Bahadur added his hymns to the Sikh text himself. Second, the resulting text was not that of the Adi Granth. And finally a third: the tradition that the Adi Granth was originally compiled in 1706 is not accurate. Manuscripts of the Adi Granth already began to appear as early as the 1680s.

We have evidence that in the late 1670s, Guru Gobind Singh while living at Anandpur felt the need to create the final text of Sikh scripture. In this, the traditional view is correct, though the dating is amiss. He therefore sought to borrow the Kartarpur Pothi. The custodians of the Kartarpur Pothi, however, could not part with it as they were in the process of moving from their quarters in Baba Bakala to Kartarpur. And it seems, this is the principal factor that led Guru Gobind Singh to prepare a new and independent text. This happened in the early 1680s, and the result is what has come to be called the Adi Granth (Kahn Singh 1995: 42–50).

The precise details of how the contents of the Adi Granth were selected are not entirely clear. This text differs slightly from both the Kartarpur version and its Lahore cousins. The presence of the Adi Granth in the areas of Anandpur and later Damdama where the Guru lived, evidently gave it an authoritative status by the turn of the eighteenth century. After the death of Guru Gobind Singh, the version represented by the Adi Granth came to be regarded as definitively codified scripture. In technical Sikh terms, it became the Guru Granth Sahib.

Tradition would have us believe that the story of the compilation of the Adi Granth came to a close once Guru Gobind Singh declared it to be the Guru. Yet earlier manuscripts did on occasions continue to be copied, and this process created texts which were not identical with that of the Adi Granth. It seems plausible that the scribes engaged in the production of such manuscripts were simply not aware of the textual differences between the Adi Granth and the earlier texts they had before them.

On the whole, there is thus no indication of any concerted attempt to redefine the emerging Sikh canon. Yet there is an exception to prove the rule. This is manifested in a manuscript dated 1713, which is presently in the custody of Manjit Singh Sethi of New Delhi. The compilation of this manuscript is traditionally associated with Bhai Mani Singh (d.1738), a major Sikh figure of the opening decades of the eighteenth century. In this, he reorganized the contents by placing the hymns of the non-Sikh saints at the end of the text rather than at the end of each subsection. For understandable reasons, this revised conception of the organization of Sikh scripture, however logical it might seem to some, was rejected by the community. It was not canonical. But the fact that such a manuscript could be compiled at all – and under the supervision of a Sikh of Bhai Mani Singh's status – merits attention.

From the early nineteenth century onward, when communication between various branches of the Sikh community became much closer, these 'deviant' manuscripts had to be explained somehow, and scholars of the 'centre' accounted for them by seeing them as being conscious in design to challenge the Adi Granth. In reality such disparities occurred primarily because the exact contents of the closed canon were not known in regions distant from the center – even when the idea of the closed canon may have been enthusiastically embraced. These 'deviant' copies continued to be generated throughout the eighteenth and nineteenth centuries. This process came to an end only with the appearance of the printed edition of the Adi Granth, in 1865. Once the printed version was prepared, the minor variants of the regional manuscripts became all too clear, and they ceased to be used.

All these 'corrections' were corrections from script to print. But there was also a contrary process. In the early part of the twentieth century, a major effort was made to correct the text of the printed Adi Granth to make it conform to the text of the Kartarpur Pothi, which had by then been accepted as the original text written under the direction of Guru Arjan. Thus the initial victory of print in the canonization process was sought to be reinforced, ironically, by a return to manuscripts – that is, the right manuscripts. The collation process lasted several decades and was the work of several major Sikh scholars. The result was the standard edition of the Adi Granth, the Sri Guru Granth Sahib published by the Shiromani Gurdwara Prabandhak Committee in 1951 – a text of 1,430 pages. And with this – only fifty odd years ago – the work of canon formation seem finally to have come to a close.

Or has it? Interestingly, minor changes have continued to appear. First, the old manuscript tradition of connected writing – a form in which word boundaries are not observed on the page, only in performance – was foregone in the early 1970s. There was strong opposition to this change. Some saw it as tearing apart the body of the Guru. But eventually this criticism was contained by arguing that it is important to separate words for those readers who might otherwise fail to make the correct breaks between the words. After some controversy, then, the new text with separated words was accepted. This text, with a standard pagination of 1,430 pages, is now in use in Sikh homes and gurdwaras all over the world.

Other unexpected developments came with the twentieth century. For the first time, whole communities of Sikhs are largely unable to read Gurmukhi. For example, the Sindhi and the Afghani Sikhs understand the language of the Adi Granth but cannot read it, and many Sikhs growing up in South East Asia or Europe or North

America can understand only a bit of its language in either written or oral form. Several options have been explored to meet this challenge. The problem was first addressed by producing editions of the Adi Granth in Devanagari, in Indo-Persian script, and also in Roman transliteration for people with purely scholarly interests. Both the SGPC and commercial publishers played a pioneering role in these efforts (Ashok 1982: 261). A new edition of the Adi Granth in which the original text, a Roman transliteration, and an English translation appear side by side has been recently released (Chahil 1995). In the 1990s, the text of the Adi Granth also became available in digital formats, produced by a variety of individuals and organizations. So even now, it seems, the sacred text continues to inhabit a state of constant evolution.

## Scriptural authority

Tradition assigns the scriptural authority of the Adi Granth to the decision of Guru Gobind Singh, but in historical reality, as we have seen, this authority seems to go all the way back to Guru Nanak himself. Guru Nanak was quite clear that his compositions represented divine revelation, and that Sikhs must follow them. As the manuscripts show, the idea that the pothi containing these hymns was also an object of authority developed early in the tradition. Interestingly, certain Sikh narrative traditions seem to take this for granted. A crucial early seventeenth-century tradition recorded in the *Puratan Janamsakhi* refers to Guru Nanak's giving his pothi to Guru Angad at the moment when he nominated Angad as his successor (Ashok 1969). The historical accuracy of this story may be in doubt, yet its existence in early Sikh literature seems clearly to reflect the spiritual authority that written scripture commanded in the early Sikh community. In fact, the janamsakhi story represents the pothi as the core symbol of succession.

The idea that scripture was requisite for *bona fide* succession manifested itself in a series of conflicts in the early years of the Sikh community. At the death of Guru Amardas, for example, the Goindval Pothis were retained by his son Baba Mohan at Goindval, and clear evidence exists that he attempted to strengthen his claim to the spiritual office of his father through his physical possession of the manuscripts containing the writings of the Gurus. Guru Arjan's authority was challenged in turn by Baba Mohan at Goindval, and by

21

Prithi Chand, his elder brother. If Baba Mohan claimed guruship on the basis of possession of the Goindval Pothis, then Prithi Chand, to support his claim to the office, claimed to possess the pothi said to have been compiled by Guru Nanak himself, the Guru Harsahai Pothi. No wonder the Guru Harsahai and Goindval Pothis remained in the custody of the descendants of these men. They represented far more than books.

The possession of early manuscripts continued to buttress claims of authority during the seventeenth century. Two major manuscripts inscribed in the seventeenth century were held by the rivals of the Gurus, by Dhirmal at Kartarpur and Ramrai at Dehradun. Later, the historical importance of many of these early manuscripts went unrecognized because of the very fact of their custody by families that had rivaled the Gurus once a proper succession had been agreed upon by the majority. At that point, the manuscripts in the hands of outsiders could safely be ignored as tainted and perhaps even heretical. But better communications and the coming of modern education caused these manuscripts once again to emerge in the light of scholarship, an important group of Sikh scholars has been arguing vehemently against accepting their authenticity, and along the same lines (Pritam Singh 1998: 228–9). Since these manuscripts are in the custody of families that opposed the Gurus, they argue that they have to be fakes – a case of guilt by association.

Guru Gobind Singh's decision to replace the office of the personal Guru with that of the sacred text may indeed have been the climactic point in the story of how the Adi Granth attained its current authority, but given what we know we must recognize that Guru Gobind Singh was working with a scriptural tradition whose authority was already established at the time of Guru Nanak. The doctrine of inerrant authoritative scripture worked side by side with that of the authority of the Guru Panth during the eighteenth century, but it eventually took over, beginning with the turn of the nineteenth century and the building of the Sikh Raj under Maharaja Ranjit Singh. And as things stand today, the Sikh community has tended to regard authority of its sacred text in a way matched by few other religious traditions.

## Conclusion

This brief reconstruction of what went into the making of the Adi Granth shows that canon formation in Sikhism was a long and complex process, one that was closely related to other developments in the community. Like the Semitic religious traditions, the early Sikhs conceived scripture as revealed, and eventually regarded it as a bounded, authoritative text – a book. Yet this conviction that Sikh scripture is a revealed, timeless, complete entity – however true one might think it to be at a theological level – has tended to mask the historical reality: Sikh scripture was shaped over time. The process apparently began in the days of Guru Nanak himself, and it continues to evolve as we speak.

## Appendix: Extant Sikh Scriptural Manuscripts

1 The Goindval Pothi. 300 folios. Vinod Kumar Bhalla, 371 Lajpat Nagar, Jalandhar; early 1570s.
2 The Goindval Pothi. Singh Bhalla, 224 folios. Sundar Kutia, Pinjore; early 1570s.
3 MS 1245. 1267 folios. Guru Nanak Dev University, Amritsar; early 1600s.
4 The Kartarpur Pothi. 974 folios. Karamjit Singh Sodhi, Kartarpur, Jalandhar; Bhadon *vadi* 1, VS 1661 (1604).
5 The Kanpur Pothi. 467 folios. Gurdwara Bhai Banno, G. T. Road, Kanpur; Assun *vadi* 1, VS 1699 (1642).
6 The Gurdwara Bhai Ramkishan Pothi. 760 folios. Sheran vala Gate, Patiala; Har *sudi* 14, VS 1710 (1653).
7 The Amritsar Pothi. 591 folios. Arjan Singh Bhalla, Gali 5, House 9, Tehsilpura, Amritsar; Phagan *sudi* 1, VS 1711 (1654). Known in the tradition as the Bura Sandhu Pothi.
8 The Dehra Dun Pothi. 651 folios. Darbar Sahib Sri Guru Ramrai; Vaisakh *vadi* 1, VS 1716 (1659).
9 The Patiala Pothi. 683 folios. Ajaib Singh Sekhon, Lovely Cottage, Sangrur Road, Patiala; VS 1718 (1661). Known in the tradition as the Kangar Pothi.
10 MS 341. 577 folios. Punjab Archives, Patiala; Harsh 20, VS 1723 (1666).
11 MS 1084. 464 folios. Guru Nanak Dev University, Amritsar; VS 1723 (1666).
12 MS 115338. 688 folios. Punjabi University, Patiala; Magh *vadi* 1, VS 1724 (1667). Known in the tradition as the Jograj Pothi.
13 MS 1229. 679 folios. Guru Nanak Dev University, Amritsar; VS 1728 (1671). Known in the tradition as the Saranke Pothi.
14 MS 1192. 605 folios. Panjab University, Chandigarh; Jeth 9, VS 1731 (1674).
15 The Anandpur Pothi. 608 folios. Bibi Narinder Kaur Sodhi, Bari Manji, Mahala Bari Sarkar, Anandpur; Jeth 9, VS 1731 (1674).
16 The Chandigarh Pothi 1. 554 folios; Man Singh Nirankari, 9 Sector 4, Chandigarh; Jeth *vadi* 10, VS 1733 (1676).

17 The Balbir Singh Sahitya Kendar Pothi 1. 638 folios; 20 Pritam Road, Dehra Dun; Assu *sudi* 3, VS 1736 (1679).
18 The Lucknow Pothi. 691 folios. Singha vali Gali, Mahala Yahiyaganj, Lucknow; Asar *vadi* 9, Samat 1743 (1686).
19 The New Delhi Pothi. 530 folios. Mohan Singh, D 913 New Friends Colony, Delhi; Assu *vadi* [1], VS 1743 (1686).
20 MS 115152. 706 folios. Punjabi University, Patiala; Magh *vadi* 1, VS 1744 (1687).
21 The Bhai ki Daroli Pothi. 684 folios. Ratan Singh Sangha, Bhai ki Daroli, District Faridkot; Bhado *sudi* 5, VS 1745 (1688).
22 MS 1189. 682 folios. Panjab University, Chandigarh; Katak *vadi* 1, VS 1748 (1691).
23 MS 6. 596 folios. Punjabi University; Patiala; Savan *sudi* 1, VS 1749 (1692).
24 The Patna Pothi. 1036 folios. Sri Takhat Harmandirji Patna; VS 1749 (1692). Known in the tradition as the Ramrai Pothi. The absence of Guru Tegh Bahadur's hymns in the original inscription of the following undated manuscripts suggests that they too were prepared prior to the mid-1670s:
25 The Gurdwara Bal Lila Pothi. 840 folios. Maini Sangat, Patna.
26 MS 1. 589 folios. The royal collection at Motibagh, Patiala.
27 MS 2. 860 folios. the royal collection at Motibagh, Patiala.
28 MS 3. 992 folios. the royal collection at Motibagh, Patiala.
29 MS 8. 564 folios. Punjabi University, Patiala.
30 The Balbir Singh Sahitya Kendar Pothi 2. 700 folios. 20 Pritam Road, Dehra Dun.
31 The Chandigarh Pothi 2. 517 folios. Giani Gurdit Singh, 56 Sector 4, Chandigarh.

## Chapter Three

# Eighteenth Century Khalsa Identity: Discourse, Praxis and Narrative

*Jeevan Deol*

Perhaps the most central event in Sikh self-construction is Guru Gobind Singh's creation of the Khalsa. As is to be expected of so seminal a moment in the shaping of the Sikh consciousness, it has spawned a number of varied representations and interpretations. Singh Sabha writers questioned eighteenth and nineteenth century versions of the Baisakhi gathering that gave a central role to the goddess Devi, while some non-Sikh writers claimed that it constituted a decisive 'transformation' of the community. In the second half of the twentieth century, some historians came to question the details of the traditional version of the ceremony itself. This paper skirts the issues of the historical and religious antecedents of the Khalsa and the problems of its historiography; instead, it seeks to examine the discourses and narratives created by the eighteenth century Khalsa as it constructed itself both as a community of believers and as a political entity. I argue that the Khalsa's perception of itself as a distinct and bounded community with aspirations to political power comes to be linked with a metanarrative derived primarily from the Dasam Granth. This metanarrative places those aspirations within a framework broadly based on the Puranic myth and cosmology, while prescriptive texts created by the Khalsa seek to define the community and the terms of its distinctiveness. Since these developments are rooted in the Khalsa's perception of its position in the ritual and social universe, the paper begins with an examination of the discursive and social contexts created by the separation of the Khalsa from the Nanakpanth.

## The Khalsa and the Nanakpanth

Although the corpus of contemporary or near contemporary sources about the creation of the Khalsa is extremely small, such sources as we do have make it clear that Sikhs of the period saw its creation as an innovation which created a rupture both with earlier Sikh tradition and with the ritual universe of maximal lineages (*biradaris*) in which most Sikhs seem to have participated. One of the most widely used eighteenth century sources for the life of Guru Gobind Singh and the formation of the Khalsa, Sainapati's *Sri Gur Sobha*,[1] dedicates two sections (*adhyays*) to the controversies that arose among the Sikhs of Delhi when they heard the news of the Guru's new order. Much of the concern in Sainapati's text revolves around the prohibition on *bhaddar*, the ritual shaving of the head after the death of a close relative.[2] According to Sainapati, when Gobind Singh created the Khalsa at Anandpur, he told his followers, 'Know in your heart, O *sants*,[3] that *bhaddar* is illusion (*bharam*) not *dharma* at all' (5:23), nearly inverting the accepted ritual universe and its discourses. New evidence suggests that he also intended to weaken the Mughal state's hold over the Khalsa. Although we have no sources to indicate with certainty when it was first imposed, a *parvana* from the eleventh year of the reign of Muhammad Shah (corresponding to 1728) abolishes in perpetuity a tax on *bhaddar* in accordance with a petition by Jai Singh of Amber (Bahura and Singh 1988: 83). The abolition of this tax thus occurs between the withdrawal of the poll-tax on non-Muslims (*jizya*) in 1722 and that of the pilgrim-tax in 1732, both of which had been imposed by Aurangzeb and withdrawn after petitions by Jai Singh. It seems likely therefore that the tax on *bhaddar* had also been imposed during Aurangzeb's reign and was in effect when Guru Gobind Singh formed the Khalsa. As such, Sainapati's text stresses what must have been a significant point of concern for urban adherents of the Sikh Panth, whose proximity to centres of state power would most certainly have made them wary of opposing themselves to the regulatory structure of the Mughal state by accepting the command of the Guru.

The consequences of this dilemma can be expected to have been particularly telling in Delhi, a city whose Punjabi Khatri population had strong commercial and social ties with the Mughal elite. Tension seems to have dominated the relationship between members of the new Khalsa and non-initiate Khatris in the city from the very beginning: a prominent Khatri Sikh was expelled from the place of worship (*dharamsala*) for refusing to join the Khalsa and another Sikh

26

for eating with him, starting a chain of further ejections. The expelled Sikhs convened a gathering of the community at which two wealthy Khatris protested against the Khalsa's social strictures, demanding that the Khalsa produce written orders from the Guru to substantiate their claim that a new code of conduct (*rahit*) had been promulgated (6:15–47). When the new Khalsa funerary practice seemed likely to impinge on the livelihood and position of the Khatris, their reaction was swift: the refusal of the family of a prominent Sikh family to perform the tonsure rite after his death led to their being boycotted by their caste fellows (*adhyay* 7), presumably as much for their flouting of Mughal taxation rules and its possible consequences as for their rejection of caste custom. The Khatri caste council (*panch*) closed the bazaar to put pressure on the Khalsa, who petitioned state officials to intervene. Despite Khatri attempts to influence the outcome through bribery, the officials eventually forced the reopening of the shops. This appeal to higher authority would appear to be an instance of the Mughal emperor exercising through his officials the Indic king's prerogative as the ultimate juridical authority of the caste *biradari*, responsible both for excommunicating and for readmitting those who violated its rules (Dumont 1980: 169). Before peace was established in the Delhi congregation (*sangat*), a situation had arisen in which 'The Khalsa was on one side and the world on the other' (7:30). The resulting fault line between a constituency of urban Khatris and the Khalsa seems to have persisted through the course of the eighteenth century: some urban Khatris, for example, welcomed and even financed resistance to Banda's army in the second decade of the century (Alam 1993: 152). It is perhaps in the context of this mutual animus that the strong hostility to Khatris in the mid-eighteenth century *rahitnama* attributed to Chaupa Singh is to be read.[4]

Another rift between the Khalsa and some other Nanakpanthi groups at the level of praxis would seem to be the Khalsa's firm adherence to the doctrine that Guru Gobind Singh had ended the line of human Gurus and vested the Guruship in the Adi Granth and in the Khalsa itself. From the eighteenth century onward, a number of *gurpranalis* listing the Gurus, their wives and their offspring were written. With one notable exception, all the available early *gurpranalis* are unanimous in their affirmation that the Khalsa succeeded Gobind Singh as Guru: indeed, the two earliest *gurpranalis*, Sita Ram's *Gur Bansavali* (VS 1831 1774) and Kavi Saundha's roughly contemporaneous *Gur Bansavali*, both accept the existence of only ten human Gurus.[5] Most other published and unpublished eighteenth and nineteenth century *gurpranalis* are equally firm in their insistence that there were only ten human Gurus, and where they state a successor either name the Khalsa or, especially in later texts, the Guru Granth.[6]

There is, however, evidence that for some eighteenth century Sikhs – urban Khatris again most likely prominent among them – the line of human Gurus did not end with Gobind Singh. The roots of this belief would seem to lie in the idea current since at least the time of Guru Hargobind that the Guruship was the hereditary possession of the Sodhi descendants of Guru Ramdas.[7] Presumably basing themselves on this belief, some eighteenth century Sikhs extended the line of Gurus to include Banda, Guru Gobind Singh's widows Mata Sundari and Mata Sahib Devi, and Mata Sundari's adopted son and grandson Ajit Singh and Hathi Singh. Rai Chaturman's geographical compendium *Chahar Gulshan* (AH1173 1760–61) claims that Ajit Singh was placed on the *sajjada*[8] with imperial permission, a move that implies significant participation by Khatris having influence at court. According to Rai Chaturman, many Nanakpanthis believed in Ajit Singh – a statement that implies that there were others who did not. The text states that when Ajit Singh grew older, he was encouraged to set up his own court and dispossessed Mata Sundari, who in turn set up her own *sajjada* during the reign of Farrukhsiyar. It adds that many Nanakpanthis followed her, the number increasing after the execution of Ajit Singh; after Mata Sundari's death, the text continues, she was succeeded by Mata Sahib Devi. There is no evidence in Sikh sources that either of the Matas ever assumed the status of Guru, although letters of command (*hukamnamas*) to *sangats* in Patna, Benares and Punjab are extant (Ganda Singh 1985: 196–231).[9] In any case, the two Matas based themselves in Delhi, a city in which Khatris were presumably prominent in the Nanakpanthi community: this would seem to indicate the importance of Khatris in their following, whatever its nature.

After Ajit Singh's death, his son Hathi Singh moved to Mathura, another city where Khatri traders can be assumed to have been prominent members of the Sikh community. He seems not to have enjoyed a very wide following, though, since Rai Chaturman admits that (AH 1172 1759–60) although 'all Sikhs had no one to worship but Hathi Singh' he had only a few hundred followers.[10] Hathi Singh is said to have died in Burhanpur, an entrepôt town whose Sikh community was again largely Khatri, and his funeral monument (*samadhi*) is located there (G.B. Singh 1944: 325–26). Written in AH 1826 1769, Kesar Singh Chhibbar's *Bansavalinama* supports some of these details: according to the text, Ajit Singh lived in Delhi and was guru for sixteen years, his son Hathi Singh sitting on his *gaddi* after his death (12:103). Kesar Singh thus places the beginning of Ajit Singh's supposed tenure as guru at the death of Guru Gobind Singh in 1708. Elsewhere, Chhibbar notes that Ajit Singh's followers tried to build and occupy a *bunga*[11] in the premises of the Darbar Sahib at Amritsar but concludes that after VS 1788 1731 they were largely confined to Delhi alone (13:22–23, 33). Kesar Singh's *gurpranali*, in turn, lists the length of the guruships of Ajit Singh and Hathi Singh (Randhir Singh 1977: 121–22). The consensus of these eighteenth-century sources, then, seems to be that a number of urban Nanakpanthis – most of them probably urban Khatris – tried with limited success to extend the line of human Gurus beyond Guru Gobind Singh.

Despite their having provided the evidence that some in the Nanakpanthi community tried to continue the line of human Gurus, there is some evidence that both Rai Chaturman and Kesar Singh are somewhat ambivalent about this attempt to extend the Guruship. In his *Bansavalinama*, Kesar Singh states clearly that there were only ten Gurus and that Guru Gobind Singh passed on the Guruship to the Granth and the Khalsa, later adding that the Dasam Granth is to be considered Guru as well (10:679–84, 14:264, 14:268). He includes in his text no independent account of Mata Sundari, and is reluctant to name Mata Sahib Devi as guru. Further, when speaking of the murders committed by the 'Turks', he separates the killings of the Gurus and their children from those of Banda and Ajit Singh, both of whom he refers to as having been 'sent by the Guru' (12:101–2). Similarly, while he admits that some Sikhs viewed Banda as the eleventh guru, he insists that Banda was not in fact a guru but is instead among those who live forever (11:12–13, 12:1). Despite this adherence to the orthodox narrative of ten human Gurus, Kesar Singh also notes that 'First the *sangat* used to go to the Presence [of Guru Gobind Singh], then they started going to Banda. Then large congregations of thousands of Sikhs started coming to the courts of Ajit Singh and Mata' (12:88). His narration of the life of Mata Sundari includes the comment that after Guru Gobind Singh's death 'she sat on the throne in the Guru's court' (13:2) and ends by remarking that after her death and that of her servants 'everything slowly passed away, and it became the Panth's turn' (13:35).

The same ambivalence is present in Rai Chaturman's text, which precedes its account of the Matas and Ajit Singh with the comment that after Guru Gobind Singh the Sikhs 'do not believe in others who sat on the *sajjada* although many respect them.'[12] It is unclear whether the *Chahar Gulshan's* ambivalence stems from Rai Chaturman's inability to distinguish different strands of the Nanakpanthi community or from divided loyalties within some sections of the Nanakpanth itself. Certainly, a Mughal document from the reign of Bahadur Shah states that some Sikhs had faith in Ajit Singh, while others did not.[13] Firm in its doctrine of only ten human Gurus, the Khalsa exhibited no such ambivalence.

## Khalsa metanarrative and the Dasam Granth

It should come as no surprise in the context of such social rifts in the Nanakpanthi community that the formation of the Khalsa seems also to have been marked by an equally striking discursive rupture. While pre-Khalsa Sikh discourse seems to have participated in the shared inheritance of Indic cosmologies and temporalities that characterised much of contemporary north Indian society, a significant strand was characterised by a high degree of eclecticism. This polysemy is most visible in the syncretic plurality of names for the Supreme Deity in the tradition – from Ram to Rahim in the celebrated formation. These various discursive strands are most clearly visible in the *janamsakhis* of Guru Nanak's life, a result of the mélange of sources that went into their creation. Harjot Oberoi has noted the fluid image of the Guru that emerges from the *janamsakhis* (Oberoi 1994: 55–56), an image most memorable in its visualisation of Nanak in the dress of Hindu ascetic (*sadhu*) and Muslim mendicant (*faqir*) accompanied by his companions, one Hindu and one Muslim.

While the Khalsa did not entirely reject the Nanakpanthi discursive universe, it did centre itself more firmly in a 'Puranic' universe than the early Nanakpanthi tradition had. The source of this Puranic metanarrative was the Dasam Granth, a compendium of theological, mythological and narrative works attributed to Guru Gobind Singh. Twentieth-century scholars have debated at length the issue of whether the mythological and the occasionally racy narrative works can in fact be attributed to Guru Gobind Singh, but the issue need not concern us here: what is important for our purposes is that in the pre-Singh Sabha period most Sikhs seem to have accorded the text reverence based on the presumption that it was in fact the work of the tenth Guru. One extant manuscript of the Dasam Granth contains portions of the text said to have been written by Guru Gobind Singh's court scribes in VS 1752 1695–96, while another at Takht Sri Harimandir Sahib, Patna bears the completion date Asar *vadi* 1, VS 1755 14 June 1698.[14] By 1724, the *Charitropakhyan* compilation of tales was in sufficient demand for it to be copied as a separate volume intended to be carried in a quiver,[15] and by 1745 the Puranic portions of the text seem to have gained a substantial measure of popularity. In that year, the writer and Mughal courtier Anand Ram 'Mukhlis' quotes a line from the *Nihkalanki Avtar* section of the Granth in one of his Persian works (Mukhlis 47).[16] Since Anand Ram was a Punjabi Khatri, his familiarity with the Dasam Granth would seem to indicate that its metanarrative had a hold on the Khatri scribal classes of Delhi and other urban centres as well as on the Khalsa. Writing in 1769, Kesar Singh Chhibbar states that the Dasam Granth was to be considered Guru along with the Adi Granth (14:268), and in the early nineteenth century it was placed next to the Adi Granth at meetings of the Panth at Amritsar that passed resolutions in the Guru's name (*gurmatas*) (Malcolm 1812: 120, 173). During the reign of Maharaja Ranjit Singh, the Dasam Granth was taken in procession along with the Adi Granth whenever Maharaja Ranjit Singh or his nobles travelled (Ali ud-Din 2:59).

Beyond the obvious theme of devotion to the Supreme Being, a number of broad motifs recur throughout the text of the Dasam Granth. The most prominent of these is the theme of warfare and conflict, which occupies pride of place in the text's versions of the lives of Chandi, Ram, Krishna and Guru Gobind Singh. A corollary of this focus on warfare is the text's tendency to visualise the Deity as weaponry (and vice versa), most notably in the invocations to *Bachittar Natak* and *Akal Ustati* and at length in the text of the *Shastra Nam Mala*:

I bow to the sword with heart and mind:
Give me your help that I may finish this book.

(Bachitar Natak, DG 11)

Akal Purakh protects me; the All-Steels protects me.
The Destroyer of All protects me; the All-Steel always protects me.

(Akal Ustati, DG 39)

The arrow is You the spear You, You the axe and sword;
Whoever repeats your name has crossed the ocean of existence.

(Shastra nam mala, DG 717)

The major continuous narrative in the Dasam Granth is the narrative of the martial exploits of Chandi and the *avtars* of Vishnu, Brahma and Rudra, the importance of which has been somewhat obscured by modern antipathy to these portions of the text. Some idea of the centrality of this narrative to the Dasam Granth and of the hierarchy of discourses in the text can be formed by reference to early manuscripts. There seem to have been at least five major variant eighteenth century recensions of the Dasam Granth, each of which had a different order and some of whose contents were somewhat different than the modern printed version.[17] Each of the manuscripts preserves an arrangement in which *Jap*, a composition in praise of Akal Purakh, heads the volume, while the Sangrur and Patna texts follow it with further compositions in praise of the Formless One. Significantly, all the volumes then have a cluster containing the *avtar* texts, beginning in each case with the text now referred to as *Bachitar Natak*. In three of the four recensions considered here, one or both of the *Chandi Charitras* is placed next. After this follows the *Chaubis Avtar* narrating the twenty-four incarnations of Vishnu and the *Brahma Avtar* and *Rudra Avtar* describing the incarnations of those deities.

*Table 1.* Contents of eighteenth century Dasam Granth manuscripts.[18]

| Mani Singh | Moti Bagh | Sangrur | Patna |
|---|---|---|---|
| Jap | Jap | Jap | Jap |
| Bachitar Natak | Bachitar Natak | Shastra Nam Mala | Shastra Nam Mala |
| Chandi Charitra 1 | Chandi Charitra 1 | Akal Ustati | 32 Savayyas |
| Chandi Charitra 2 | Chandi Charitra 2 | Bachitar Natak | Bachitar Natak |
| Chaubis Avtar | Chaubis Avtar | Chandi Charitra 2 | ChaubisAvtar[19] |
| Brahma Avtar | Brahma Avtar | Chaubis Avtar | Gian Prabodh |
| Rudra Avtar | Rudra Avtar | Brahma Avtar | Chandi Charitra 2 |
| | | Rudra Avtar[20] | Rudra Avtar |

In both the published text of the Dasam Granth and the eighteenth-century manuscripts (Jaggi 1965: 73–76), the rubrics at the end of *Bachitar Natak, Chandi Charitra 2, Chaubis Avtar, Brahma Avtar* and *Rudra Avtar* all state that the texts are part of the *Bachitar Natak Granth*. Modern exegesis, on the other hand, understands only the portion of the text containing the account of Guru Gobind Singh's life, referred to in the text itself as *Apni Katha* ('My own story'), to be *Bachitar Natak*, viewing all the rest of the compositions as independent from it. Restoring the intended unity of this extended *Bachitar Natak Granth* yields an organic whole which progresses from praises of Akal Purakh through an account of the life of Guru Gobind Singh to Chandi and the incarnations of Vishnu, Brahma and Rudra. In this extended text, the Puranic *avtar* narratives are subordinate to the text's account of the life of Guru Gobind Singh. In this context, *Bachitar Natak*'s contention that Gobind Singh was sent from his devotions on the peak of Hemkunt to this world as the son of Akal Purakh 'to propagate the Panth, spread *dharma* everywhere and keep people from foolishness' (DG 57) becomes part of a larger mythical and cosmological narrative of incarnations dominated by warfare and contests with demons. Like the incarnations of the gods in other ages, then, Guru Gobind Singh has taken birth to continue the cosmic struggle between good and evil.[21] Indeed, the text's statement of the Guru's mission consciously evokes Krishna's explanation of his *avtars* in the text of the *Bhagvadgita*:

> I came into the world for this purpose: the Lord sent me for the
>   sake of *dharma*:
> 'Spread *dharma* everywhere and seize the evil and slanderers and
>   destroy them.'
> Understand, virtuous ones, that I took birth for this reason:
> To propagate *dharma* and save the *sants*, and to uproot evil
>   doers.[22]

(DG 57–8)

According to the grand narrative of the Dasam Granth, then, at the centre of Khalsa self-construction lie the worship of weapons and the perception of partaking in the Guru's mission to reestablish *dharma*, a mission that is itself embedded in a wider cosmological cycle of battles against evil that extends back into mythical time. At the same time, the Khalsa's own context places a new burden on the narrative: Khalsa praxis rejects and redefines the traditional notion of *dharma*. Early *gurbilas* texts such as Sainapati's *Sri Gur Sobha* broaden this Khalsa reinterpretation of *dharma* by adding to it the imperative to win political sovereignty, in this case over Anandpur:

> *Siddhas*, devotees, *sants* and *mahants*[23] will joyfully sing praises;
> Hearing them, ghosts, spirits, demons and fairies will repeat the
>   formula and find salvation.

33

> The music of rejoicing will play happily in every home.
> You will be fortunate in that moment: we will reinhabit the fort
>   of Anandpur (19:12).

The last line of the verse – and of seven of the other eleven in the
*adhyay* – is itself a reference to the Dasam Granth: its first half is a
modification of the refrain of *Nihkalanki avtar*'s account of the
coming of Vishnu's final incarnation, whose birth will lead to a new
Satiyuga. According to *Sri Gur Sobha*, then, the establishment of
the Khalsa's rule is intended to fulfill the Puranic metanarrative of the
*Bachitar Natak* by marking the beginning of a new era.

The various strands of Khalsa discourse come together rather
dramatically in a letter from Banda to the *sangat* of Jaunpur. The letter
reads:

> You are Akal Purakh's Khalsa. Put on the five weapons and
> come to the presence in accordance with this command. Follow
> the *rahit* of the Khalsa: do not consume cannabis, tobacco,
> opium, poppy, alcohol or any other intoxicant. Do not eat meat,
> fish or onions. Do not thieve or have illicit sexual relations. We
> have created the Satiyug. The Guru will assist whoever follows
> the Khalsa's *rahit*. Dated Poh 12 the first year.
>
> (*Ganda Singh* 1985: 194–5)

Many familiar elements of Khalsa discourse appear here: an
insistence on the *rahit*, an attention to weapons, and the contention
that the Khalsa enjoys the special favour of Akal Purakh. Most
interesting of all, though, is the letter's insistence that 'we have
created the Satiyug', that the promise implicit in the Dasam
Granth's Puranic metanarrative has been turned into reality.
Unfortunately, the letter does not attempt to describe the features
of the Satiyug beyond its injunctions to follow the Khalsa *rahit* and
refrain from anti-social behaviour. The letter is dated 'the first year'
rather than by the usual *vikrami* calendar, most probably in
imitation of the imperial practice of giving the regnal year of the
incumbent emperor on official documents. The tone of the letter
implies, however, that the date on the document is also to be taken
as the first year of a new Satiyug as much as of a new reign.[24] That
Banda should choose such explicitly Indic symbolism is interesting
in the light of his reported attempts to induce Jai Singh of Amber to
join him in *dharamyudh* against the Muslims[25] and his strong links
with mendicants and 'Hindu' religious establishments (Alam 1993:

153). It is almost paradigmatic in the light of its Khalsa precedents and antecedents.

## Community formation and narrative in eighteenth century *Rahitnamas*

While the central narrative of the Dasam Granth and the Indic resonances of Banda's letter demonstrate the extent to which Khalsa discourse was embedded in a broader cultural universe, a significant strand of eighteenth century Khalsa discourse spurned these wider associations. The defining texts of the eighteenth century Khalsa are the *rahitnamas*, the codes of conduct written by and largely for the Khalsa. While some *rahitnamas* discuss the relationship between Khalsa and non-Khalsa Sikhs or define some of the rituals of non-Khalsa life, their main concern remains the Khalsa, its rituals and the minutiae of its everyday life. As such, these texts are probably the closest we can get to an exclusively Khalsa discourse, moderated by and influential upon the Khalsa itself. Although most of the extant *rahitnamas* present themselves as having been written during the lifetime of Guru Gobind Singh, these claims seem somewhat difficult to accept. Indeed, some of the texts appear to be late eighteenth or nineteenth century productions.[26] In the absence of a solid basis upon which to date the entire corpus of texts, I will here consider the three *rahitnamas* for which eighteenth-century exemplars exist: the *Tankhahnama* attributed to Bhai Nand Lal, extant in a manuscript dated VS 1775 1718–19, and the *rahitnama* attributed to Chaupa Singh with its appended *Sakhi Rahit Patshahi 10* (also attributed to Nand Lal), found in a no longer extant manuscript dated VS 1821 1765.[27] Before the discovery of the 1775 VS manuscript introduced in this paper, the *Tankhahnama* was generally believed to be a late eighteenth or nineteenth century production (McLeod 1989: 37; McLeod 1982: 117). Although the *Tankhahnama* is therefore the earliest extant dated *rahitnama*, the length and detailed nature of the Chaupa Singh text means that much of what follows will necessarily derive from it.

Each of the *rahitnamas* begins by highlighting those concerns which it believes to be central to the definition of a member of the Khalsa and the community of which he is a part. For the *Tankhahnama*, this means recognising that the central duties (*karam*) of a Sikh are attachment to the ideal of *nam dan isnan*[28] and obedience

35

to the Word (*bani*). At the centre of Sikh identity is the community of believers, constituted through worship and commensality:

> Whoever doesn't go to the assembly of true believers (*satisang*) in the morning will be called a great reprobate;
> Whoever allows his mind to wander in the *satisang* will not find a place in this world or the next.
> Gobind Singh says that whoever speaks while listening to the praises of Hari will go to the city of the god of death (Yam).
> He will be called a complete reprobate who does not sit the poor man next to him.
> Whoever speaks of anything but knowledge of the Word (*shabad*) will obtain nothing.
> Whoever does not bow his head at the end of a recital of the Word will not meet the Supreme Lord.
> Whoever is greedy when giving out sacramental food (*prasad*), a little here and a lot there, will always experience sorrow.
>
> (*Tn* 56)

The *Sakhi Rahit* with its characteristic stress on the separateness of the Khalsa and the need to reinterpret the discourse of Indic life-cycles is rather more laconic in its definition of a Sikh: 'He who is my Sikh will believe in nothing but the Khalsa. Worship nowhere but where the *shabad* is, and do not go to memorials for the dead (*marhis*) or cremation grounds. Do not take instruction from a pandit, ritual priest, Muslim or *mahant*. Take instruction only from the Guru' (*SR* 133).

As is perhaps to be expected with a text of its length and detail, the Chaupa Singh *rahitnama* manages to embody in its initial definition of a Sikh many of the central themes of the eighteenth-century *rahitnamas*' discourses of community formation. After situating the *rahit* within the context of the *bani* through scriptural quotation, the text outlines the daily duties of a Sikh, '*kesdhari* or *sahajdhari*':[29] he is to bathe, recite the *bani* and join the *sangat* at the *dharamsala*. Returning home, he should either feed a Sikh or keep aside a portion of food to give away. In the evening, he should again recite the *bani* before going to the *dharamsala*, being careful after his return home not to soil the first of the last quarters of the night by having sexual relations with his wife.[30] In the last quarter of the night, he should clean his teeth, bathe and recite the *bani* again. His daily routine, therefore, is intended to supplement a strong focus on personal purity and discipline with communal worship; put another way, the purified

36

Sikh is enjoined to renew his bond with the community of Sikhs at least twice a day. Significantly, the *rahitnama* follows its explication of the daily duties of a Sikh with a warning against associating with the five reprobate groups (*panj mel*), here defined as the Minas, Ramrayyas, Dhirmalias, *masands* and the followers of *masands* (CS 57–58). If the Sikh is to create a bond with his fellows through his worship and actions, the *rahitnama* is keen at the same time to delineate sharply and with immediacy the boundaries of the community: all those who have contested or opposed the orthodox line of Gurus are to be spurned. The Khalsa is, therefore, a community which defines itself as much by exclusion as by fellowship.

This rhetoric of definition by exclusion lies at the heart of the eighteenth century *rahitnamas*. The Chaupa Singh text stresses that in giving his Sikhs sword baptism (*khande ki pahul*), Guru Gobind Singh was 'separating out the Panth', although it does not specify from whom (CS 82–83). The text's numerous injunctions against associating with or trusting Muslims and its repeated renarrations of Muslim treacheries make it clear that the Panth is to be completely aloof from Muslims. The early *rahitnamas* are equally insistent that the Khalsa must keep itself separate from the realms of popular piety and Brahman-centred ritual as well. The *Sakhi rahit*, for example, repeatedly warns Sikhs against following or reverencing Brahmans, also forbidding them to worship tombs, repeat the *gayatri* or perform worship of deities (*puja*) (SR 133–38). Instead, the ritual universe of the Khalsa is to centre around the *shabad*, and the Sikh sacred universe around pilgrimages to sites associated with the lives of the Gurus (CS 72).

The presence of *sahajdharis* within the wider Panth problematizes and sharpens this rhetoric of distinctiveness. For the compiler of the Chaupa Singh text, the shaven Sikh (*mona*) is ritually impure compared to the *kesdhari*: thus, the *kesdhari* is instructed not to drink from a *mona*'s vessel without cleansing it and not to distribute food at gatherings of *monas* (106–7). His solution is to offer the *sahajdhari* a latitude not available to the *kesdhari* Sikh: he is permitted to wear the forehead mark (*tikka*) and sacred thread (*janeu*) and may conduct non-Khalsa funeral rites, although he is enjoined to give them a Sikh colouring by reading from the Granth and feeding Sikhs (CS 60, 63). It would seem, then, that the boundary between the Khalsa and the Nanakpanth is to be as firm as that between the Khalsa and the non-Sikh world. Indeed, the Chaupa Singh text repeatedly insists that the *rahit* and the Guru's message are not to be preached to outsiders: it states that its contents 'are directed to Sikhs, not to the world', adding that 'these techniques, *rahits* and punishments are directed to the Guru's Sikhs, not to *sevaks* or the worldly' (*CS* 78, 114).[31] By excluding both non-Sikhs and non-Khalsa Sikhs from the Khalsa's sacred universe, the *rahitnamas* buttress its distinctiveness and ensure that it remains the territory of the Khalsa alone.

The most prominent marker or sign of the Khalsa's distinctiveness is, of course, the *rahit's* insistence that each Singh bear arms and keep his hair long. Not only does this mark out a Singh as a member of the Khalsa community but it also inscribes a collective narrative on his body. Explicitly and ostensibly a political discourse, this narrative places both the individual Singh and the community within a number of temporal frameworks and systems of meaning at once. On the one hand, the marking of the Singh's body inserts him into the historical narrative of the formation of the Khalsa, which explains the very existence of the *rahit* he follows and enjoins upon him a duty to remain distinct: on the other, it inserts him into a vision of the future which promises sovereignty to the Panth. The path to political sovereignty, in turn, eventually reintroduces the Khalsa into mythological time, since the Khalsa metanarrative is part of a cosmic cycle that inevitably leads to the depths of Kaliyug and the destruction of moral and social order. This dual narrative is reflected in the structure of the Chaupa Singh *rahitnama* itself: a self-contained explication of the *rahit* is followed by the story of the formation of the Khalsa, leading to a second explication of the *rahit* as a collection of prohibitions and a concluding section that narrates the chaos to come.

As is to be expected, the Chaupa Singh text contains a fuller expression of the narratives that surround the formation of the Khalsa than the other two *rahitnamas* under consideration. According to the text, the Guru's anger that his Sikhs were able to hide themselves at the martyrdom of his father causes him to dictate a new identity for his followers. His determination to prevent his Sikhs from being able to hide themselves in future leads him to create the Khalsa: '[Guru Gobind Singh] said, "A Singh is he who bears weapons." In this way, the Lord began to separate out the Panth. *Kes* was given as the symbol of faith (*sikhi*). The words he had spoken in anger were fulfilled' (*CS* 83). At this point the compiler of the text inserts a number of injunctions regarding weapons, ending with a statement of the narrative contract that those weapons imply:

38

The Lord desires warfare. The *kes* and weapons he has given are for the sake of warfare. If they fight, they will obtain rule (*raj*). ... He will take revenge on the barbarian (*mlecchh*) Turks by giving *raj* to the Panth. The Turks have tangled with the Guru's people from the very beginning. A Singh or Sikh is he who takes revenge on behalf of the Guru (*CS* 85).

Just as in the Chaupa Singh text the ultimate meaning of the Khalsa is its pursuit of political sovereignty, the theme of the Khalsa's military prowess and its eventual attainment of sovereignty forms the much quoted climax of the *Tankhahnama*:

> He is a Khalsa who rides a horse. He is a Khalsa who always fights.
> He is a Khalsa who bears weapons. He is a Khalsa who kills the Turk.[32]
> He is a Khalsa who protects *dharma*.[33] He is a Khalsa who has an umbrella over his head.
>
> . . .
>
> The Khalsa will rule and no one will be against it:
> All will be destroyed, save those who seek its protection.[34]

The inscription of Khalsa identity on the body of the individual Sikh, then, marks each member of the Khalsa with a narrative that links him to his past at the same time as it promises him a glorious future. In turn, he is to attend to his weapons, fight bravely when called upon to do so and ensure that the Khalsa remains distinct.

## Conclusion

The inscription of narrative on the body of the individual Khalsa Sikh assimilates him into a collective identity at the same time as it inserts him into the Khalsa metanarrative. These acts in turn place the individual Khalsa Sikh – and through him the community – within a number of temporal and narrative frameworks at once: the historical entailments of the narrative of the formation of the Khalsa enjoin it to be distinct, while the Puranic metanarrative of the Dasam Granth situates the Panth within a longer mythological time-cycle in which it is part of a larger design to fight the forces of evil. Most early texts express this cosmic struggle in terms of the Indic notion of the re-establishment of *dharma*, although the Khalsa's construction of the term differs from the usual classical conception. In particular, the Khalsa notion of *dharma* valorizes ideas of rule and political sovereignty in a way that classical definitions and others contemporary to the Khalsa do not. This stress on the struggle for political sovereignty is unusual if not unique in the north Indian religious context of the period and transcends the usual strategies of Indic identity formation to embrace wider political and cosmological claims. As such, this reinterpretation of *dharma* must lie at the heart of any explanation of the Khalsa's distinctiveness as surely as it forms the discursive context within which the eighteenth century history of the Khalsa is to be read. A fuller understanding of this notion and the concepts allied with it must form an essential part of any discussion of the formation of Khalsa identity.

# Notes

1  Although *Sri Gur sobha* seems to be an eighteenth century production, the actual date of its composition is far from clear. The text itself states that it was composed on Bhadau *sudi* 15, VS 1758 1701 (*adhyay* 1:6), although it contains events up to Guru Gobind Singh's death in 1708. Writing in 1882, Bava Sumer Singh dates the composition of the text to VS 1768 1711 (Bava Sumer Singh 1882: 713), while Akali Kaur Singh suggests in his 1927 and 1935 editions of *Sri Gur Sobha* that the word *athavan* ('fifty-eight') in the line containing the date be amended to read *athanav* ('ninety-eight'), yielding the date VS 1798 1741 (Ganda Singh 1980: 22). The manuscript evidence is inconclusive: Ganda Singh does not identify the manuscripts on which his edition is based so their dates are uncertain (Ganda Singh 1980), and 'Ashok' uses two undated manuscripts which he states elsewhere are from the nineteenth century (Ashok 1967:8 and Ashok 1968: 348–49). *Sri Gur Sobha* itself does not contain the name of its author, and it may well be that the source of the attribution to Sainapati is also Bava Sumer Singh. Two texts which do identify their author as Sainapati are extant in manuscript, a translation of the *Chanakya Rajniti* and a medical text known as the *Sukhsain* or *Sukhchain Granth* (a translation of the Sanskrit *Ram Vinod*). Both identify their author as a Man Jat and speak of his association with the Guru's court (see for example Punjabi University, Patiala ms. 90284, f. 22a and Guru Nanak Dev University, Amritsar ms. 596, ff. 1b–2a respectively). Verse references to *Sri Gur Sobha* are to the 'Ashok' edition throughout. Common era dates are given according to the Julian calendar before 2 September 1752 and according to the Gregorian calendar from that date onward.

2 Usually written as *bhaddan*, the term also refers to the shaving of a child's head during the sacred thread ceremony. In this context, it is usually referred to as *mundan*.

3 *Sant*: one who knows the truth, pious person.

4 It may also be the case that the branding of offenders against the *rahit* as *tankhahias* (those who draw a government salary) by both the Chaupa Singh text and later Khalsa tradition stems in part from ambivalence to the presumably largely Khatri contingent of Sikhs in government service.

5 For Sita Ram's text, see British Museum ms. Or. 2762, ff. 168–83; for Saundha, see Randhir Singh (1977: 90–8) and Guru Nanak Dev University, Amritsar ms. 824, ff. 289b–95a.

6 For texts which enumerate a line of ten Gurus but do not nominate a successor, see: two anonymous texts published by Randhir Singh (1977: 123–31, 143–61); Ram Singh, *Satigur ka Vansu Varnanam* (Randhir Singh 1977: 233–39); Shivdayal, *Gurpranali* (Guru Nanak Dev University, Amritsar ms. 291); *Sir Gur Jas Panchasika* (Guru Nanak Dev University, Amritsar ms. 571, ff. 1a–13b); *Gur Bansavali* (Guru Nanak Dev University, Amritsar ms. 571 ff. 14a–18a); Gian Singh, *Gurpranali*, dated 1930 VS/1873–74 (Guru Nanak Dev University, Amritsar ms. 28); and four anonymous undated texts (Punjabi University, Patiala ms. 115037; Guru Nanak Dev University, Amritsar ms. 1171; Punjab State Archives, Patiala ms. 386 and Punjab State Archives, Patiala ms. 887). For texts which name the Khalsa alone as Guru Gobind Singh's successor, see four anonymous texts: a text published by Randhir Singh (1977: 123–31); Guru Nanak Dev University, Amritsar ms. 605, ff. 202a–3a; Punjab State Archives, Patiala ms. 396, ff. 266a–71b; and Punjab State Archives, Patiala ms. 684, ff. 213b–15a. For texts which name the Guru Granth alone, see: Kavi Gulab Singh, *Gurpranali* with its prose commentary (Randhir Singh 1977: 164–210, 211–32) and Kavi Tara Singh, *Sri Guru Nanakadi Ista Vansavali*, Guru Nanak Dev University, Amritsar ms. 18. For a text which nominates both the Guru Granth and the Khalsa, see Guru Nanak Dev University, Amritsar ms. 605, ff. 201a–2a. Most of these manuscripts appear to be nineteenth century texts.

7 For a brief note on the early roots and consequences of this conception, see Deol 1998: 174. Compare also the *Apni Katha* portion of *Bachitar Natak* in the Dasam Granth, which attributes the Sodhi Guruship to a boon promised to the Sodhis by the forebears of Guru Nanak (Dasam Granth 53–54). For a very general treatment of self-proclaimed successors of Guru Gobind Singh to the late nineteenth century, see Ganda Singh 1946.

8 The term *sajjada*, literally 'prayer carpet', usually symbolises the succession to a Sufi *shaikh*, the successor being known as the *sajjada-nashin*, 'he who sits on the prayer carpet'. Both terms are used to designate the orthodox succession of the Sikh Gurus in seventeenth and eighteenth century Persian texts, for example in Sujan Rai Bhandari's *Khulasat ut-Tavarikh* (written in 1696) and Rai Chaturman's *Chahar Gulshan* (Sujan Rai 69–70; BM Ms. Or. 1791, f. 128b). Punjabi texts often use the term *gaddi* ('cushion, throne') in the same context as Persian documents use *sajjada*.

9 None of the extant letters attributed to the Matas refers to them as Guru. Ganda Singh publishes a letter dated sometime in the VS 1780s (from the period 1723–32) in which Mata Sahib Devi admonishes members of the Phulkian family for ceasing to send contributions and attaching themselves to Mata Sundari alone (Ganda Singh 1985: 209). Since he does not give a photograph of the letter, it is impossible to determine whether or not it is authentic.

10 British Museum ms. Or. 1791, ff. 129a–30a. There are a number of references to Ajit Singh in Mughal court newsletters (akhbarat), some of which imply that as Banda's rebellion became more serious, the imperial authorities attempted to use Ajit Singh to garner support. The court newsletter of 30 October 1708 records the grant of a dress of mourning (khil'at-i matami) to the son of 'Gobind Rao Nanakpanthi'. An undated document reporting the Khalsa's occupation of Sarhind suggests that patronage be extended to Ajit Singh and 'the family of Guru Gobind Singh', presumably to use their influence to draw their followers away from Banda. Ajit Singh was brought to the emperor on 26 September 1710 by Raja Chhatarsal Bundela and remained in the custody of various nobles until 30 December 1710, when he was released and granted Chak Guru (modern Amritsar) (Ganda Singh transcriptions of Jaipur akhbarat, Punjabi University, Patiala ms. 332176, ff. 34, 123–4, 48, 64–5, 88, 115). This grant seems to have been an attempt to increase his standing in the Nanakpanthi community. According to Muzaffar Alam, the strategy was tried again on 16 August 1715, when Ajit Singh was granted a fresh khil'at-i matami by Farrukhsiyar, which 'signified the extension of official patronage to those who could possibly be put against Banda' (Alam 1993: 175). He appears to have remained in contact with the imperial court, since he is mentioned in connection with a hunt on 7 August 1716 (Punjabi University, Patiala ms. 332176, f. 200). Mirza Muhammad Harisi's Tarikh-i Muhammadi (c.1748) records that 'Guru Ajit Singh' was executed 'for rebellion' on 4 Jamadi ul-avval 1137 AH/8 January 1725 (Mirza Muhammad 55), while two Adi Granth manuscripts formerly at Purani Sangat, Burhanpur recorded Ajit Singh's death date as Friday, Magh sudi 5 VS 1781 (G.B. Singh 1944: 330–1). The latter date appears to be of the elapsed year (gat samvat) since Magh sudi 5 VS 1780 was a Sunday but Magh sudi 5 VS 1781 (gat samvat 1780) corresponds to Friday 8 January 1725. According to the Chahar Gulshan, Ajit Singh was captured by the troops of Qamar ud-Din I'timad ud-Daula for killing a Muslim faqir and executed by being tied to the foot of an elephant in AH 1134 in the fourth regnal year of Muhammad Shah, corresponding to 1722 (BM Ms. Or. 1791, f. 129a). Kesar Singh states that Ajit Singh died of fright in VS 1780 1723–24 after being captured by imperial troops for the offence of killing a faqir (12:89–99). For a traditional Sikh account of Ajit Singh and Hathi Singh, see Santokh Singh's Sri Gurpratap Suraj Granth, ain 2, ansu 28–34 (Santokh Singh 6352–85).

11 A resthouse or mansion built around the Darbar Sahib to accommodate pilgrims and visitors, often containing an educational establishment.

12 BM ms. Or. 1791, f. 129a.

13 The document is an undated addendum to an *akhbar* containing a brief account of the Khalsa. It erroneously identifies Ajit Singh as the actual son of Guru Gobind Singh and notes that he had received a *khil'at* from the emperor before coming to Delhi with 'the family of Guru Gobind Singh' (Ganda Singh transcript of Jaipur *akhbarat*, Punjabi University, Patiala ms. 332176, f. 122).

14 The first manuscript, referred to in the literature as the 'Anandpuri *bir*', seems to consist of texts of individual compositions written by a number of scribes, some of whom may have been scribes from Guru Gobind Singh's court. Some portions of the manuscript appear to be in a later hand, and the following portions are reported to be in the hand of court scribes: *Krishna Avtar, Chandi Charitra* 1, *Chandi Charitra* 2, *Charitropakhyan* and the miscellaneous verses (*asphotak chhand*). The manuscript is said to have been given to a reader of the scriptures (*granthi*) at Maharaja Ranjit Singh's court whose son was the tutor of Maharaja Dalip Singh. The manuscripts subsequently travelled to Amritsar, Sangrur and finally Mumbai (Padam 1982: 28–30; Balbir Singh 1967: 162–6; Jaggi 1990: 11). The fullest description of the manuscript is a report compiled by Mahan Singh on 1 January 1957 entitled *Dasam Granth di Hazuri Bir di Riport (kujh bhag 1752 da likhat)*, Dr. Balbir Singh Sahitya Kendra, Dehra Dun ms. 269. I saw the second manuscript at Takht Sri Harimandir Sahib, Patna in November 1998 but was not able to examine it in detail. It is thus unclear whether the text actually dates from 1698 or is a later production.

15 Panjab University, Chandigarh ms. 783 is a small-sized volume of the *Charitropakhyan* that its colophon describes as '*tarkas ki pothi*' (presumably meaning a volume to be carried in a quiver). The colophon states that the volume was completed by Chhona Singh on 6 Vaisakh 1780 VS/1723 (f. 842a). It adds the corroborating date 'in the fifth year of Muhammad Shah's reign', which also yields the year 1723, since the beginning of the first regnal year of Muhammad Shah was fixed on the date of Farrukhsiyar's deposition on 19 February 1719 rather than of the date of Muhammad Shah's formal ascension to the throne on 28 September 1719. Padam notes that one of Guru Gobind Singh's court scribes was named Chhauna Singh (Padam 1976: 256), although it is of course unclear whether this volume was written by the same individual.

16 In describing the mosque of Sambhal, Anand Ram notes that the Hindi quotation '*bhaga bade sambhala ke ki haraji hara mandala avenge*' refers to the building, which had been converted from a Shiva temple known as the 'Har Mandal' during the reign of Akbar. The line '*bhalu bhaga bhaya iha sambhala ke haraji hara mandala avahinge*' is the refrain of *savayyas* 141–56 in the published text of *Nihkalanki Avtar* in the *Chaubis Avtar* (DG 581–3).

17 For descriptions of the individual manuscripts comprising four of the main recensions, see Jaggi 1964. The Moti Bagh and Sangrur manuscripts no longer appear to be extant.

18 The first three columns of the table are based on Jaggi 1965: 345–6. I have based the fourth column on two manuscripts I saw at Takht Sri Harimandir Sahib, Patna in November 1998, the first the 1755 VS/1698

text and the second an undated eighteenth-century volume. I have only included in the table the portion of each text up to the last of the *avtar* compositions. I have not included the 'Anandpuri *bir*' since Mahan Singh's description of the text raises the possibility that the major portion of the text may have been written by a later hand (*Dasam Granth di Hazuri Bir*, 9, 14–15).

19 *Chandi Charitra* 1 has been included in the text of the *Krishna Avtar* section of *Chaubis Avtar*.

20 This section of the text is incomplete (Jaggi 1965: 346).

21 The text itself anticipates the danger of extending the metaphor and equating Guru Gobind Singh with Akal Purakh: it warns that 'Those who call me Parmesur will fall into the pit of hell' (DG 57).

22 Compare *Bhagvadgita* 4:7–8:

> *yada yada hi dharmasya glanir bhavati bharata*
> *abhyutthanam adharmasya tad atmanam srjamy aham*
> *paritranaya sadhunam vinashaya cha duskrtam*
> *dharmasamsthapanarthaya sambhavami yuge yuge*
> Whenever *dharma* is in decline
> And *adharma* rises up, O Bharata, I create myself.
> I take form in *yuga* after *yuga* for the protection of the good (*sadhu*),
> The destruction of the evil doers and the firm establishment of *dharma*.

23 *Siddha*s: the eighty-four personages said to have attained immortality, often conflated with the Nath *yogi*s; *mahant*: the head of a religious institution.

24 Ganda Singh takes the date of the letter to be 12 Poh VS 1767 12 December 1710, implying that the sack of Sarhind in May 1710 marked the beginning of Khalsa rule (1985: 194–5). Unlike the extant letters of the Gurus and the Matas, Banda's letter bears a seal, itself a declaration of political significance. An undated news report from the reign of Bahadur Shah notes among the 'strange practices' of the Khalsa the facts that they are said to have struck a coin, 'enter the first year on their *hukamnamas*' and use a seal that refers to Guru Nanak (Ganda Singh transcript of Jaipur *akhbarat*, Punjabi University, Patiala ms. 332176, f. 65).

25 J.N. Sarkar's transcripts of the Jaipur Kapaddwara records contain a letter that may be from Banda to Jai Singh of Amber. The letter begins with Banda's characteristic salutation '*Fateh darshan*' and expresses the writer's surprise at Jai Singh's having 'forsaken Hindu *dharma*', especially since 'Akal Purakh has commanded that the time of the Turks has reached its end and it is the turn of the Hindus.' The letter states that 'the foundation of *dharma* must be strengthened' and asks Jai Singh to join the writer in marching on Delhi 'to kill the oppressive Turks.' It ends by stating that 'I do not need sovereignty (*shahi*) but have been sent by Akal Purakh to strengthen the foundations of *dharma*' (National Library, Calcutta, Sarkar transcripts, notebook 105, p. 2). The exact nature of the letter is problematic, especially as the original is not listed in the latest catalogue of the Kapaddwara collection (Bahura and Singh 1988). The grammar and

diction are occasionally irregular, and the transcription bears the name 'Guru Gobind' at the bottom, although it is unclear whether the words are an addition by Sarkar or by a Jaipur scribe or record-keeper. It is of course also possible that the letter represents a transcript of a forged letter sent to Jai Singh in the name of Banda.

26 Scholars seem to have missed a possible criterion for setting the date before which a *rahitnama* could not have been written: the presence or absence of an injunction forbidding the wearing of red (*suha*) clothing. The injunction is present even in the most recent of *rahit* texts (*Kharara* 25). In the note to his translation of the relevant injunction in the Chaupa Singh text, McLeod accepts Kahn Singh Nabha's contention that red is forbidden because it is associated with women's clothing and 'inappropriate for the manly' (McLeod 1987: 236, n. 338). This supposition does not seem reasonable. It is much more likely that the colour red has been forbidden because of its use by the Bandai Khalsa, the followers of Banda (see for example Bhangu 1984: 191), and as such the latest date for the inclusion of the injunction would be the defeat of the Bandais by the Tat Khalsa at Amritsar. Kesar Singh Chhibbar places the Bandais' defeat after the death of the Guru's uncle Kirpal Singh in VS 1784 1727–28, while Seva Singh puts it eight years after the death of Banda, in the years VS 1780–1 1723–5 (Kesar Singh Chhibbar 11:9; Seva Singh 81)

27 The earliest manuscript containing the *Tankhahnama* is Guru Nanak Dev University, Amritsar ms. 770, part of a larger text dated VS 1775 1718–19. The earliest version of the Chaupa Singh and *Sakhi rahit* texts was Sikh Reference Library, Amritsar ms. 6124 dated VS 1821 1765 (McLeod 1987: 20). For the text of the *Tankhahnama*, I have used Padam 1989, supplemented by Guru Nanak Dev University, Amritsar mss. 770 and 29; the text of the other two *rahitnamas* is taken from McLeod 1987. The texts are abbreviated in references as *Tn*, *CS* and *SR* respectively.

28 'The Name, charity and bathing/purity', a mnemonic formula attributed to Guru Nanak describing the essence of Sikh belief and praxis. It is used in the *Siddha gosti* (AG 942) and in the *janamsakhis*.

29 The *kesdhari* is the Sikh, Khalsa or non-Khalsa, who keeps unshorn hair (*kes*); the term *sahajdhari* normally denotes a follower of the Gurus who does not keep *kes*.

30 The Sikh addressed by the early *rahitnamas* is almost invariably male. An exception is the section of the Chaupa Singh text containing injunctions for female Sikhs (*CS* 114–6).

31 The term *sevak* appears to refer to non-Khalsa or *mona* Sikhs (*CS* 60). Ganda Singh noted a similar distinction among the Sikhs of Afghanistan (many of whom would presumably have been Khatris and Aroras) in the 1950s, with those who had not been initiated into the Khalsa but did not follow another religion being called *sevaks* (Ganda Singh 1960: 51). Writing about the first decades of the twentieth century, the novelist Nanak Singh notes that the same distinction obtained among the largely Khatri followers of the Sodhis of Haranpur, district Jhelum (Nanak Singh 1962: 41). McLeod mistranslates the term as 'servants' (McLeod 1987: 188).

32 Padam alters the text to read 'He is a Khalsa who kills the evil-doer (*dusata*)' (Padam 1989: 59).
33 The manuscript reads 'He is a Khalsa who finds *dharma*' (Guru Nanak Dev University, Amritsar ms. 770, f. 36a). I have corrected the reading against an undated nineteenth-century manuscript, Guru Nanak Dev University, Amritsar ms. 29, ff. 6ab.
34 Guru Nanak Dev University, Amritsar ms. 770, ff. 35b–6b. The published version rearranges the verses (Padam 1989: 59).

## Chapter Four

# Thinking Differently about Religion and History: Issues for Sikh Studies

*Arvind-pal Singh Mandair*

If we find ourselves thinking, speaking, even writing of God, it seems embarrassing, horribly embarrassing – even when our inquiry is critical. All of this God stuff was to have been over a long time ago. Why do we still search, still probe, still question? What calls us to respond? What disrupts the present? Unless our work is 'academic' in the worst sense of the word, something else haunts the search that is our research. What is this 'something else' and why will it give us no rest?

*(Taylor 1999: 30)*

Few people in the field of South Asian studies would need any reminder of how the relatively short history of attempts to establish Sikh studies in Western universities has been overshadowed by a fundamental disagreement between two opposed camps. At its peak this disagreement assumed the proportions of a bitter international dispute between proponents of the University's unnegotiable stance as the bastion of secular scholarship, and representatives of the community with its desire for a traditional religious programme. At times the kind of arguments put forward seemed to echo the political crisis in Punjab between advocates of Sikh ethno-nationalism and those of the secular state. To give an example, the prevailing view in academic circles is that the current problems are due solely to the intransigence of a small but vocal minority of fundamentalist Sikhs who appear incapable of adjusting to the secular and democratic ideals espoused by Western universities. Having hijacked the Sikh community's agenda on education these fundamentalists are bent on destroying any Sikh studies programme that does not conform to a nationalist ideology. The opposing perspective from the community paints an equally grim picture. Western academics have, it is argued, deliberately or otherwise contrived to distort the true teachings of Sikhism, thereby presenting a false picture of Sikhs and Sikh tradition to the outside world. According to this view, secular scholarship by its very nature will inevitably undermine the faith of ordinary Sikhs.

While there have been various articulations of this impasse over the last decade or so, a particularly notable statement is provided in a recent article by W.H. McLeod (McLeod 1994). The importance of this article resides in the fact that the author, whose work has been at the centre of the entire controversy in Sikh studies, is also regarded by his peers as the premier Western scholar of Sikhism, and certainly one of the finest historians of South Asian religions of his generation. The paper in question which began as a public lecture delivered at SOAS, is at the same time a remarkably revealing self-disclosure by someone whose scholarly output is widely recognized as having shaped the nature and direction of modern Western Sikh studies. Writing primarily in defence of secular scholarship and by implication his own oeuvre, the paper contains an unusually explicit statement of the theoretical assumptions that continue to underpin the contemporary form of Sikh studies in the West. Moreover, it allows an insight into the central issue that has fuelled the divergence of opinion between University and community to the extent that, in North America at least, their agendas have often appeared to be irreconcilable.

Although it has not been stated explicitly in these terms, the issue concerns the nature of the object being studied; more precisely whether this object is a religion, a tradition, or simply an aspect of society. But as the subtitle of McLeod's essay suggests – 'History versus Tradition in the Study of the Sikh Community' – the nature of the object has already been settled well in advance: it is a community. Insofar as it is a community or society that is to be studied, the only issue of any relevance concerns the appropriate methodology to be deployed for the study of a society. Note, however, that I say methodology not methodologies. Indeed, it becomes patently clear on reading the paper that there are no methodologies, only a single methodology with which any Sikh studies must be consonant. This methodology is located in the work of history or the historical approach, that is to say, in the task that is appropriate to the critical or secular historian. Yet, not only does historicism become the foundational criterion in the humanities and social sciences for the task of representation, the very means by which it is empowered allows us an insight into why the object of study cannot be something like religion (or tradition). Why, in other words, religion is no longer a question that asks about itself (e.g. 'What is Religion?'). Or why the only relevance of religion in secular education is in terms of the phenomena which it is able to supply for the ultimate task of academic inquiry, namely classification and its corollary, social contructivism. The reason is that the secular historian already has the answer to the question 'What is Religion?' in terms of a presupposition or a classificatory hypothesis as to what counts as religion. Because we are already supposed to know what religion is, it is meaningless to question it further. Furthermore, we know that we know, for otherwise we would not be able to carry out Sikh studies, nor could Sikh studies be an object for knowledge.

What I want to contest in this chapter is precisely this view: that the rules of engagement in respect of Sikh studies have already been prescribed and cannot be altered – specifically the rule that history must govern any proper representation of religion in the academy. I shall contest this view by providing an alternative reading of the nature of the problem. My argument is relatively simple, although it will follow a circuitous route. The problems encountered in the establishment of Sikh studies do not exist at the level of individual personalities and their motivations irrespective of whether these are leading academics or members of the community – although I do not wholly discount this as a factor which may have fuelled the situation. Nor is it a problem that afflicts Sikh studies alone. Following a mode of critical thinking inspired largely by the work of Martin Heidegger and in a different, though not unrelated manner by Michel Foucault, I attempt to locate the problem as part of what has been variously described as the current intellectual and methodological crisis or rupture in the human and social sciences (Spanos 1989). This rupture is in turn the result of an increasing disclosure of the humanities as a knowledge production industry which from the outset has concealed a certain complicity between truth, power and the dominant socio-political order. One of the central functions of this industry has been to render forms of difference and intellectual dissent in terms of a subversive threat from incommensurable constituencies such as tradition and religion which must be disarmed, either by accommodation into a benign pluralism, or by overt exclusionary tactics.

Although this mode of thinking – where criticism is directed back towards the grounding principle of inquiry – has normally been considered anti-thetical to the question of religion or the religious, recent scholarship working at the intersection between philosophy of religion and cultural theory has shown that this is far from being the case (Milbank 1990; Jantzen 1998). Based on the deconstruction of traditionally irreconcilable opposites such as 'theism' versus 'atheism', 'sacred' versus 'secular', these studies have provided a much needed corrective to the belief that we cannot think about religion except insofar as this thinking is grounded in history, or that movements such as post-structuralism and anti-imperialism necessarily undermine religious and traditional perspectives. A case in point is the widespread misinterpretation amongst social scientists and historians that Foucault's 'repressive hypothesis' is directed primarily against religion and theology (Carrette 1999). By contesting the ground rules through which secular reason has been placed in a position of super-vision in respect of any possible inquiry into religion, a major consequence of these studies is to have opened up a way of reading religion as a site of difference (Van der Veer 1996), or in the case of minorities such as the Sikhs, as a site of political resistance. As Peter Van der Veer has shown, such a reading has potentially significant implications for the study of South Asian religions (Van der Veer 1994). Although regarded as a subdiscipline of South Asian studies, Sikh studies has remained largely immune to this new debate. Part of the purpose of this chapter will be to show why this has been so.

The following exposition is divided into two parts. I begin by analysing McLeod's argument, which is articulated by way of two related moves: (i) an ontological devaluation of tradition, (ii) a rebuttal of tradition's appeal to transcendental authority. Each of these moves will then be explored and contested in relation to an alternative genealogy of history and religion in the overall context of the human sciences. The focus of my critique is McLeod's claim to be free of transcendental or metaphysical premises, a claim that is shown to be untenable given that the prerequisites of any 'genuine scholar', namely scepticism and disinterestedness, possess a distinct ontological status of their own. By revealing that the transcendental premises of secular scholarship are dependent on similar metaphysical and transcendental structures that authorize normative theology, the way is cleared for opening the discourse on religion as a *question* ('What is Religion?') as opposed to a ready made answer. One important consequence of this is that translation, more precisely cultural

50

translation, becomes an ethical issue in the reception of non-Western cultures within the humanities, rather than a transparent process normally taken for granted by epistemological classification.[1] Far from being a thinly disguised nostalgia for uncritically reproducing the 'piety of believers' or traditional forms of religiosity,[2] the critique of humanist scholarship – in this case secular historiography – helps to expose a deep rooted complicity between the normally opposed principles of religion and secularism, a complicity that is grounded in the form of an ontotheologic[3] manifesting itself in surprisingly similar political practices whose coercions in both tradition and modernity are concealed in the illusion of the sovereign subject or of centralized self-consciousness. The chapter ends with a brief outline of some pointers towards a more nuanced future debate on the nature of Sikh studies as a field of inquiry.

# Redefining the rules of engagement[4]

## 1 The ontological devaluation of tradition

As McLeod's title suggests, 'Cries of Outrage' (hereafter *CO*) reads like any classic exercise in contrapuntal criticism – history and historians being counterposed to tradition and traditionalists. 'The disagreement' we are told, and by implication the root of the entire problem

> comes down to the simple difference between these two approaches. On the one side stands the historian who trusts traditional sources, and on the other the one who views such sources with scepticism. It really is as simple as that (*CO* 124).

The difference between these two types of historians is a question of attitude: the certainty of belief or trust in tradition against the insecurity of doubt generated by scepticism. But is it quite as simple as McLeod suggests? Is it even clear that there are two types of historian, the traditional versus the sceptical? A closer look at his argument suggests that this distinction is no more than a subterfuge since an evaluative premise regarding what counts as history is already at work here. This value or standard is 'scholarly analysis' (*CO* 124). It is the idea of scholarly analysis – and by implication who counts as a scholar – that gives the measure for one's being a historian. To count as a historian 'one is required to apply a certain range of techniques

51

which qualify for the description of scholarly analysis' (*CO* 124). However, if one probes further and asks what is meant by scholarly analysis the circularity of the argument becomes plainly evident. 'Scholarly analysis' as such can only be defined in relation to an already existent evaluation that privileges history over tradition. Consequently the difference between scholarly or analytical history and traditional history resides in their being two very different attitudes that are ontologically distinct, or as McLeod himself states, these attitudes constitute 'separate existences' (*CO* 125).

It would seem perfectly logical at this point to probe further into the origin of these attitudes. For example, what does it mean *to be* sceptical or *to be* faithful? If these attitudes are no more than modes of existence or settled ways of thinking, how do they originate? Do they occur naturally or are they acquired? Instead we encounter a remarkable reluctance to question further:

> The argument of this paper does not really concern the origin of the two attitudes. The fact seems to be that they certainly do exist and that one must come to terms with their separate existences (*CO* 125).

If it were not already obvious, one of the dangers of questioning the origins of attitudes such as scepticism and trust would be to expose McLeod's argument (up to this stage at least) as set within, and taking its essential moves from, a classical and –dare I say – very traditional way of thinking inaugurated by Descartes' *Meditations* and the *Regulae*. Such questioning would lead us to conclude that in themselves neither scepticism nor doubt possess any ontological status. They do not, as McLeod suggests, constitute 'separate existences', but are part of an overall strategy that involves both the simultaneous overcoming and devaluation of tradition as that which has been handed down,[5] and a search for that which cannot be doubted, namely self-certainty.

Thus although the sceptic will begin by doubting everything, this doubt must ultimately be grounded on something which cannot be doubted. That is, the doubter cannot doubt that he is present, and he must be present in order to doubt at all. Though as a sceptic I am able to doubt, I must nevertheless admit that 'I am', that I exist at this very moment. Yet I can only admit this in so far as I am able to posit my existence to myself; that is to say, in so far as the 'I am' is simultaneously an 'I think'. Accordingly the 'I' as an 'I think' is indubitable and becomes, courtesy of Descartes, not just the central standpoint of modern thought, but, in as much as the 'I think' is the fundamental act of reason, it becomes axiomatic of thinking per se. As a result, modernity, as the very adventure of sceptism and doubt, inaugurates the possibility of history as a break with tradition. Doubt is therefore linked to the project of modernity: *modus hodiernus*, beginning anew, just now, of today. As such, history is one particular name for the new beginning that modernity is, and that tradition, by default, is not.[6]

Briefly then, any questioning that is directed towards the origins of scepticism, as opposed to simply accepting it as given, threatens to delay this new beginning that only history and the historian can bring about. By definition, therefore, there can only be one type of historian. Furthermore it threatens to make visible the transcendental basis of history as 'scholarly analysis'. The disagreement between 'History' and tradition belongs therefore to a very traditional narrative of modernity' as the freedom to choose between two apparently irreconcilable ways of being: reason versus faith. Stated differently, this entails conformity either to the principle of reason ('every fact requires believable evidence to support it' (*CO* 124) or to the principle of faith.[7]

## 2  The rebuttal of the traditionalist's resort to transcendental authority

Anticipating a hostile response on the part of his opponents – mainly those who purport to uphold the Singh Sabha tradition – McLeod posits what will continue to be the most consistent objection to the above formulation. The objection which simultaneously constitutes both a rejection of the purely secular notion of history and a defence of the standpoint of faith, concerns the precise nature of the object being studied, i.e. Sikhism. The objection is that although both sides agree that what we are discussing is a 'religious faith' or 'a religion', nevertheless 'all that we have said so far views Sikhism from the perspective of history' (*CO* 131). The question for the traditionalists is whether 'history' which relies on the work of 'the intellect' and therefore reason, is sufficient for the study of religion. 'Religion', it is argued, is a reality to which historical analysis alone is ill-suited. History within the limits of reason alone can at best only partially measure the true nature of religion which comprises an 'intuitive reality that transcends both.' (*CO* 132). According to another proponent of tradition cited by McLeod:

> The study of religion involves a study of the spiritual dimension and experiences of man, a study that is beyond the domain of sociology, Anthropology and History. Therefore, Religion has its own tools, its own methodology and principles of study which takes cognizance of a higher level of reality . . . The study of religion requires sharp insights into the totality of life including transcendental knowledge concerning God, the universe and the human spirit (*CO* 132–3).

In keeping with the idea that religion is *sui generis*, the traditionalists' central argument clearly depends on a metaphysical claim to a special category of knowledge that transcends time and space. The special 'transcendental' knowledge is not available to persons or approaches which rely on ordinary, temporally 'limited' faculties of understanding such as reason. One must possess a special faculty that is attuned specifically for the reception of religious knowledge, a faculty that enables us to cognize a higher level of reality associated with the essence and nature of religion. As McLeod effectively demonstrates, the trump card of the traditionalists against secular history – their claim to possess or to participate in a religious experience which cannot be explained by those who do not possess it, nor experienced by those who have not already experienced it – is no more than a heuristic device to limit the power and reach of the academic standpoint itself. What is in essence an ontological problematic, i.e. one's being religious or one's participation in tradition, is articulated in terms of a cognitive epistemology, i.e., the insider's possession of a special faculty of perception.

McLeod's answer to the argument from transcendental experience is emphatic, though as we shall see, disarmingly deceptive. Instead of prolonging an impossible debate on the metaphysical nature of religion – impossible because it is already out of reach, unsolvable, involving an impasse in knowledge itself – he candidly confesses his primary limitation: that he is largely devoid of any religious or spiritual experience, and that he *lacks* a sense of the numinous or any other religion for that matter:

> I approach Sikhism as a historian, one who is devoid of any pretence to that spiritual sense which many Sikhs (and Christians too) assure me is vital to its understanding. I simply

do not possess it neither in relation to the Sikh faith nor to any other faith (*CO* 133).

At this point traditionalists might be forgiven for entertaining the hope that having confessed to what sounds like the standpoint of methodological atheism – one's non-attachment any faith or tradition – McLeod has thereby renounced his claim to study the cherished object – Sikh religion. Not so fast, says McLeod. What I confess to is not having any pretence to being religious, or any claim to have access to it. As it happens I am perfectly happy to confess that my 'primary limitation is an inability to comprehend the need for a spiritual interpretation' (*CO* 133). But this by no means suggests that I cannot study it, nor that the fundamental discipline for such research should not be history. In fact the message from McLeod is clear: as long as 'truth and a strictly impartial understanding' (*CO* 134) are the objectives of historical research, then not only is history empowered to study religion, but as a historian I am perfectly justified in adopting a stance of indifference or disinterestedness towards the claims of metaphysics vis-à-vis such terms as 'the numinous', 'the spiritual', 'transcendental knowledge', etc.

As the last statement suggests, the real *coup de grace* for McLeod, his final riposte to the Singh Sabha traditionalists, is not simply that he disagrees with the standpoint of faith and tradition. It is rather that he stands absolutely assured that a combination of two intrinsically related elements will enable him to overcome the constraint which ordinarily limits the perspective of faith and tradition. One is history and its continued position of empowerment despite fundamental objections. The other is the standpoint of impartial and disinterested scholarship, the standpoint that constitutes the *being* of a 'genuine academic' (*CO* 134).

This of course begs a whole series of questions. How are these two elements 'history' and 'disinterestedness' related? What is it that empowers them in overcoming the metaphysical claims of religion? Why is it that even when the discipline of study is not history per se but other disciplines in the humanities such as philosophy, sociology and particularly religious studies, the historical approach remains dominant and transparent? Is there a link between the humanities, indeed the very notion of humanism, and historicism? Extending the debate to non-Western cultures, why and at what point does history assume a paradigmatic role in relation to the study of Indic cultures, and specifically in relation to the interpretation and self-interpretation of Indic cultures as religion(s)? Why is it that history and/as the academic standpoint can so easily override the most vigorous of metaphysical claims?

In answer to this nexus of inter-related questions I shall venture the following 'formula': History *is* the metaphysical. History *is* metaphysics itself. As metaphysics history *is* religion.

The logic of this 'formula' will not be immediately evident. In view of the foregoing discussion it may even appear ridiculous. However, at the risk of pre-empting the discussion which is to follow, I would maintain that the lumping together of history with metaphysics with religion is neither arbitrary nor accidental. There are historical antecedents for it which occur as part of the ongoing debates and polemics between the Western religious and philosophical traditions and consequently as part of the intellectual framework in which the study of religions has been transmitted. It is of immediate relevance here that this debate also takes place at the intersection with the ongoing encounter with Indic cultures. More precisely, the nexus history-metaphysics-religion is determined in relation to the classification of Indic cultures as religions within the fledgling disciplines of the human sciences. In this debate between philosophy and religion on the one hand, and Indology on the other, one of the pivotal figures is Hegel.

Despite the importance of Hegel in bridging so many disciplines, Anglo-American scholarship has by and large tended to underplay his role and significance.[8] It will therefore be instructive to outline some of the key moves in Hegel's reworking of the ontotheological tradition, moves which aimed to establish firstly a firm theoretical standpoint for conceptualizing religion in general in the face of a plurality of religions, and then as a result of this, the classification of Oriental cultures according to a reworked ontotheological schema. In effect I am proposing to sketch out the barest outlines (given the space available) of a genealogy of religion, broadly after the manner of Foucault, in which the classification of Indic cultures is of more than marginal interest. This alternative genealogy will help to clarify some of the issues that have been raised so far, such as the collusion between history and the attitude of disinterestedness, the dominance of the historicism and social constructivism in the humanities (especially religious studies), and lastly why the standpoint of methodological atheism in the very act of denying any attachment to faith or belief ends up utilizing intellectual resources which are ultimately rooted in the very structure of faith and belief. As scholars such as Grace Jantzen

56

and Richard King have convincingly demonstrated, developing a Foucauldian genealogy of religion in this way makes it possible to demonstrate that technologies of power were not only historically involved in making the structure of belief central to both religion and methodological atheism, but continue to operate in the work of Indologists and historians of South Asian religions.

## Hegel's reconstitution of religion (and Indology)

Apart from a brief note in Cantwell Smith's acclaimed study *The Meaning and End of Religion*, it has become common practice to overlook Hegel's role as the instigator of some of the leading contemporary problems in the study of religion. Most earlier accounts follow a well known excursus that at the very least includes reference to Kant's first and third critiques and to Schleiermacher's reinterpretation of faith in terms of artistic sensibility towards the divine. More recent accounts, while taking their cue from Schleiermacher's notion of a core religious experience, have developed their own variations on this theme. These include a variety of different schools that continue to influence the nature and direction of modern religious studies including the history of religions, philosophy of religion and comparative religion. Common to all of them is that they generally follow William James's influential account of mystic experience as an intensely subjective or psychological state that is outside of spatio-temporal limitations (James 1928). Based on this mode of privatized experience the defining characteristic of religion is then taken to be the idea of a central mystical core that is in essence, if not in form, common to all religions (Jantzen 1990).

Although figures such as Kant and Schleiermacher have been instrumental in redefining religion in an age dominated by its 'cultured despisers', one of the problems inherited by Hegel was that their formulations of religion had become a major liability in the war of cultural politics between Occidentalists and Orientalists, a war that had important implications for European identity and the future direction of the human sciences. The problem for Hegel was twofold. First, while Kant's and Schleiermacher's theories certainly advanced the discussion beyond the deistic preoccupation with rationalized religion, they tended to leave religion confined to the private sphere of subjectivity with no connection to time or the lived world. That is to say, they merely accentuated the founding premise of modernity: the dichotomy between the sacred and the secular, and between religion and politics. Secondly, in the hands of the Jena Romantics[9] (themselves avid readers of Indological materials, not committed to an exclusively Christian-European viewpoint, and deeply critical of modernity) the then prevailing definition of religion was brought dangerously close to the Oriental variety of pantheism, a situation which threatened to displace the dominant vantage point of European identity and its exclusionary claims to scientific knowledge.

Hegel's response as formulated in the 1824 and 1827 *Lectures on the Philosophy of Religion* provides a rigorous redefinition of the nature of religion, one that would render an all-encompassing 'Concept of Religion' (Hegel 1987a: 185) where the concept provides the mechanism whereby religion can represent itself without needing to rely on anything outside of it. As such, the 'Concept' provides the theoretical standpoint for the passage to (the representation of) all other religions. Hegel's definition would simultaneously render 'Determinate Religion' (Hegel 1987b), that is, a system for classifying or ordering the plurality of religions as concrete phenomena in time and history.

In order to reconcile the all too obvious dichotomy between Religion and religions, or Concept and phenomenon – the dichotomy between that which is beyond time and history as opposed to that which appears in time and as concrete forms of knowledge – it was necessary to formulate some kind of connection, or better still a passage, from Concept to concrete knowledge, that is, from universal to particular.[10] But at the same time Hegel had to avoid the dangerous possibility that this passage could render a displacement of the field of identity proper to Western self-consciousness. Which meant that the temporality of the passage needed to coincide with the temporality of representing. More simply stated, the purity of the (Western) self, and therefore the identity of the European Indologist, needed to be safeguarded in the face of cultural otherness, i.e. being subjected to the influence of Oriental ideas.

Recognizing the centrality of time to this problem, Hegel's solution was to make the temporality of the Concept – 'the necessary moment of the concept itself' (Hegel 1987b: 157–8) – and thus the ontological status of representation, coincide with the definition of 'the metaphysical' as the essence of history. In other words, the passage from Concept to phenomena is redefined as the movement of history: history as the movement of time itself. The metaphor of movement here represents the nature of 'the metaphysical' as exaltation or elevation from nature to spirit, from physical to meta-physical.[11] Hegel's interpretation of passage in terms of 'the metaphysical' means that the criterion for what counts as religion is the same as the criterion for that which counts as history. Which is to say that religion can only emerge in and as history, or alternatively, that the movement we comprehend as history is in essence religious, the history of mankind's religious experience.

One other move was required for the system to become complete. This was the connection of 'the metaphysical' to the activity of proving God's existence. In Western ontotheological tradition the operation of providing proof, of proving, constitutes the essence of rational thinking, of a thinking which gives reasons for why something exists rather than nothing (Heidegger 1987: 1). Since rational thinking can only begin at the point where the Deity enters thinking at its ground, this means that insofar as God exists, God cannot *not* be thought (Taylor 1991). As a result rational thinking is necessarily theistic, or alternatively, theism is necessarily rational. The consequences of this particular ontotheologic are far reaching. I shall focus on the two that are of specific relevance to this discussion.

Firstly, religion and history are absolutely metaphysical, which means that the standpoint of religion and history is absolute self-consciousness, which in Hegel's terms is reason itself. History as what is past is coextensive with theism. History is therefore religious history, the history of the progressive overcoming of the nihil by the movement of reason. Moreover, because history is the history of thinking, and because all thinking is coextensive with the need to prove God's existence, the extent to which any culture can think God's existence becomes the central criterion in the historical classification of religions. Consequently, for the first time, the terms pantheism, theism and monotheism become standardized world-historical categories for classifying non-Western religions. Which means that the implicit schema of the religious history of mankind constitutes a linear graph where history and religion (i) co-originate with the sublation of pantheism, (ii) progress dialectically as theism, and (iii) culminate in monotheism or revealed religion. Paradoxically,[12] however, the culmination of the religious history of mankind (theism) signals the *beginning* of secular modernity, the era of Man.

Secondly, this paradox is perfectly illustrated in the task of the post-Hegelian Indologist (Sharma 1988).[13] As already stated, one of Hegel's aims in reformulating the standpoint for the study of religion was to render the influence of Indology – and through Indology any competition from non-Christian religions – politically harmless. The results from Indology would no longer prove troublesome to the field of Western self-consciousness. The problem of passage between concept and concrete phenomena – which in turn raised the problem of conflicting ontologies, i.e. of multiple identities – is solved by adopting an absolutely theoretical, or to use Taylor's terminology, a theo-aesthetic standpoint (Taylor 1992), which would allow the Indologist to carry out his work as an Indologist, and at the same time remain committed to Christianity or to Western self-consciousness. Stated differently, the Indologist can simultaneously be a theologian and an anthropologist without there being any contradiction between the two positions. Lack of contradiction implies infinite or perfect translatability between the Indologist's identity (who or what he is) and his intellectual work (what he does). Moreover, since history and religion are intrinsically metaphysical, the law by which one position translates into the other is the law of thinking itself.

Not surprisingly the problem that will now dog future studies of religion – the problem of separate or conflicting ontologies – is averted or rather circumvented since, being always involved in perfect translatability (as one who has by definition always-already-crossed-over), the Indologist is absolutely involved in the object of his inquiry. In theological terms absolute involvement (*inter-esse*) is the same as absolute immanence. Yet even a cursory reading of theology will show that absolute immanence is a transcendental concept based on the Aristotelian notion of time as a point-now that is absolutely present to self-consciousness: the standpoint of history itself.

## Faith in reason: the transcendental foundations of disinterested inquiry

Though it is not generally recognized, the paradoxical outcome of the Hegelian ontotheological schema continues to prefigure the study of religion within the educational infrastructure of the modern secular university. This can be seen in the two broadly distinct disciplines under which the study of religion has been housed since the 1960s: departments of Religious Studies, versus departments and faculties of Social Sciences and Oriental Studies. Though somewhat exaggerated, this distinction allows a useful comparison between the respective ideologies from which each is drawn: theology and anthropology. The popular conception is that theology and anthropology are irreconcilably opposed, the latter having historically displaced the former. Yet closer scrutiny of their underlying premises suggests that these ideologies are not simply heirs to a common intellectual heritage. As thinkers with intellectual projects and sensibilities as widely divergent as those of Heidegger and Foucault[14] have shown, they are intrinsically linked to each other by the very factor which supposedly divides them, namely, logic, metaphysics or reason (Heidegger 1991).

In the recent history of the modern university, changes at institutional and theoretical level in the way that religion is studied serve to remind us of the continuing legacy of nineteenth century philosophy's ambivalent relationship to Indology. At the institutional level the transformation of departments of religious studies has signaled a weakening of Christianity's claim to dominance in the university and to be the national religion. At the theoretical level, a shift from the exclusive concern with a Christocentric theology to the problem of conceptualizing the nature of religion in the context of a plurality of religions.

Although this theoretical shift comprises several independent strands of thought, including those associated with such names as Eliade, Ricoeur, Van der Leeuw and Cantwell Smith, it can be said with considerable justification that the basic theoretical standpoint of these schools converges on the age-old problem of truth as it arises in an irreduceably plural context. The apparent problem with any theory of religious pluralism is this: upon what basis can one theoretically inquire into the nature of religion in the face of competing truth claims? Given that anything less than eternal truth suggests relativism, anarchy and nihilism – for it seems nothing is fixed and stable any longer – how can we reconcile the radical difference of religious traditions and cultures and their unique context of meaning and truth?

Clearly, however, the metaphysical assumptions within such a form of questioning – the privileging of eternity over time, universal over particular, necessity over contingency – has already predisposed the principal theorists in modern religious studies into adopting a particular way of asking 'What is Religion?' At the risk of over-simplifying, the essential criterion for what counts as religion is that all religions possess a central and unifying mystical core which can be characterized in terms of the quality of experience evoked between Man and God. The basic understanding of 'mysticism' or 'the mystical' in modern religious theory tends to follow William James's reference to a form of experience that centrally involves an intensely subjective state of pure interiority, usually brief in duration, which has privileged access to an ultimate (transcendent) reality (Jantzen 1989). As such, this so-called 'mystical' consciousness is radically distinct from 'ordinary' consciousness which is situated in time and world (Hick 1989). Despite the supposedly absolute difference between the two states, there must nevertheless be a means of transferring or translating between the divine and the human, eternity and time. The interface between these two mutually exclusive states is provided by the structure of faith or belief. More importantly, in addition to being central to virtually all discussion concerning mysticism, mystical experience, and thus to the very core of what counts as religion, modern theorizing in religious studies has elevated the structure of faith to an all-encompassing transcultural principle of humanity and humanism irrespective of cultural differences. An important issue arises here. Faith is normally conceived as a specific attitude or disposition through which a person exists both in the world and in relation to a transcendent dimension. But how exactly can faith/belief extend *beyond* world and time in order to participate in the transcendent without itself being a transcendental or grounding principle?

The difficulty of even conceptualizing the problem in this way is partly due to the common definition of faith as that which must be contrasted with reason. Faith and reason, it is often said, belong to different sources or are irreconcilably opposed. To speak of faith as a subjective attitude means that I have faith in something or someone. But whatever I have faith in must firstly exist. It must have being in order for that faith to be justified. Secondly, it must be an object which as far as possible conforms to our belief in it. There are two aspects to this. First, to say that I have faith in something means that I hold that something as true. The true is that which is in-being. In the Western ontotheological tradition, being has been defined according to a notion of time that privileges the present (the point now) as the basis on which we can take what lies before us as fixed and constant. Hence the being or truth of an object is that on the basis of which I can say it is present to me, and is able to remain present as the same object. Any change in the way that this object is re-presented to me would constitute a change in its truth or being. Thus being and truth are defined by excluding time as successivity, by infinitely compressing time to the point now of presence. Hence the assurance of faith lies in the affirming decision whereby the object of our faith is posited beforehand as always fixed and constant. To impose continuity and self-sameness *a priori* is to impose an identity on the object. It is to posit the object as identical. However, as Heidegger has shown so convincingly, such positing of identity is nothing natural. The essence of rational thinking is in fact to think in abeyance of the principle of reason. To have faith is therefore to trust in reason, or to trust in reason's ability to re-present the object of faith as the very same object, and not as something other. Consequently faith presupposes the exclusion of difference (as time or becoming) in order that identity as eternal self-preservation can be maintained.

There would certainly be strong objections to the equating of faith and reason from various quarters. The object of religious faith is no ordinary being but the highest being, the first cause or *causa sui*, the ultimate Reality. This ultimate Reality, it is argued, grounds all existence. To ground means to transcend, and as transcendent this ultimate reality transcends all human impositions such as culture and logic. But as Heidegger argues in *The Metaphysical Foundations of Logic* (Heidegger 1991), what this objection crucially overlooks is that the Transcendent as a grounding principle had already been anticipated within the scholastic doctrine of *scientia dei*: God's knowledge is the naturally necessary knowledge since it belongs to the nature of God as absolute self-consciousness or self-presence. Furthermore the totality of knowledge is always already anticipated within God's *scientia visionis*, where *visio* is a conceptual grasping in the manner of present intuition – *praesens intuitus* (Heidegger 1991: 64). According to Aquinas the word *praesens* is understood from the perspective of an eternity which exists without succession – *aeternitas, quae sine successione existens totum tempus comprehendit* (Heidegger 1991: 37–41). In contrast to *successio*, *praesens* means that God's intuition realizes itself in the eternal 'Now', the *nunc stans* as the totality of times in which God is absolutely present. Far from being opposed to the notion of transcendence, absolute presence or pure identity becomes the measure of transcendence and therefore ultimate Reality itself. Thus transcendence, as this notion is received from scholastic theology, through the history of modern Western philosophy, to the more recent project of religious studies, is indicative of the attempt to overcome what is effectively the same problem: the insecurity of time as succession or becoming and/or the threat posed by an irreducible difference between religions and cultures.

All difference *per se* comes to be grounded in identity. Yet, as already mentioned, that identity can be a ground in this way presupposes a standpoint that is identity-positing, that gives reasons, or affirms absolutely. That is to say from a standpoint of faith as absolute certainty which, as we have seen, is framed from within the structure and field of self-consciousness. In faith defined as absolute certainty of the transcendent, we are no longer threatened by other cultures or by cultural difference. In the awareness of faith we stand still in the *nunc stans*, having risen to the highest (transcendent) viewpoint (*visio dei*) from where we are able to over-see the global history of mankind *sub specie aeternitatis*. Faith is therefore an ontological distancing device in the sense that its theo-aesthetic standpoint keeps other cultures at a safe distance, from where we can safely observe them without our existence being threatened. Insofar as the privileging of transcendence is the privileging of self-consciousness, theology from the outset presupposes a form of humanistic thinking. Theology is thus a closet anthropology!

Such a statement might appear to blatantly contradict received opinion. Its significance is missed, however, if we continue to comprehend the issue at the level of a mere opposition between *theos* and *anthropos*. It is the simplistic opposition between Man and God that has largely been responsible for fostering the climate in which methodological atheism supersedes faith, becoming thereby the byword for locating all teaching of the world under a science of Man – variously called anthropology, disinterested or humanistic inquiry. Yet the ground of methodological atheism is essentially historical, or as we have already seen in reference to Hegel and Descartes, historical reason, or reason in and as history. Thus while appearing to be at odds with faith or religion, the disinterestedness of humanistic inquiry with its claim to pursue knowledge for the sake of knowledge – to impart a 'strictly impartial understanding', to 'understand simply for its own sake' (*CO* 143) – is in fact the other side of the same coin.

The faith of the religious believer, represented intellectually by theology (the science of God), relies on the same metaphysics that grounds the certainty of methodological atheism, represented intellectually by historicist anthropology (science of Man).

The metaphysics that is proper to historicism or historicist thinking suspends and spatializes the temporal process into an identical whole that can be seen all at once from the superior vantage point that is history. In thus reifying time, in bringing time to light, metaphysical historicist thinking achieves the essential criterion of disinterested inquiry, i.e. objectivity. Objectivity here is defined in terms of a dis-stance that the historian must maintain from the

64

originative experience of the object. This space allows anyone who thinks historically to become a privileged observer who from a dis-engaged position – or as Thomas Nagel aptly puts it, 'a view from nowhere' (Nagel 1986) – overlooks the lived experience of the event as if it were a completed narrative. Clearly the narrative articulated by humanistic inquiry is determined by resort to a transcendental method that remains beyond the reach of criticism. The only real difference between theological and humanistic inquiry is that the latter's great achievement has been to render invisible its determining transcendental structures and methods by concealing them in a rhetoric of renunciation, confessionalism and self-absolution that could almost pass as religious.

The concealment of transcendental presuppositions will therefore be at work whenever historicism in general provides the central approach to the study of religion or religions. McLeod's scholarly rhetoric of self-confession in 'Cries of Outrage' is no exception. The rhetoric is centred around a candid acknowledgement of the historian's limitations in regard to the study of a different culture. His own 'primary limitation' resides in an 'inability to comprehend the need for a spiritual interpretation in research on the Sikh religion or for that matter in anything else' (*CO* 135). The reason for this 'inability to comprehend, we are told earlier, is due to the fact that as a historian he is largely devoid of this religious or spiritual experience, or that he is 'devoid of any pretence to that spiritual sense', that he 'lacks a sense of the numinous'. It is something which he simply does not possess (*CO* 133).

Given that what is at stake here (by McLeod's own admission) is the question of limits or borders, the use of denegatory terms – 'devoid', 'lack', 'inability' – is methodologically significant. It indicates the use of the transcendental *epoche* – the classic phenomenological strategy of self-effacement, a form of renunciation where the scholar self-consciously brackets his identity and by implication conceals his faculty of judgement. In confessing that I am *devoid* of, that I *lack* something, or that I am *unable* to comprehend the metaphysical-transcendental etc, the historian conveniently absolves himself from making any judgement about the truth or reality of the metaphysical. In fact he has no need to deny it since his identity/'I' – as that on the basis of which there could be any *relation* to the metaphysical – is negated or voided. This dissolution points to more than a simple denial or confession of one's 'primary limitation'. It represents the fundamental act of *being* disinterested: the essence of

65

humanistic inquiry and the true disposition of any 'genuine academic' as someone for whom the object of inquiry must be infinitely representable but who can bracket his own existence at will.[15]

Although the acknowledgement of 'primary limitations' is clearly a pointer to the existence of cultural boundaries, this does not mean, so the argument goes, that the existence of cultural boundaries should in any way hinder the work of historical research, nor that the historian should have to apologize for its results (*CO* 135). Although the historian may suffer from personal limitations, the work of history itself should not be hindered by cultural boundaries. Indeed the historian's mode of inquiry signals that as long as there is a prior display of academic honesty – where one openly confesses to having no relation or trafficking with the metaphysical on the basis that this not what the 'genuine academic' does – cultural borders can be crossed infinitely and at will. That is to say, the historian's self-effacement in disinterested inquiry is synonymous with an infinite ability to translate cultural borders. This is especially true for the historian of Sikhism for whom cultural translation has never been a problem since as a historian of religion he is (and always has been) in possession of a classificatory hypothesis, namely, the presupposition 'What Religion is', and as a consequence, of what Sikhism is or where it can be installed within the already defined schema of the history of religions.[16]

It is clear in light of the above discussion that a reliance on transcendental and metaphysical structures continues to determine the historian's practice. For how is it possible to differentiate between phenomena – one religion from another, religion from non-religion, history from non-history, etc. – and then to organize them without a clssificatory hypothesis, an overall and totalizing concept called 'history', and without a privileged moment in which this overall concept 'history' is grounded? Once there is a realization of the absolute reliance of history on metaphysical presuppositions, then, notwithstanding objections from a significant body of opinion within the humanities, it becomes evident that the mode of disinterested inquiry proper to historical research reflects the socio-political ethos of the dominant culture. As a result the historian, irrespective of ethnic, cultural or religious background, has no choice but to maintain a certain complicity with the standpoint of the majoritarian ethos of the cognitive elite. Contrary to what many historians themselves think there is no ethical escape route here. The question of ethics cannot arise here since the standpoint of the dominant culture – whether defined as modernity, humanism, globalism, or liberal democracy, etc. – defines the ethical as such as the universal, and as universal it applies to everyone and at all times.

## Conclusion: pointers to a future debate

Attempts to criticize the field of representation proper to secular academic scholarship tend to be rebuffed in two ways. The usual way is to portray such criticism as an attack on freedom associated with critical thinking in contradistinction to the closed mind of traditionalists who either seek refuge in an other-worldly mysticism or an escape from the reality of hard facts into ascetic ideals that can be desired but never achieved. The other form of rebuff – articulated mostly by social scientists inspired by Habermas – regards criticism directed against secular inquiry as a misguided anti-Euro-centrism, an anti-realism or 'magical realism' that relies on the very rationalism that it seeks to undermine.

However, it should be clear by now that this is far from being the case. Indeed, it is quite misleading. As the foregoing argument has shown the promise of a proper method ('genuine scholarship') is no more than a secularized version of theology's desire for transcendental principles. That is, if both history and theology are merely alternative technologies of concealment (disinterestedness versus mysticism), to deploy a form of critique which deconstitutes the logic underpinning both secular history and theology, is to take the first step outside the domain of a form of thinking limited to reason, logic, rationalism and its main technology, i.e. representation. To take such a step does not mean to detach oneself from Western thinking. Rather it is to contest the orthodox belief that thinking as such can be reduced to the rule of reason, that there is no other form of thinking except by way of logic and reason. As already alluded to, even the history of Western philosophy has not been entirely closed to the possibilities of thinking in any other way than via subservience to the law of reason. By turning scepsis against itself, possibilities of a different thinking arise, which take critique much more seriously than the theologian or the sceptical historian. The result is a foundationless thinking, a thinking based on non-representation, a thinking that does not necessarily obey the law of non-contradiction A=A. Such thinking – traditionally dismissed by secularism as non-worldly, escapist, nihilistic and incapable of providing an ethical-political standpoint – finds more fertile reception in Eastern 'spiritual' traditions regarding it as an entry point, a qualification for entering into a dialogue with texts such as the Adi Granth. As Charles Winquist tells us, the problem is not that religion and thinking are intrinsically incompatible, but rather that the demand for a religious way of life, a way of thinking religion differently, is in conflict with the formulation of the basic concepts by means of which the discourse on religion continues to be regulated (Winquist 1995: 6). It would therefore be misleading to suggest that non-representative thinking, thinking that does not have to answer to the rule of reason, is alien to the West. Indeed some of the most influential strands within recent European philosophy take the critique of pure secularism not as an escape from the rigours of academic scholarship into irrational non-utile thinking, but as a political strategy for resisting dominant power structures, the most pervasive of which is the centrality of reason.

It should not surprise us therefore to find (amongst others) the work of thinkers such as Foucault, normally associated with militant forms of atheism, being used in a new wave of scholarship in the study of religion (Carrette 1999). Foucault was in fact fascinated by new religious and spiritualist movements, particularly those that mani-fested a demand for a new subjectivity. He felt he had discerned a very different imperative to the Socratic 'know (= control) thyself', an imperative that went beyond the simplistic opposition between theism and atheism, and which he formulated in terms of an existential concern or care of the self: 'above all we have to change ourselves. Our way of existing, our relationships with others, with things, with eternity, with God'. What does it mean, Foucault asks elsewhere, for people 'to seek out, (often) at the price of their lives, that thing whose very possibility we Europeans have forgotten at least since the Renaissance and the period of the great crises of Christianity – a spirituality. I can hear the French laughing at these words, but they are making a mistake' (Foucault 1997: xxiii).

Although ideological transformations such as these have been steadily taking hold in Anglo-American universities over the past two decades, such bastions of orthodox secularism as Asian and Oriental studies continue to resist their destabilizing influence. This is hardly surprising given that what is at stake – certainly in the case of Sikh Studies – is the displacement of a purely objective, i.e. classificatory, and infomatic regime that has sustained a museum culture of 'experts', 'expert witnesses', archivalists, etc., with an educational culture in which the study of Sikhism is at once a form of self-discovery, no less spiritual than political, no less therapeutic than classificatory. Given that the propriety of 'Sikh studies' is intrinsically linked to the privatization of desire – the desire to be and think from within a Sikh experience – and the repression of this desire to one's interior, to the home or gurdwara where it remains harmlessly irrelevant to the 'real' world – it seems likely that strategies which threaten to displace the boundary between public and private would be regarded as a desecration of the purity of academic space. There are increasing indications, however, which suggest that desecrations of this sort will become part and parcel of academic scholarship, and not least in Sikh studies.

I shall conclude by citing only two of the more pressing ones. The first is a need, based on the aporetic experiences of the Sikh diaspora, to reinvent a theory and practice of communication based on the experience of a body that houses multiple and often incommensurable identities – Sikh and Western – resulting in the remaking of Western identity and theory in a manner not dissimilar to the way that many Jewish and other minority writers and thinkers have done. In other words, a theory and practice of communication that is amenable to a cross-cultural context and not automatically reducible to mimetic responses irrespective of whether these are *dialogues* of the interfaith type, or *apologies* to secular orthodoxy. The second is related to the spread of digital telematics and internet web-based technologies for distance learning and teaching. Combined with the significant expansion of the university and higher education sectors, these developments promise, yet at the same time threaten, to drastically alter the structures of normative pedagogy. Although their full implications remain to be explored, the possibilities for challenging both ecclesiastical and secular academic authority, are considerable. Given the pace at which technology has been transforming the way we live, think and interact, it might not be unrealistic to suggest the creation of symbiotic as opposed to the previously hierarchical relationships between the university and community networks by the first decade of the twenty first century – an age of virtual *sangats*.

# Notes

1 The topic of translation is treated at length in my forthcoming monograph *Religion and the Translatability of Cultures* (Manchester University Press).

2 I refer of course to the Singh Sabha tradition and in particular to its theology. A rigorous criticism of this theology, its underlying premises and intellectual borrowings constitute the point of departure for this essay. A question that will be probed in detail elsewhere but which I can only take for granted here is how and why Indic cultures came to be translated (and continue to translate themselves in the scholarly and other work of the indigenous elites) in terms of an ontotheology (see note 3 below) or more broadly speaking 'religion', and what the multiple consequences of this are.

3 The term was first used by Kant and following him by Hegel. In this chapter the term ontotheology is meant to depict two related things: (i) following Heidegger's essay in the volume *Identity and Difference* it refers to the entry of the Deity into any discourse based on reason, i.e. the circular dependence of the principle of reason on God; (ii) the essential continuity of the Greek (*onto*), mediaeval (*theo*), and modern humanist (*logic*) traditions as components of the broader Western religio-cultural-philosophical tradition. In this sense it is essentially continuous with the term metaphysics.

4 Throughout this chapter the terms history/historicism, methodological atheism, humanism/humanistic inquiry/disinterested inquiry will be used interchangeably, given that underpinning all of them is the work of secular reason.

5 It is interesting to note that for both Descartes (philosopher) and McLeod (historian), doubt and scepticism are *already* posited in relation to tradition as false opinion, as uncertain, as that which is by default doubt*able*. Thus whereas Descartes refers to the received tradition of scholastic theology as the 'false prejudices of our childhood education', McLeod suggests that the Singh Sabha tradition (again by default) entertains and perpetuates unexamined opinions relating to material sources and opinions that must be doubted, and that cannot be regarded as factual until believable evidence can be found to support it.

6 The connection between modernity and the project of history as a break with tradition is pursued in different ways by Martin Heidegger and Walter Benjamin. Limitations of space preclude any sustained analysis of this connection beyond the few remarks made above. For a sustained reading of the inter-relatedness of methodological doubt, modernity and history see Benjamin (1995).

7 McLeod does state in his paper that there are varying degrees of skepsis and trust, but it should be clear from the Cartesian origins of this problem that methodological doubt and self-certainty based on the mathematical, implies a clean break with the alleged prejudice of tradition and the past. In addition there has to be an ontological forgetting involved which makes the break all the cleaner.

8 An exception is Wilhelm Halbfass (Halbfass 1988) who devotes an entire chapter to Hegel. It needs to said however that there is no close reading of Hegel or any other philosopher in Halbfass's book. His comments remain rather general and it is of use mainly to Indologists and to a lesser extent to historians of ideas.

9 The people I have in mind include Herder, the early Schlegel, Schelling and Schopenhauer (Clarke 1997).

10 In terms of classical theology this passage corresponds to the relationship between God as Transcendent and God as involved or immanent in the world. For Hegel, as is well known, immanence is defined by history.

11 There is a remarkable passage in the first volume of the *LPR* in which the activity of 'the metaphysical' as the essence of religious consciousness is described by resort to a series of metaphors such as: *Erhebung* (elevation), *Übergehen*, (passing over), *Ausgehen* (going out), *Fortgehen* (progression), etc.

12 Paradoxically, because as a result of this Hegel was constantly rebutting charges of atheism from Protestant theologians.

13 As Krishna Sharma argues, the work of Indologists such as H.H. Wilson, Albrecht Weber, Monier Williams, and George Grierson, must be read in light of the dominant religious and philosophical currents of the day (Sharma 1986). This point is taken up argued at length in my forthcoming *Religion and the Translatability of Culture*.

14 As Jeremy Carrette has recently argued, Foucault's *Order of Things*, long considered by social scientists as anathema to theology/religious thinking, can be read *religiously* as a negative theology (Carrette 1999).

15 To the somewhat obvious objection that words such as 'devoid', 'lack', 'inability' are being used in a perfectly ordinary (methodologically non-significant) way, it can be said that this would indeed be the case, were it not for McLeod's insistence on and argument for the disinterested standpoint of genuine academic inquiry. What is significant here is that the defence of the scholar's standpoint (what it means to be a 'genuine academic' by adoption of the skeptical attitude) coincides with the necessity of being seen to have have *no relation* to the metaphysical. As I have already explained, to dissolve one's relation to the world is premised on an ability to efface one's identity. It is this effacement of historical and existential being which creates the possibility of distance, i.e. the purified space of disengagement that is so vital to disinterested inquiry or to impartial and objective understanding.

16 What is often overlooked is that after the publication of his *Guru Nanak and the Sikh Religion* the conceptual programme of McLeod's work reads as a series of extended footnotes to this early volume. Hence it is usually forgotten that this volume provides the only sustained interrogation by the author of the meaning of Sikhism in terms of a theological statement that is adequate for consumption by a Western readership. In virtually all of his later publications (most if not all in the area of history and anthropology) a classificatory hypothesis – 'what Sikhism is' – is always ready to hand.

# Chapter Five

# On the Hermeneutics of Sikh Thought and Praxis

*Balbinder Bhogal*

On the first page of the Adi Granth (AG),[1] one comes across the following passage:

> *sochai soch na hovai je sochi lakha vara* (AG 1)
> Having thought deeply (comprehension of Reality/Truth) will
>    not occur even if I think a hundred thousand times.

In the effort of comprehending the above verse, one's own hermeneutic thinking suddenly becomes profoundly questionable. Furthermore:

> *kare vakhianu janai je koi, amritu pivai soi ...*
> *manu ki mati matagalu mata, jo kichu boliai sabhu khato khata*
>    (AG351)
> He alone can discourse (on the Word) who knows (it); for he
>    alone drinks the nectar.
> The mind's understanding is like a drunken elephant; whatever
>    is uttered is all totally wrong.

Is it then necessary to 'drink the nectar of the world' to speak meaningfully about it? Or are we doomed to a drunken stupor? Guru Nanak goes on:

> *nanakn janai sacha soi*
> *je ko akhai bolu vigaru ta likhiai siri gavara gavaru* (AG 5)
> O Nanak! That True One alone knows (Itself).
> If any loudmouth says (he knows), then he is marked a fool
>    amongst fools.

Can there be anything academically known about the teachings of the AG, or are we soberly led to silence?

> *chupai changa nanaka vinu navai muhi gandhu* (AG 1288)
> To be silent is good, O Nanak, without the Name (the words of) the mouth produce a stench.

Being in great danger of being labelled as the utterance of a fool, babbling drunkenly and speaking but foul works, the following chapter contemplates how to study the teachings of a sacred scripture whilst acknowledging the importance of self-understandings internal and external to the scripture's context. Are the above words hermeneutically and ethically significant, or are we simply to ignore them in favour of a Eurocentric method?

What would a 'hermeneutics' of *gurmat* look and sound like? What contextual horizons are fusing? Are there broader horizons, such as those understood by pre-modern, modern and modern-*post-modern*[2] paradigms, at work? Indeed what one finds in Sikh studies is a predominantly historical framework that spans both academic and traditional interpretation. This has emerged from the material changes brought about by imperialism, modernization, the effects of missionary Christianity, and most important of all, the interpretive formulations of Sikh thought and praxis by the indigenous elites of those times. It is through these colonially inspired interpretive processes that the question of hermeneutics becomes central to Singh Sabha exegesis of the AG. Given this interpretive history, then, in what ways are second and third generation Sikhs in the diaspora predisposed to understand the AG?

## Hermeneutics: translation, interpretation and praxis

One of the primary issues of this chapter concerns the interpretation of Sikh thought from within a diasporic context. It limits itself to the works of Guru Nanak and asks whether the words of Nanak can 'speak again' – more specifically, whether they can speak (and thereby be heard) in English. Following Gadamer's understanding of hermeneutics 'as the art of bringing what is said or written to speech again' (Gadamer 1981: 119), the necessity of translation and interpretation is brought to the fore. Given the impact of colonialism and oriental scholarship, perhaps the most important idea guiding this interpretive exploration is Ricoeur's argument that it is not so much who is 'behind the text' (i.e. Punjabi Nanak) as who is 'in front' of the text (second/third generation British Sikhs) that matters in interpretation. The romantic belief that the intentions of the author, their 'original meanings', are somehow magically present in the text waiting to be rediscovered by the interpreter has been roundly criticized since Schleiermacher. If 'I' am to meaningfully engage with the text, then my present (post-modern British–English) context cannot but influence the textual interpretation, so that to understand at all I will have to understand differently from previous scholars who operated in different colonial, oriental or modern contexts.

Gadamer has shown how one's prejudices not only influence interpretation but do so in entirely natural and even creative ways (Gadamer 1993: 265–300). In other words, understanding is predicated upon the existence of prior judgements and under-standings (the heurmeneutic circle). Furthermore, the translation from Guramukhi[3]/Punjabi into English predisposes a different understanding, despite any conservative and metaphysical claims that may be entertained.[4]

Most second/third generation Sikhs in the diaspora, by the mere fact of their location, are directly and indirectly led by the presuppositions carried by their cultural-linguistic context. These predispositions are unavoidable when approaching the AG, not only because such Sikhs think in Western thought forms and categories, but also because the received tradition, articulated by the Singh Sabha elites, was itself formed by a mimetic internalization of such Western–Semitic ideas. Difference (in understanding the AG) then, is inherently built into any shift in context, most visible in the translative move from Gurmukhi to English. This difference, born out of a conflation of contexts, manifests in a diasporic hybridity, where an 'internally translative self' challenges any thinking based on the simple either-or assumption between a Western outsider who is 'capable of reason' (*theoria*) and an Eastern insider who is 'advantaged by faith' (*praxis*), since these hybrid Asians are both and neither. Therefore the self-imposed polarization between Singh Sabha exegesis and Western academic narration operates within a false dichotomy that elides their shared assumptions, i.e. colonialism, English education and migration. In the Western diaspora, the north Indian contexts of the AG are in a relationship of conflation with the European contexts of the interpreter, as they have been since the Singh Sabha period (*c.* 1870–1970). One of the aims of the paper therefore is to 'bring together', or simply acknowledge the interdependency of, reason (objective or theoretical interpretation) and faith (intuitive or community-praxis). But beyond this reciprocity, this paper further investigates how *praxis* can lead *theoria*, challenging both colonial and traditional accounts for their modernist assumption of the reverse, that doctrine dominates practice. The focus here then is to make a preliminary attempt at addressing the problematic and often ignored issues of translation and interpretation.

Translation and interpretation are central not only in the broadest sense to understanding, but also in the specific sense of textual exchange and transformation. Roman Jakobson categorises three main areas of translation (Gentzler 1993: 1): the *intralingual* reworking of signs in one language with signs from the same language; the *interlingual* interpretation of signs in one language with signs from another; and the *intersemiotic* transfer or transformation of signs in one language to non-verbal signs, i.e. from language into art or music. In the case of the AG, all three are inter-related; the *intralingual* translation of the AG is seen in various indigenous interpretive traditions (*pranalis*) and day-to-day exegesis (*katha*); the *intersemiotic* translation consists of devotional singing (*kirtan*), backed by the musical performance of the AG's thirty-one melodies (*ragas*), into meditative repetition (*jap, simaran*) and oral exegesis (*katha*) and vice versa; and finally the *interlingual* translation from written Gurmukhi to written English, comprising various Western orientalist, as well as indigenous Sikh, translations. With the focus on Western Sikhs, this paper limits itself to the last category of *interlingual* translation – the most problematic given the complexity of the cross-cultural encounter. Though the intralingual and intersemiotic are not directly engaged with, they form a part of my own Sikh praxis, and have thereby been brought to bear on the interlingual translation. It is acknowledged however that my own experience, as a diaspora Sikh trying to understand the AG *in English*, is largely focused on the interlingual dimension of semantic translation and interpretation. Nevertheless, given this interlingual context of diaspora which includes conventional academic study, there is a danger, without treatment of the other two modes, of reducing translation into a semantic process which sacrifices form on the altar of content. The focus on content alone with scant regard for the contextual form or forms has been noted by Sontag as a modernist strategy:

By reducing the work of art to its content and then interpreting *that*, one tames the work of art. Interpretation makes art manageable, comfortable ... But it should be noted that interpretation is not simply the compliment that mediocrity pays to genius. It is, indeed, *the* modern way of understanding something, and is applied to works of every quality.

(*Sontag* 1994: 8–9)

This hermeneutic method has been paradigmatic for Western scholars translating and interpreting the AG. If this paper were to treat the AG as though its only import was its 'meaning', then a reductive injustice would ensue. There are obviously various integrated levels of intralingual and intersemiotic engagement, although a vital link between the sung and recited words and their meaning is often missing for diaspora Sikhs. Therefore the semantic level is without doubt of primary importance in a western context – especially given the Gurus' own criticism of the ritualization of religious practice.

Steiner would see Sontag's *Against Interpretation* as oxymoronic, given the ubiquity he places on translative interpretation:

Translation is formally and pragmatically implicit in *every* act of communication, in the emission and reception of each and every mode of meaning, be it in the widest semiotic sense or in more specifically verbal exchanges. To understand is to decipher. To hear significance is to translate ... This general postulate has been widely accepted.

(*Steiner* 1992: xii)

The philosophical detail of what occurs in cross-cultural translation is beyond the scope of this chapter. Nevertheless, it is largely accepted that translation is inseparable from interpretation, and that it is not without reason that hermeneutics involves both as forms of understanding, as well as including a practical dimension where 'understanding always involves something like applying the text to be understood to the interpreter's present situation' (Gadamer 1993: 308).[5] This was not, however, the case in early hermeneutic theories which paralleled the scientific paradigm of the Enlightenment. Here texts were treated as fixed, objective realities that could be interpreted via the appropriate methods, and their 'truths' or 'meanings' could be elicited by a prejudice-free application of those methods. Such assumptions led to the naïve belief that a text carries its own truths and that these can be accessed and translated into any language and context without significant change. But any treatment of interpretation that elides translation and the diversity of interpretation due to different contexts and times, is inherently problematic. This is primarily because it promotes an academic theorization of hermeneutics as a method which allows convenient access to the 'truths' of different cultural texts, without any ethical acknowledgement of the contexts in which those very 'texts' themselves are current. Thus in opposition to Schleiermacher's hermeneutics as an 'art of objective understanding' of all texts, sacred and secular,[6] the Gadamerian or 'philosophical hermeneutics' negotiated here follows Heidegger, whose critique of an ideal subjectivism led him to postulate the temporal nature of human being as a being-in-the-world that is always already 'thrown' into existence. Hermeneutic understanding is here not then something additional that human beings can do alongside other acts, but is integral with, and the most basic feature of, that existential structure of understanding itself.

As with Gadamer, the approach taken here attempts to couple thinking with acting, and reflects upon what aids a meaningful engagement with the AG from a Western contextualized space. This chapter argues that the taking into account of the self-understandings of the AG would reveal a context of engagement where one is not only to read the text, but to be transformed by it. It is in this respect that a 'philosophical hermeneutics', with its linkage between understanding, interpretation and praxis, provides a useful tool for the diaspora Sikh to bring his or her own lived experience into the context of interpretation. Understanding then involves the fusion between the horizon of the text and the horizon of the interpreter.

Due to the complexity of interlingual translation concerning cross-cultural incommensurability, the chapter attempts a tentative investigation which uses Western ideas heuristically, not metaphysically. That is to say, whilst the universality of hermeneutics is not accepted, hermeneutic ideas are understood to provide a fruitful and appropriate avenue of discussion. The intention is not to take Gadamer's 'philosophical hermeneutics' as a method – something he himself has repeatedly warned against – but as providing an approach for diaspora Sikhs that affords an accessible point of engagement with the AG from their own Western context. But to begin to do so one has not only to contextualize one's present hermeneutics in accordance with the text's own interpretive claims, but also critically to re-understand the various contexts of past Singh Sabha interpreters. If 'understanding is, essentially, a historically effected event' (Gadamer 1993: 300), then one has to become aware of tradition as an 'effective historical consciousness' (*Wirkungsgeschichte*). Without such a critical awareness, the legacies and prejudices of past interpreters, both academic and Sikh, will be unthinkingly reproduced, and their interpretations left to alienate further an already distanced diaspora Sikh culture.

Given the colonial context of the Singh Sabha interpreters, the main argument here relates less to the actual linguistic process of translation and more to the ideologically interpreted constructions; for it matters little how Nanak's words are *translated*, but what his words are *interpreted* to mean: into which contexts is Nanak made to speak, and for what purposes? For example, the highly valued Singh Sabha constructions reveal the stamp of orientalist history, having been forged under the trope of post-Enlightenment modernism and sealed with the idea of 'monotheism'. Suffice it to say here that beyond this turn to a modernist metaphysics of *theoria*, there was a significant shift in the classification of Sikh thought from Trumpp's 'atheistic' and 'immoral' characterization, to Macualiffe's and all subsequent Singh Sabha reactionary interpretations of 'Sikhism', as not only 'theistic' but 'monotheistic' and 'moral'.

## Colonial modernism as a hermeneutics of possession

Whilst there is no single origin of the Enlightenment nor one modernity, there are persistent themes that characterize and are associated with these terms. Europe and North America, with their 'advanced' mechanization and industrial modes of production, developed technologies to study and exploit the resources of nature. This 'modernization' was a product of the largely secular culture of liberal democracy, built upon the notion of the individual and his 'need' to order and rationalize his life. Humanism, science, industry, the free market, etc., were the means to achieve 'social progress' and 'freedom', if not 'liberation' and 'truth'. Yet the cost of such 'advances' of the modern project, integral with imperialism, was primarily borne by the exploited lower classes and those colonized – apart from the concomitant bureaucratization of life, the destruction of nature and rise of communalism and nationalism.

Interpretive theories and themes embedded in Enlightenment thinking cannot be separated from these material outcomes, and can be summarized as comprising a Eurocentric and theocentric bias towards the written Book and literature in general; the absolutization of reason in an atomized individual, culminating in science and the

78

search for universal laws; a progressive and linear understanding of history with authority of authenticity invested in a past foundational origin; the unitarization of phenomena into fundamental substances; and finally the belief in transcendent verities (Truth, Beauty, etc.,) as self-evident facts. The above characteristics of the modern episteme are underpinned by a metaphysics which inhibits engagement with the difference of the Other.

Reason is assumed to be normative, beyond the contingencies of history, or those of subjectivity, language and translation. This meant that the 'truths' of an Eastern 'text' regardless of its context could be accessed by any western scholar who had mastered the particular language. In contradistinction to such an epistemological approach, the ontological inclination of philosophical hermeneutics challenges any form of inquiry that tries to deny its own interpretive nature by masking its own historicity, and thereby puts into question any claim to have 'discovered' ahistorical truth or truths.

Cross-cultural and interlinguistic translation is therefore profoundly problematic, since it involves not only great loss and gain but endless distortions and instrumental appropriations of foreign ideas in the terms of one's own classificatory system. For example in thinking about religion, 'what modernity provides for the naming of God, therefore, is a series of seemingly endless debates on the correct ism, that is, that correct set of abstract propositions which name and think God' (Tracy 1994: 307), e.g., deism, theism, monotheism, pantheism, atheism, agnosticism, panentheism – irrespective of a tradition's own understandings and terms.

The ahistoricity of modern rationality in its theorizing of such isms, is challenged by acknowledging that one's position and discourse is situated, subject to context and always negotiated. Accepting the temporal conditions integral with contextual analysis, the modernist finality of interpretation and translation becomes over-ambitious and oppressive:

> Despite modernity's belief, there is no set of abstract propositions, no rational, clear, and distinct ideas, no sublating concept, no rational prepositional doctrine – in a word no *ism* – that is ever adequate for naming and thinking God ... For the modern to think God is to try to find the right abstract name – the right ism – for affirming or denying on modern rational grounds the existence and nature of God.
>
> (*Tracy* 1994: 309)

Backed by imperialism, modern scholarship sought knowledge of other cultures through a process of domination that turned the difference of the Other into an expression of the European Same, albeit a 'mediocre' and even 'subconscious' version. It will be shown below how the differences of the AG soon get overwritten by a colonialist/modernist discourse that transforms Guru Nanak and the AG into advocates of 'monotheism'. Such a modernist discourse manages this by prioritizing an abstract and scientific knowledge, gained from instrumental translation of texts, over an actual engagement with the Other (here practising Sikhs) via an equal and mutually co-determining praxis. This paper makes a preliminary attempt to move away from a universal 'hermeneutics of possession' to a contextual 'hermeneutics of praxis', 'defend[ing] the practical experience of reality *from the hegemony of autonomous theory*' (Smith 1996: 316). In order to understand and deconstruct the modernist presuppositions at work in the translation and interpretation of the AG, McLeod's systematization of Guru Nanak's teachings (*gurmat*) will serve here as a case in point. His work discloses a characteristically modern interpretation, revealing how *theoria* (his 'systematic theology') of the AG as written text has overdetermined Sikh *praxis* with the text as Guru.[7]

## McLeod's classic interpretation of *gurmat*

McLeod's assertion, commonly replicated by both Western and Eastern scholars, that 'the whole of Guru Nanak's thought revolves around his understanding of the nature of God' (McLeod 1996: 148) requires questioning. Such a conclusion seems eminently natural if superficial similarities are valued over the more complex realities of difference. The presence of a revealed text, expressive of 'the unity of God' is not grounds enough for theories of equivalence. The colonial inculturation aided a 'theologization' of Nanak's ideas which were formulated under the rubric of 'monotheism', wherein a 'belief in God' displaced the practice of the Word (*shabad*). This is in stark contrast to Nanak's persistent expression of resistance to any reification of his teachings independent of praxis. McLeod himself knew this only too well, when he consciously constructed a theology focused on 'beliefs' based on the Enlightenment presuppositions. In so doing he duly provides us with a 'creed of modernism' that tries to tame and capture the spirit of Nanak's genius:

The purpose of systematic theology is to construct a consistent framework, to develop a coherently integrated pattern out of what is dispersed throughout the record of an individual or corporate religious experience. In order to do this it is necessary to extract, analyse, and rearrange in a pattern which serves this particular purpose. By itself, however, such a pattern must be inadequate, for it will inevitably lose much of the spirit which prompted the original record.

(*McLeod* 1996: 176)

What 'systematic theology' has to do with Sikh praxis (of the Word) is an issue that remains unaddressed. Nevertheless, the obvious problem with 'extracting' and 'rearranging' a text to fit a 'coherent and consistent pattern' is that it simply does not fit; the presuppositions of the modernist creed make the choices of what is to be selected and presented, not the individual academic, nor the categories of the text itself. It is not surprising then to see that McLeod unknowingly finds himself in the modernist quandary over which ism provides the 'correct representation' of Nanak's teachings, just as Trumpp was in the 1870s with his classification of 'atheism' – though this time McLeod swings to the other extreme of 'monotheism':

If we are compelled to choose between these two polar conceptions our choice must settle upon the former [i.e., monotheist] alternative ... Guru Nanak's thought cannot be made to conform to the categories of *advaita* doctrine without equating his concept of God with the ultimately unreal of *Ishvara* of Sankara's philosophy. The total range of Guru Nanak's thought makes this equation manifestly impossible and accordingly requires us to reject the monistic alternative ... Strict pantheism is also excluded, for immanence is accompanied in the thought of Guru Nanak by a notion of transcendence. If a label must be applied then monotheism is the label we must use, but it should be remembered that the vital expression of the One is through the many, through the infinite plurality of the creation.

(*McLeod* 1996: 164–5)

Why must a label be applied? McLeod is by no means the only one who seems unable to detect where the motivation for 'correct classification' comes from. Such an argument, spun by assumptions of monolithic and abstract unities, is underlined by a desire to possess

81

the oriental Other. Sankara's advaitic Ishvara is unreal. Pantheism must be *strict* for it to be excluded. Identities must be internally consistent and 'made'. Nanak's thought is thus cast as monotheistic, attaining complete identity with that theological label, after the 'total range' of Nanak's thought has been analysed. Justification for such conclusions is judged by a measurable quantity not quality. McLeod's choice is reduced to an Aristotelian dualism: *either* monotheism *or* monism, no in between is possible for to own a teaching it must be made into a complete object of knowledge.

Nanak's understanding is then totalized and transformed into an unambiguous system, purged of its 'irrational' contradictions. Such a translation-interpretation need only be done once for it to be academically inscribed. There is no reason to reunderstand his teaching, once its basic pattern as (constructed) 'beliefs' have been elicited, classified and written. Furthermore, any system worth its Enlightenment salt must be rid of inconsistency or contradiction, or else, under the power of the either-or logic, it is simply rendered incomprehensible if not backward. Thus even though McLeod sets up the opposition between Nanak's religion of experience, of the 'real' rather than the 'notional', he claims that

> The latter can, however, do much to impart an understanding of the former ... For the purpose of *our own* understanding an integrated pattern can do much to clarify the nature of Guru Nanak's belief and accordingly the intention of this section is to seek such a pattern.
>
> (*McLeod* 1996: 149, emphasis added)

This systematization therefore clearly *belongs* to McLeod, yet the paradigm he is working on is so insidious that while he states, 'the fact that Guru Nanak's thought is not set out systematically does not mean that it is necessarily inconsistent', he forgets who is making the pattern. Soon after he states, 'the system developed by Guru Nanak is essentially a reworking of the Sant pattern' (McLeod 1996: 149, 151). Not only does Nanak *systematize his own* thought, he makes it in the pattern of monotheism, as too do the Sants. The academic's 'divine' ability to define *correctly* reaches absolute closure and Sikh difference is turned into more of the Imperial Same.

Though McLeod shows obvious reluctance to simplify Nanak's thought, it is clear that the modernist episteme has the final say. One last example of a modernist presupposition will suffice. Throughout Nanak's works there are obvious strands of his thought that can be understood under the themes of grace (*nadari, bakhasi, dati*) and *karma* (*karamu, likhia*). McLeod again feels compelled to make a choice between them, despite his insightful observations on both:

> *Karma* is one theory and the other is divine grace ... The latter theory is the one we must accept, but not at the cost either of maintaining that Guru Nanak denied the relevance of *karma* as far as this initial perception is concerned, or of admitting that at this point he was inconsistent ... The quotation ["If it is inscribed in the record of one's former deeds then one meets the True *Guru*". (AG 421)] implies an inconsistency, but when the paucity of such references, direct or implied, is compared with the very considerable weight of emphasis which he lays upon his concept of divine grace there can be no doubt that in the last analysis it is this grace which must decide the issue. The solution which he himself provides to the seeming inconsistency is a compromise which does accord a necessary place to *karma* as far as the initial apprehension of the Word is concerned, but which specifies grace as the ultimate determinant.
>
> (*McLeod* 1986: 204–5)

McLeod here seeks to resolve textual tensions and differences into conceptual unities; relations between such reified unities are then understood hierarchically, where one is dominant and ultimate and the other derivative and subservient. Rather than understand Nanak nondualistically as speaking at different levels simultaneously, the modernist discourse creates a unified and level playing field where all can be seen and classified systematically – and so finally: 'from his extensive hymns ... it is possible to frame a system which is complete in every respect' (McLeod 1997: 87). If the hidden depths and levels cannot be made visible, and/or are inconsistent with that which can be seen, then they are ignored as irrelevant if not irrational. It is noticeable that Nanak did not polarize *nadari* and *karamu*, nor did he make a compromise as McLeod claims. McLeod succeeds in transposing what is essentially a modernist problem to be Nanak's own dilemma. 'Solutions', 'inconsistencies' and 'compromises' do not feature in Nanak's thinking, but are part and parcel of a modernist academic discourse.

As can be seen from McLeod's studious considerations over the correct 'ism', it matters very little in the end which label is used, be it atheism or theism; what does matter is *how* that label is understood. Though politically charged, it seems dogmatic, if not futile, to argue which label is the correct one. The conundrum at the heart of the modernist discourse reflects a situation where scientific knowledge, to be scientific, must on the one hand accept interpretation but on the other deny its very existence. The greater the diversity of interpretation, the more fixed and occlusive definitions must become. No matter how much the closure of classification pretends to achieve in the abstract, it is undone in practice where interpretive application is required.

What McLeod and Singh Sabha interpreters (in their emulation of things western and modern) failed to see, was the text's own 'hermeneutic' claims. Rather than seek an external methodology validated by science to understand the AG, the Gurus' own clues about how to interpret the Word (*shabad*), in the text as well as in life, go unnoticed. The next section therefore investigates a contextual hermeneutics which seeks the interpretive intimations external and internal to the AG.

## A contextual hermeneutics of the AG:
### *satguru*, *shabad* and praxis

The Indian poet and philosopher A.K. Ramanujan sees the Western focus on the text as being based on a 'context free' hermeneutic, which is practiced through a rational discourse that formulates into a philosophical system building. This in turn leads to the familiar tendency to universalize one's theoretical constructions beyond the context from which they arose – the typical modernist enlightenment objective. This rationalistic emphasis and approach relies on a dis-embodied mental reasoning which, more often than not, results in a decontextualized metanarrative – a discourse that has 'forgotten its own metaphorical birth' as Derrida would have it, a discourse described by Nietzsche as one in which 'truths have forgotten their illusory nature.' This context-freedom is contrasted to Indian perspectives where action and thought are understood to be 'context-sensitive', involving engagement and praxis. Such modes of praxis often involve understandings of language and text not (only) as representations of meaning, but as (ritually) used: to evoke emotion (*bhav*) or heightened states of consciousness (*samadhi*), or to exact internal purgings (*tapa*).

The AG is not then a fixed document abstracted out of time and space, but is understood more as a process linking various levels of personal and social engagement. The text is not uniform and linear in structure, but 'circular' and interwoven in its themes, allowing repetition in use – a site for praxis and transformation. Rather than reified objectifications, one finds that within Indian traditions, embodiment, commentary, transmission and performance are emphasized. The text here then is inseparable from various activities linking the devotees and a tradition of interpretive exegesis, with the most revered figure and ideal being the Guru:

> For Hindus generally, scriptures play a secondary role ... A Hindu is 'saved' by a guru rather than by a scripture. From this point of view I am rather inclined to claim that 'Hinduism' has no single scripture, but innumerable scriptures, since the teachings and instructions of the guru are absolutely binding on the disciple-student ... Access to the Veda or to any other religious sources, such as the *puranas* or epics, was usually given to a disciple through the guru, and even here the scriptures play only a supportive role and they functioned within the instructional framework of a guru.
>
> (*Sundararajan*, cited in *Smith* 1993: 305)

A scriptural truth is only true if it can in some sense be engaged with, if not actualized. The guru's instruction is aimed at achieving this. The text is therefore the guru's means, a secondary tool. The AG becomes primary only after the tenth Guru's edict (as traditionally understood) and then primarily because it is understood as the 'Guru' itself. Though most Western scholars note that a text has content and form, here a third aspect of the (textual) guru must be appended. For it is not only *what* is said that matters, but *how* it is said and *who* does the saying. Without the lived experience of the truths of a text, the content and form reveal little in way of transformative understanding. Alper states:

> Respect for the well-uttered word is central for traditional Indian culture. The concepts of guru, mantra, and *shabda*, the institutions of preceptorial authority, mantric utterance, and commentarial exegesis inform and support each other ... In India, the word of the guru – par excellence the mantra – has often been thought the most effective form of 'truth-telling'.
>
> (*Alper* 1991: 413–4)

The guru's voice is efficacious due to his/her insightful perception and understanding. Meaning is thus not necessarily located in the text but in the guru's ability to interpret the text and relate it to the individual or group. The guru does not speak timeless truths, but truths the devotee can hear and enact. Thus there is no abstraction, but a retelling in pedagogy and praxis. Scholars may make claims about Nanak's words, but to claim in the Enlightenment paradigm means to assert the prepositional truth of a statement. Nanak's proclamations, however, lead one to believe that the truth of a statement does not depend on its descriptive accuracy, but how it affects the listener. It is the challenge and embodiment of knowledge, not only its representation, that is the focus in the contexts of orthopraxy.

To perceive the AG as simply a collection of various timeless truth-claims is to romanticize and formalize its textual-semantic content over and above its situational and often pedagogical-phonetic context. The teacher-student relation (Guru-Sikh), keeping the company of saints (sadh-sangat), singing and interpreting the hymns (kirtan-katha), repetition of (jap) and meditative reflection (dhian, vichar) on the divine Name, all provide the contextual tone, sound, feeling and meditative sense within which the former meaning should be understood. The focus being not on the text per se but the activity generated with and around it. Such textual praxis is not something to be thought about under the strictures of logical argument, but understood as an activity people do. The concern then is not in believing the once interpreted meanings of words but living by the word-as-communicated by an authority. The Word of the Guru is a communication that occurs through the words of the text but does not wholly reside in those words themselves; the communication speaks of an attitude and action not only of statement and abstraction.

There are then three basic senses of the Word in Sikh thought: the Word (shabad) as the hidden communication of the cosmic, everpresent True-Guru (satguru), which can take any form, internally and externally; the textual Word as the actual recorded hymns (bani) of the AG; and the Word as a site for engagement. The latter includes the former two senses; from those practices which are more closely associated with shabad, where the Word beyond the text is made (ghariai), practiced (kamaiai), recognized (pachhaniai) and reflected upon (vichariai), to those practices which relate more to bani where the textual Word is experienced through repetition (jap), reading (path), interpretation (katha) and singing (kirtan). Both of these engagements (relating to shabad and bani) taken together should lead to an effortless and beatific (sahaj) mindfulness (surat) of the Word as the Name (nam).

Since the assassination of the tenth Guru, the emphasis has shifted from the esoteric shabad to the exoteric bani, assisted by the conflation between the communication of the *satguru* (*gur-shabad*) with the hymns of the Adi Granth, to make a textual guru, the Guru Granth Sahib, which gives the 'illusion' that the material *bani* is actually the all-pervading *shabad*. This 'illusion', not entirely mistaken, only becomes meaningful however when there is true *praxis* of the Word.

This argument must not, however, be misconstrued. The importance of written words as exemplary means to accessing the Word is in no way undermined but positively encouraged:

> *gura bachani sachu shabadi pachhata* (AG 154)
> Through the words of the guru, the truth in the Word is
>     recognized.

Yet 'providing access to' does not mean that those words *themselves* are the Word, such that simply by reading them (*bani*) one would be reading the Word (*shabad*) – the danger of 'textolatry':

> *pariai nahi bhedu bujhiai pavana* (AG 148)
> Not by reading (but) through understanding is the secret found.

For Nanak there is no place without the Name because all creation is fashioned from the Name:

> *jeta kita teta nau, vinu navai nahi ko thau* (AG 4)
> As much as has been created, that much is the Name; there is no
>     place without the Name.

Given that the Name shares a basic identity with the Word, then at every point of engagement one can find the *satguru* teaching through *shabad* in/as a *gur-shabad* praxis. One crucial praxis across most bhaki traditions and hitherto regularly neglected, is singing the praises of the Divine.

## The musical text and *kirtan*

Guru Nanak's words were delivered in song, accompanied by Mardana, a Muslim rebeck player. Indeed, the AG is structured according to thirty-one melodies (*rag*), which have largely been ignored by western scholars and assumed not to have any bearing on the meaning of the hymns. Music demands participation through listening and singing; and a song, unlike a concept held in the mind, is immediately embodied affecting a person's attitude directly. It is,

87

therefore, hardly surprising that the importance of the evocation of *bhakti* emotion, inspiration and the creation of texture through the music of the *rag*, has been hitherto ignored by a reason-led Enlightenment hermeneutic.

As Nanak's poetic Word was musically born, given and understood, it is understandable that he did not systematize it into an abstract philosophy. It is notable that the earliest Sikh commentaries, for example those of Bhai Gurdas, also reciprocated the verse style of the Granth. Indeed any change in style to aid systematization would miss the point of praxis, like any poem turned into prose, or any song that is read. Hence *rag*, as 'a melody that charms' (Daniélou 1968), works directly to predispose the listener's attitude and orientation. Emotion and tone contextualize speech and thought as *praxis* orientates and directs interpretation.

Mood affects not only the quality of voice but also intention. The predisposition of thought by mood-emotion has, within the scientific paradigm, been denounced as something wholly negative, irrelevant and obfuscating, colouring one's judgement of the meaning of a text. In the *bhakti* context of loving-devotion, however, these objective biases appear to be hermeneutically confused on account of their privileging of thought at the expense of emotion, reason at the expense of intuition, thus separating feeling from thinking. The indigenous self-understandings dictate a contrary idea: the *bhakta* who does not feel the *ras* (refined taste, delicacy and feeling) of the *rag-kirtan* is considered to be lacking sensitivity – the aim not being only to analyse but to feel, and harmonize with, the message through its singing. This reflects not an ownership of knowledge but a participation with it. Fixing a rationalized semantic translation as superior to an emotionally engaged interpretation is to confuse hermeneutic priorities, to privilege the written form over embodied praxis, and to dogmatize a way. For a song speaks beyond its words, not only through them. The performance of *kirtan* is therefore hermeneutically significant for the exegesis of *katha*.

## The Word as hermeneutic praxis: diasporic *katha*

*adisatu disai ta kahia jai, binu dekhe kahana biratha jai* (AG 222)
(When) the Unseeable One is seen, then what is said (about it)
   is of value.
Without seeing (that One), vain is one's speech.

It is of paramount hermeneutic importance to understand that Nanak's starting point as Guru is quite different from that of the 'average' human being. It is his awakened Guru-state that gives value to his words, not just the words themselves. His egoless condition allows spontaneous (*sahaj*) hermeneutic access to the Word; whereas, for those afflicted by the false I (*haumai*), any hermeneutic ability is veiled, i.e. fundamentally selfish. *Haumai* is then the most formidable hermeneutic obstacle – not language, grammar, knowledge or experience, but the self's own conditioned nature:

> *haumai mare gura shabade pae* (AG 228)
> He who destroys the false I, finds (it) through the Guru's Word.

When the false I is present, one's understanding is empty:

> *eko ek kahai sabhu koi haumai garabu viapai*
> *antari bahari eku pachhanai iu gharu mahalu sinapai* (AG 930)
> Everyone says that 'He is One, just One,' but each is engrossed
>     in pride and the false I. Let him recognize the One within and
>     without; in this way he will realize (the One) in the court of
>     his own home.

The mere saying, or representation of a truth is not what interested Nanak, for such a metaphysical approach does little to challenge, dislodge or transform the false I. Indeed a translation that simply represents the 'truths' of the AG in another language, without an engaged praxis, is a futile exercise. The focus falls not on a descriptive and explanatory knowledge, but a transformative knowledge through becoming:

> *jini jata so tisa hi jeha* (AG 931)
> He becomes like the one whom he knows.

Knowing through the praxis of discernment of the Word and its application is integral with a philosophical hermeneutic self-reflexive in understanding. However, living the Word is understood to be a serious enterprise, for it leads to the destruction of the mind and its worldly delusions about the world as well as the ego:

> *shabadi mue manu mana te maria* (AG 796)
> He who dies by the Word destroys the mind through the mind.

As sounds contains silence, so *bani* accommodates *shabad*; as desire houses the desireless, so the noise of the egoistic mind contains within it the serenity of an egoless mind. An understanding that 'destroys' the bound mind leaves the free mind 'open' to be 'spoken through':

> *kia hau kathi kathe kathi dekha mai akathu na kathana jai*
> *jo tudhu bhave soi akha tilu teri vadiai* (AG 795)
> What should I say? Whilst talking of You I see that I cannot describe the indescribable. Whatever pleases You, that alone I speak and that is but an iota of Your greatness.

Nanak does not take refuge in silence due to the ineffability of that which he wants to communicate. Nor does he get lost in an endless, and self-defeating attempt at metaphysical description, but speaks that which is spoken through him by a source beyond the ego-self. This intimates that his words are not to be taken as a philosophical discourse – be it monotheism, atheism or pantheism, but as ways and means to transform the self in praxis. Nanak is fearlessly blunt in his expression: to communicate with the Word the self has to die (*ap gavai*):

> *antari shabadu nidhanu hai mili apu gavaia* (AG 228)
> Within lies the treasure of the Word: having acquired it the self is destroyed.

A further obstacle to a hermeneutic engagement with the Word occurs when one assumes the existence of another to be present, whether taken as a worldly or a divine particularity. The world is but a passing show, episodes of which one selects and attaches to in vain; for nothing remains for long:

> *jo disai so chalasi kura nehu na vekhu* (AG 61)
> Whatever is seen shall depart. Contract not affection for the false show.

This 'false show' can also be of the divine, if the absolute is reified. But Nanak's Ultimate resists the succour of fixed abstractions:

> *sahibu mera nita nava sada sada dataru* (AG 660)
> My Master is perpetually new, and ever and ever the Giver.

In Nanak's thinking both the Master Giver and the world are dynamically conceived and are not two. It seems then that it is not what one attaches to, be it physical or metaphysical, but attachment itself that creates the dualism (*dubidha*) of the self and other. The point is certainly not to exchange attachment to the world for attachment to 'god', where insecurity remains constant; nor to 'forget the world' and 'remember god', since what can be remembered of 'god' is always an aspect of this world. The unsatisfactoriness of such attitudes rests on a dualistic interpretive framework, and it is precisely this dualistic way of reading (that posits the reality of 'others') that Nanak singles out as a root problem in interpreting the world and the Word:

> *duja mari shabadi pachhata* (AG 223)
> Destroying [attachment to] the other, the Word is realized.

The Word, as the supreme Reality, is nondualistically identified with the world and is simultaneously a rejection of it. Duality either polarizes both absolutely so that their relation becomes incomprehensible, or unites them categorically, making any particularity idolatrous. The nondual understanding of the Word and the world thus demands a skilful way of eliciting the Word from the world in all its 'worldliness'.

Rather than from the quality of any particular object, practice or belief, it is from the state of one's conditioned consciousness and the quality of one's engagement with life, that the Word may be discerned and realized:

> *beda gandhu bole sachu koi* (AG 143)
> If anyone speaks the truth he establishes a link with the scriptures (Vedas).

Hence the practice of virtues, serving those in need, take on hermeneutic importance. But even beyond this, the *satguru* imparts a way of interpreting and listening to the world that reveals that any experience or interaction with the world may provide an opportunity to hear the teaching of the Word. This parallels the hermeneutic circle. For instance, Nanak says:

> *dubidha chukai ta shabadu pachhanu* (AG 1343)
> When duality is removed then recognize the Word.

Here there is an obvious circularity that supplements this statement with an understanding that it is only through the Word that duality can be removed. As with the self and Word above, the Word is accessed only when the self is destroyed, yet it is only through the Word that the self can be overcome. Though apparently a catch-22, this is not a vicious circle. The circularity here between the Word (*shabad*) and praxis (*seva*) occurs in such a way that:

> *jaisa sevai taiso hoi* (AG 223)
> One becomes as one serves.

91

*jai siu rata taiso hovai* (AG 411)
One becomes like that in which one is immersed.

Thus the hermeneutic circle of *shabad* and praxis can spin both ways. If one is immersed in the sin of worldly pursuits and not practiced in renunciation and virtuous living, then the Word can only appear opaque. Yet, this obscurity is lifted through a reversal:

> *nanaka auguna jetare tete gali janjira; je guna honi ta katiani se bhai se vira* (AG 595)
> O Nanak, there are as many chains (around) the neck as there are sins.
> If there are virtues, (which are) as brothers and friends, then (the chains) are cut.

Virtue must outweigh vice if the Word is to be perceived (regularly?). Again, one is to practice virtue to perceive the Word, and it is through perceiving and employing the Word that virtue arises:

> *nanaka avagana shabadi jalae guna sangami prabhu pae* (AG 764)
> O Nanak, he who burns his sins through the Word, obtains the Lord by associating with virtues.

This circular process between the Word and praxis, being revealed in an applied self-reflexive understanding, leads to a process whereby one eventually enacts the truths one interprets:

> *kari bicharu acharu parata* (AG 415)
> Thinking deeply [on the Word] good conduct is attained.

> *jehe karama kamai teha hoisi* (AG 730)
> As are the deeds one does, so will one become.

Praxis is therefore at the core of any understanding of the Word. The ethical and personal implications of such a hermeneutic may be briefly stated as operating under the axiom that the *quality and focus of attention determines the nature of the Word*. Such a hermeneutic would obviously be contextually defined and relationally actualized – and above all, open to re-understanding differently. Nanak specifically relates the understanding of the Word to the practice of truth (*sach achar*) over and above any knowledge of the truth (*sach*), revealing his key hermeneutic principle that establishes the focus on *praxis* over *theoria*:

*sachu orai sabhu upari sachu acharu* ...
*nanaka namu na visarai chhutai shabadu kamai* (AG 62)
Truth is the highest of all virtues; but higher still is the living of
   Truth ...
Forget not the Lord's Name, O Nanak, for one is freed (only) by
   practising the Word.

The exegete that does not apply what he interprets from the AG to his
own context will not be interpreting the Word but only the words of
the text. Scientific objectivity that attempts to curtail all subjective
involvement is wholly misplaced in such an endeavour. The context in
which this Word-praxis is likely to happen if at all, is in the company
of saints or true human beings (*sadh/satsangat*):

*sadha sangati mahi hari rasu paiai gura miliai jama bhau bhaga*
   (AG 598)
In the Society of the Saints, Hari's Nectar [Word/Name] is to be
   found, and meeting with the Guru, the fear of Yama/Death
   departs.

Another of Nanak's underlying hermeneutic principles is therefore
that: *one arrives at the truths of a religious text not by technical study
alone but by associating with those who embody those textual truths.*
Those who associate with the company of saints (*sadh-sangat*) acquire
the appropriate hermeneutic abilities, otherwise the truths of a text are
simply reflections of one's own ego-understanding (i.e., self-
produced). What is emphasized therefore, is a different kind of
learning and interpreting, involving a 'being-and-associating-with', a
'doing-through-imitation' that overrides and informs technical study.
To understand the Word as integral to social engagement in a specific
community is to comprehend the Word as a communication, a
dialectical 'speaking' and response. Guru, time, audience and personal
context, in part, determine the meanings a text can 'speak'. The
communicated Word then is not the fixed written words themselves,
but how those words are understood and recontextualized. It is in this
light that Nanak refers to the Guru's Word (*shabad-guru*) as
something to be practiced (*shabad kamai*) in a social context of the
saintly community (*sadh-sangat*) and as something that is privately
made (*ghariai shabad*) in a more yogically austere fashion, as well as
something to reflect on (*shabad vichar*) and recognize (*shabad
pachhan*):

93

*jatu pahara dhiraju suniaru, aharani mati vedu hathiaru*
*bhau khala again tapa tau, bhandha bhau amritu titu dhali*
*ghariai shabadu sachi takasal* (AG 8)
The control (of the senses) is the goldsmith's workshop,
   steadfastness the goldsmith;
The mind is the anvil and knowledge the hammer;
Fear (of God) the bellows and severe austerities the fire;
Love (of God) is the crucible, in that melt the immortal nectar;
Thus is the true mint of the Word to be fashioned.

Such a fashioning of the Word leads to true action (*achar*):

*bhitari amritu soi janu pavai jisu guru ka shabadu ratanu achara*
   (AG 1256)
That man alone obtains the inner Nectar [of the Name] whose
   right living (applies) the Jewel of the Guru's Word.

Nanak's works should not be read as though they were in some
quantitative sense comprehensive, nor in some rational sense
systematic, but as providing locations of engagement that may reveal
truths that have temporal and spatial significance.

A modernist hermeneutic strategy entails a myth of closure which
presumes to see things, rather simplistically, 'as they really are',
which often works to ignore how things could be; to translate a
couplet 'how it is meant' can deaden how its meaning can 'continue
to speak'. Absolute interpretation denies interpretation itself. To
accept any finality in interpretation as facts of scholarship can signal
the death of thinking-on and thinking differently. In neglecting the
challenge of thinking differently, the result may lead to the
possession of descriptions as simple markers of 'correct' truth and
belief, which in turn may result in ideological conflict and the
political dominance of one view over another. The culture of final
representation leads to the creation of phantom structures of the real
as totalized ideals, logically organized and unambiguously fashioned.
The movement of a hermeneutic praxis however suggests that,
diachronically, today's interpretations are the future's misrepresenta-
tions, just as synchronically, one group's translation is another's
misinformation. The truth of the Word cannot be shared as the
same because it demands personal transformative engagement. The
AG's textual truths therefore demand the responsibility of a
continual recontextualization:

*sachu purana hovai nahi* (AG 955)
The Truth does not get old.

The truth does not age because it is forever dying in its re-contextualization and expression. Understanding and finality do not sit together except in the (political) silence of closure:

*sacha ki mati sada nautana shabadi nehu navelo* (AG 242)
The understanding of the True One is ever new and ever fresh
   is the love of the Word.

As with the Buddha's Dhamma (teaching) which is likened to a raft to be used provisionally as a skulful means, so too is Nanak's *gurmati* wherein the Guru is a raft:

*guru pauri beri guru guru tulaha harinau* (AG 17)
[To reach] Hari's Name the Guru is the ladder, the Guru is the
   boat and the Guru is the raft.

And the Word is the means by which the soteric praxis is enacted:

*satiguru hai bohitha shabadi langhavanaharu* (AG 1009)
The True-Guru is a boat, through the Word one is delivered
   across.

This would mean that the Word for Nanak, also like the Buddha's Dhamma, is a medicine not a metaphysics:

*guru ka shabadu daru hari nau* (AG 1189)
The Word of the Guru, Hari's Name [are] the remedy.

A hermeneutics of the AG therefore needs to engage this *gurshabad* praxis, if the desire to conquer, tame and own the AG is to be exorcized, and the text's medicine not refused.

## Notes

1  All quotes from AG are from Guru Nanak (M1). The standard text of the AG used here is the *Shabadarath Sri Guru Granth Sahibji*.
2  This unwieldly phrase is used to highlight that there is no postmodernity without modernity. To make post-modernity into another 'ism', like modernism, is to misunderstand it; 'postmodern' thinking resists generalization and so is not paradigmatic but parasitic upon all paradigms and therefore inherently context-sensitive.
3  *Gurmukhi* strictly refers to the script, not the various 'languages' of the AG.

4 It is for this reason that the indigenous interpretive traditions or *pranalis* (*sahaja, bhai, paramartha, udasi, niramala,* and *sampradai/giani,*) are not appropriate for reference in this paper except for the Singh Sabha tradition, with its English translations and orthodox dominance.

5 Gadamer notes the three traditional forms of hermeneutics: understanding (*subtilitas intelligendi*), interpretation (*subtilitas explicandi*) and application (*subtilitas applicandi*) and stresses the latter. For a historical genesis of hermeneutics see Palmer 1969, Ormiston and Schrift 1990.

6 Or even Dilthey's romantic hermeneutics which distinguishes itself from the explanatory bias of the natural sciences (Naturwissenschaften) as a method of understanding in the social and human sciences (*Geisteswissenschaften*).

7 Due to the beguiling, unnoticed and all-pervasive nature of a paradigm, any one individual cannot be held responsible for employing its presuppositions. However in the light of a sudden crack in the glass of a paradigm's self-transparency, it becomes ethically important to re-understand one's position and views.

## Chapter Six

# Making Punjabi
# Literary History

## *Christopher Shackle*

In a magisterial aside to his recent discussion of the interpretation of
the janamsakhis, J.S. Grewal remarks:

> In fact they have continued to exercise perceptible influence
> upon the style and imagery of later generations of Punjabi
> writers. Together with the *Adi Granth*, the works of the Sufis,
> and eventually the western models, they rank as a major
> influence in the development of Punjabi literature.
>
> (*Grewal* 1998: 159)

At least among modern Sikh writers, who have played the leading role
in its creation, there would probably be very general agreement that
twentieth century Punjabi literature owes its inspiration to a
combination of these three sources: Sikh scripture and the texts
closely associated with it; the pre-modern Punjabi poetry produced by
Sufi authors; and Western literature. It is the purpose of this chapter
to explore the original construction of this composite scheme of
cultural reference and to reflect on some of its implications, through a
contrastive examination of the work of two early twentieth century
pioneers of Punjabi literary history.

While the chapter is deliberately directed towards data rather than
theory, its general approach is informed by recent general understandings of the nature of literary history (Perkins 1992; Brown 1995),
above all by the clear modern perception that all literary history is an
exercise in highly selective memory and arbitrary definition (Bassnett
1993: 48–91). It also draws upon the polysystem theory of the Israeli
critic Itamar Even-Zohar, particularly that theory's emphasis upon

the special role of translation in helping determine many developments within a given literature as well as establishing inter-relationships between literatures (Gentzler 1993: 105–25).

The chapter is also motivated by a conviction of the need for a greater attention to the Islamic component of the religious polysystem in which Sikhism has evolved, and by a belief that investigations of the long and complex relationship between Sikhs and Punjabi Muslims as religious communities can be significantly nuanced by parallel approaches from a comparative literature perspective. Such a viewpoint leads naturally to a foregrounding of the primacy of Urdu examples[1] in the following section, as a necessary preliminary to understanding the patterning of the early literary histories of Punjabi to which the chapter is mainly devoted.

## Urdu models: Azad and Hali

Urdu was the premier literary language in the complex linguistic and cultural polysystem of nineteenth century northern India. Urdu was therefore the language and the literature with the greatest direct exposure to the operations of the colonial state. Against the powerful ideological challenge of Western ideas, however, Urdu writers also proved uniquely capable of evolving significant defences through reinterpretations of their historic cultural resources, which in turn provided an influential model for the evolution of several other literatures linked to Urdu in the Indian polysystem, notably including Punjabi.

The promotion of Urdu in the Punjab after its conquest by the British and their destruction of Mughal Delhi in 1857 combined to give Lahore a new significance as a centre for Urdu. A particularly energetic role in this development was played by Dr G.W. Leitner (Bruce 1933: 10–32), both in his official capacity as Principal of the new Government College and as founder of the influential Anjuman-i-Punjab, a society designed to further Leitner's Orientalist aim of developing an educational system based on classical and vernacular Indian languages rather than English.

It is the meeting of the Anjuman on 9 May 1874 (Pritchett 1994: 34–7) which has famously come to symbolize Lahore's moment of unique cultural importance as a site of historic West-East encounter. This was addressed (in English) by Colonel W.R.M. Holroyd, Director of Public Instruction, who called as an aim of official educational policy for a remodelling of Urdu poetry and the traditional poetic symposium (*musha'ira*) which was its chief social institution:

> This meeting has been called to find ways and means for the development of Urdu poetry, which is a state of decadence today ... Let us lay the foundation of a new *mushaira* today, with this special feature that instead of a hemistich we should announce a certain subject on which the poets should write poems ... I propose that we should hold monthly meetings, and that next month the poets should write on the 'rainy season'.

> (*Sadiq* 1984: 290)

To understand just how radical a challenge was represented by these proposals requires some reference to the elite literary norms long established in Persian and largely transferred to Urdu as its Indian heir (Matthews *et al.* 1985: 16–27, Shackle 2000). These found their prime expression in the *ghazal*, a short love lyric with strict rules of rhyme and metre providing a formal frame for end-stopped verses which often appear semantically diverse from one another, but which always draw for their conceits upon a common store of rhetorical devices and an accepted if vast range of conventional symbolic patterns, like the relationship between rose (*gul*) and nightingale (*bulbul*).

The practice of the poetry combined an important oral dimension – as in the competitive recitation of *ghazals* at a *musha'ira* – with an intrinsic written tradition, including the copying and circulation of individual poems and alphabetically arranged poetic collections (*divan*). The continuity of the tradition was ensured by the practice of apprentice professionals or amateurs submitting their verses as pupils (*shagird*) to the correction of a master-poet (*ustad*); and it was always developed with continual reference to the endlessly studied and reworked masterpieces of the great poets of the mediaeval Persian canon. Thus for the *ghazal* the fourteenth century Persian *divan* of Hafiz continued to provide a major reference point, supplemented by the later example of Urdu masters like the eighteenth century Mir Taqi, and comparable models existed for all the other recognized poetic genres.

Prose was always subordinate to verse in this literary hierarchy, and the sophistication of the poetry was never remotely matched by Persian or Urdu literary history. Besides the circulation of oral anecdotes, a parallel written record of the craft's practitioners was also maintained in collections of prose memoirs of earlier and contemporary poets. In this genre, called *tazkira*, no very special order governed the presentation of the notices of individual poets, which were normally confined to quotations of representative extracts prefaced by unsystematic critical comments and by brief biographical sketches. These often highlighted the poet's affiliation with earlier poets through the master-pupil (*ustad-shagird*) relationships which were seen as the main link between poets, besides the intrinsic self-reflexivity of the poetic tradition itself which was so obviously manifested in the admired practice of deliberate *imitatio* (Losensky 1998: 100–313).

All the elaborately linked parts of the complex and self-reinforcing literary system were now challenged by the new agenda adumbrated in Holroyd's Anjuman address. Emerging from the Orientalist concerns of senior British members of the colonial bureaucracy, this challenge predictably appealed mainly to Indian subordinates whose positions in that same bureaucracy helped condition them to provide a suitably Westernizing response. Because these subordinates included the two most interesting Urdu writers of their generation – Muhammad Husain Azad (1830–1910) and Altaf Husain Hali (1837–1910) – who were both working for the British in Lahore as cultural refugees from the collapse of Delhi, the Westernizing response to the Orientalist challenge was of unique significance not only to the later development of Urdu poetry but also to the reconfiguration of Urdu literary history (Pritchett 1994).

Although Azad, as a very close associate of Leitner's, was the more intimately linked to the agenda of the Anjuman's new style of *musha'ira* (which ran for about a year), the poems which he contributed to it were artistic failures. The significance of Azad was instead to emerge through his outstandingly creative response to the colonial state's demands for vernacular textbooks. Azad's success in this new literary genre was nowhere greater than in his immensely influential history of Urdu literature, *Ab-e Hayat* (The Water of Life), which has been continually reissued (Azad n.d.) since its original publication in 1880. Written in a wonderfully crafted style which cunningly adapts many resources of the old rhetoric to the simpler expectations of Victorian India, this builds on the old *tazkira* tradition in consisting primarily of a set of notices of Urdu poets with examples of their work, but also achieves a transformation into something substantially new.

The novelty of *Ab-e Hayat* is superficially due in part to its scale, occupying some five hundred pages; in part to its methodical organization, beginning with an extended introduction dealing with Urdu language and poetics and their relationship to Persian and to classical Hindi, called 'Bhasha'; to the apparently systematic organization of the poets into five periods (*daur*); even to the use of sometimes extended footnotes. More significantly, *Ab-e Hayat* is differentiated from the *tazkira* tradition by the context of its production in a colonized society, looking back across the great cultural divide of 1857 to a literary and cultural world whose achievements Azad celebrates from a distance which also allows him to mourn its passing. *Ab-e Hayat* is thus a work of retrospective literary history which gives a radically foreshortened perspective of the more distant past in order to focus upon the most recent of Azad's five periods (*c.*1830–57), with an unashamedly disproportionate treatment of his own *ustad*, the Delhi poet Zauq (d.1854).[2]

Hali, who was by far the greater poet, did manage to produce for the Lahore *musha'ira* several rather successful thematic poems (*nazm*) on the unpromising-sounding topics prescribed: 'The Rainy Season', 'The Delight of Hope', 'Patriotism', 'Dialogue of Mercy and Justice'. After his departure in 1875 from Lahore, where his task had been to revise Urdu translations of English textbooks, Hali developed the new poetic style in his great *Musaddas-e Madd-o Jazr-e Islam* (The Flow and Ebb of Islam) of 1879, a long poem produced under the influence of Sayyid Ahmad Khan's reformist modernism which combines a celebration of early Arab Islam with a condemnation of the degeneracy of Islamic society in contemporary India (Shackle and Majeed 1997).

The enormous impact of the *Musaddas*[3] was in part due to the appeal of its grand theme, in part to the revolutionary nature of its style of 'natural poetry' (*necharal sha'iri*), the product of a deliberately modernist agenda (Sperl and Shackle 1996: 1, 231–40), which aimed to address the urgent needs of the present by jettisoning the tired Persianate rhetoric of a discredited and degenerate literary past in favour of an aggressively stripped down style which looked to daily life for its homely images. Although in practice himself hardly less ambiguous than Azad in his equivocal relationship to the magical appeal of the Urdu literary past, Hali went on to produce a lengthy prose justification of 'natural poetry' in his *Muqaddama-e Shi'r-o Sha'iri* (Foreword: On Verse and Poetry) of 1893, which is of unequalled significance as a pioneering literary manifesto.

Basing itself on a Bloomian strong reading – with an obvious if unstated debt to Wordsworth – of a translation of Milton's 'Poetry is simple, sensuous and passionate' (Steele 1981: 30), Hali's definition of good poetry is that which possesses the virtues of simplicity (*sadagi*), the power to inspire emotion (*josh*) and a firm basis in reality (*asliyat*). Itself spurning the stylistic resources of which Azad availed himself, Hali's *Muqaddama* is a somewhat confusingly arranged compilation of many short sections, and makes its points by emphatic repetition rather than strongly linear argumentation.

Although the *Muqaddama* is not designed as a literary history, its need to address the profound temporal rupture of the colonial experience means that its argument is continually underlain by a powerfully historical vision very much in keeping with that which Hali had earlier articulated in his *Musaddas*. Whereas Azad celebrates the final culmination of a literary tradition in its last flowering, Hali is a critic for whom aesthetics is not to be divorced from morality. So he continually castigates the perverse refinement of Persianate rhetoric in those same Urdu poets of the mid-nineteenth century who are so differently described in *Ab-e Hayat*. Hali instead always prefers earlier to later poets with an especial exaltation – in the name of his translated Westernizing ideals – of the simplicities he particularly associates with the early Arab poets of the Prophetic epoch. As is typical of any modernism which has little truck with the immediate past, Hali's justification of the new therefore rests upon the idealized exaltation of the ancient and the sacred.

In any society not overtaken by the hypertrophy of contemporary Anglo-American academia which so easily risks privileging criticism over creativity, the chief function of literary history is to help align present literary practice with parts of the literary heritage of the past. In the later development of Urdu literary history through the colonial period and beyond, the combined role of Azad and Hali has been extraordinarily significant in encouraging the coexistence of *ghazal* poetry alongside the looser Anglic style of the modern *nazm*, and allowing both the moral imperatives of Islamic example and the cultural appeal of Indo-Persian courtly civilization to continue to function as vehicles for a succession of responses to first the colonial, and now the postcolonial situations.

## Mechanical translation: Maula Bakhsh Kushta

Since a knowledge of Urdu was so widely disseminated by the educational system devised by the British for the Punjab, it is hardly surprising that early attempts to construct modern Punjabi literary history should have been explicitly and profoundly indebted to both Azad's *Ab-e Hayat* and Hali's *Muqaddama*. Almost by definition, however, it is hardly possible for schemes of literary history to be exactly copied from one language to another, and what makes these attempts so interesting are the consequences of the translation of models from one part to another of the complex cultural polysystem of the Punjab in which Urdu and Punjabi co-existed alongside several other languages.

Perhaps the most obvious factor inhibiting any straight translation of the Urdu models into Punjabi is the very different historical status of the two languages. The marginal place in the precolonial educational systems of the Punjab of Punjabi literary texts – as opposed to the partially overlapping category of Sikh religious texts – is readily apparent from the wonderfully rich data provided in Leitner's 1882 *Report on Indigenous Education* (Leitner 1991). Punjabi had never been the vehicle for very sophisticated courtly or learned literature, and there are no premodern prose records of earlier poetic traditions.

The first significant records of the Punjabi poetic past appear as part of the mid-nineteenth century elaborations of the narrative romance (*qissa*) in which this traditional Punjabi genre was increasingly overlaid by Persianate example. One manifestation of the increased selfconsciousness of these later *qissa*-poets is their practice of including lists of their predecessors. The earliest major example of this *tazkira*-style evocation occurs in the massive *Saif ul Muluk* (1855) composed soon after the British conquest on the northern boundary of the Punjab by the Sufi poet Mian Muhammad Bakhsh (1830–1907) of Mirpur. As part of his lengthy epilogue to the narrative of his poem – which has itself long enjoyed a uniquely canonical status as a popular classic across the northern Punjab – Mian Muhammad includes a long list of Punjabi poets. For the most part these are briefly memorialized in a single verse, although some of those nearer to his own time are more fully discussed.

Organized in a loose chronological order, this Sufi author's catalogue of some seventy verses (Muhammad Bakhsh 1983: 448–52) concentrates almost entirely upon Muslim poets,[4] and gives a natural precedence to Sufis. So Baba Farid Shakarganj, particularly associated in later scholarship with the Farid-verses included in the *Adi Granth* (Shackle 1993: 268–89), here stands first as the primal saint-poet of the Punjab, and is closely followed in the third verse by the great eighteenth century Sufi poet Bullhe Shah, then a dozen verses later by Bullhe Shah's near contemporary Varis Shah, himself often counted as a Sufi on the basis of his *Hir* (1766), the greatest Punjabi *qissa* of them all (Shackle 1992). It may readily be seen that the mode of citation is primarily devotional and eulogistic:

> First stands Shaikh Farid, the saintly Shakarganj:
> Each word he spoke a guide to truth and righteousness ...
> Bullhe Shah swam in the sea of Unity:
> His hymns remove all unbelief from every heart ...
> Who dares to criticize Varis the lord of poesy?
> How may we point a finger at one word of his?

The importance of the *qissa* to the publishing trade which developed so rapidly in later nineteenth century Punjab with its main centre in Lahore is reflected in a massive growth both in the numbers and the size of new romances (Shackle 1995). For a variety of reasons, both cultural and economic, Urdu soon claimed the active allegiance of the great majority of literate Punjabi Muslims, a position which it continues to enjoy in Pakistan over a century later. While the traditional position of Persian was rapidly eroded, a small minority of Muslim poets wrote from choice in Punjabi, and some were open to the new trends signalled in Urdu by Hali and his contemporaries.

The Amritsar poet Maula Bakhsh Kushta (1876–1954) was an unusually interesting member of the small minority of Punjabi Muslims who continued to prefer Punjabi to Urdu as a vehicle for poetic expression (Kushta 1949: i–vi, *Panj Darya* 1969). Born in Amritsar into a Bhatti Rajput family, Kushta was enrolled in the Government School but later withdrawn by his father for fear of his being converted to Christianity. He then left home for Lahore where he earned his living in the publishing business and where he developed a precocious poetic reputation as an extempore performer in the muscular urban arenas (*akhara*) of Punjabi poetic performance in the then fashionable Persianizing style. Victor in a challenge match which he had boldly issued to all comers through the press, his poetic ambition was further signalled in his publication in 1903 of the first Punjabi *divan*.

This was a deliberate attempt to give Punjabi a proper *divan* on the complete Persian model, i.e. a collection of *ghazals* arranged alphabetically by the last letter of the rhyme, with at least one poem for every letter of the Persian alphabet.[5] This mechanical coverage of the poetic alphabet may be interpreted as part of a general agenda designed to bring Punjabi up to Persianate speed. Its stylistic strategy is equally evident, for instance, in Kushta's macaronic adaptation of the famous first *ghazal* in Hafiz's *Divan*, which ingeniously changes the first hemistich of each verse into a Punjabi substitute. So Hafiz's sixth verse has a striking image:

A pitch-dark night, a fear of waves, a frightful whirlpool –
Lightly laden on the shore, how should they know our state?

Kushta keeps the Persian metre but loses Hafiz's wonderful asyndeton as he artfully works in an apt reference to the romantic heroine Sohni drowning in the river Chenab when the pot she has used as a float turns out to be unfired (Kushta 1964: 179):

*Ghara khurya pae ghumman chutarfi te kahe Sohni*
*'Kuja danand hal-e ma sabukbaran-e sahilha'*

The pot dissolved, around the eddies swirled, and Sohni says:
'Lightly laden on the shore, how should they know our state?'

Besides *ghazals*, Kushta's *Divan* also contains examples of other Persian genres as well as *nazms* in more modern style. It thus provides an interesting illustration of time lag within the polysystem. Whereas in Urdu the extreme Persianization of poetic styles had reached its mid-nineteenth century peak in time for Hali's harsh retrospective criticism in favour of his new Anglicized aesthetic ideals, in Punjabi Persianization and Anglicization proceeded more or less simultaneously, usually refracted through Urdu models. So when Kushta ends his *Divan* with examples of the Persian-derived *ruba'i*, made familiar in English by Fitzgerald, he nativizes the name of his Punjabi quatrains to 'four-footers' (*chaupaian*) but exactly copies Hali's adaptation of the *ruba'i* (Matthews and Shackle 1972: 168–71) to prosaically sent4entious ends.

Kushta's poetic reputation in the non-elite urban milieu in which Punjabi was cultivated was further consolidated by the publication in 1913 of his version in some 6,500 verses of the *Hir* story, whose immortalization by Varis Shah acted as a continual spur to later imitation. Attention needs to be drawn here only to prelude of Kushta's *Hir*. This includes the by now fairly customary list of earlier treatments (Kushta 1949: 3–5), but with a striking shift from simple memorialization to a more elaborately precise mode of versified literary history which covers, besides Persian versions, the Braj Bhasha re-telling in the *Dasam Granth* (*Triya Charitra* 98, *DG* 942–4), and a sequential account of the many versions by Punjabi Muslim poets:

In 1753 (VS) on Sunday 9 Bhadon
  The *Triya Charitra* was written for Guru Gobind Singh.
Then, eighty years ahead of Varis, came Chiragh
  Who sat in D. G. Khan to tell the tale of *Hir.*
Then, forty years ahead of Varis, Muqbil wrote
  A *qissa* whose few verses tell so much of love;
Muhammad Shah was king when his pure style was formed
  It was 1100 (AH) when he told of Hir . . .

Here a new consciousness of the literary past is strikingly evident in the way these verses strain the metre in order to convey a textbook objectivity of detail. The most remarkable feature of the first edition of Kushta's *Hir* is, however, the fact that it includes as an appendix a short survey in Urdu prose of Punjabi literature, entitled *Chashma-e Hayat* (The Spring of Life) in open imitation of Azad's famous *Ab-e Hayat.* Although actually written by one Mir Karamatullah of Amritsar, this was done expressly at Kushta's invitation and is heavily indebted to him for much of its information. Kushta himself later claimed credit for *Chashma-e Hayat* (Kushta 1960: 353), and most of its themes are reiterated in his later writings, so it may be effectively regarded as having been ghosted on his behalf.

In its lesser and less tidy fashion, *Chashma-e Hayat* (Kushta 1913: 156–86, hereafter *CH*) resembles *Ab-e Hayat* both in its formal attempt to group earlier poets into some form of coherent history – though one which is very careless of specific dates – while preserving something of the *tazkira*'s life-giving core of anecdote and brief quotation. After general reflections on Islamic literary history, it groups Punjabi poetry into five periods (*daur*). The number is itself a significant imitation of Azad's scheme for Urdu, but the periodization is significantly defined in quite different and rather suprising terms (*CH* 158):

1  From Amir Khusrau to Maulawi Ghulam Murtaza;
2  From Ghulam Murtaza's time to Ranjit Singh;
3  From Ranjit Singh's time to the Annexation of the Punjab;
4  From the Annexation to Dr Leitner;
5  From Dr Leitner's time to the Land Alienation Act and beyond

The description of the enormously long first period includes a prefatory discussion of the principal genres of Punjabi literature, on which it bestows a suitably grand pedigree by loose association with

the great Indo-Persian poet Amir Khusrau (d. 1325), but the early
Punjabi poets themselves are quickly disposed of. So, after a brief
comparison of the status of the Adi Granth to that of the Quran and
the Avesta, the method of its compilation by Guru Arjan is
summarily explained with special reference to Farid, the primal
figure of most significance to all Muslim critics of Punjabi literature:

> While including the hymns of the preceding Gurus, he also
> included particular works by other saints in order that a world
> with a vision free of bigotry might on the one hand read the
> hymns of Guru Nanak, while on the other not be deprived of
> the sweet treasure (*ganj-e shakar*) of Baba Farid (*CH* 160).

When the living tradition comes nearer with the shift to the second
period, led by Varis Shah and Bullhe Shah, the treatment becomes
more enthusiastic in tone but remains very summary, so that Bullhe
Shah's poetic quality is hurriedly captured by comparing the imagery
of one of his verses to a conceit in a verse by the Urdu poet Mir Taqi
(*CH* 167).

Actually, what makes *Chashma-e Hayat* so peculiar as literary
history is the small attention it gives to recognizable literary classics. It
soon becomes apparent from the much greater detail given to the
following periods, beginning with the now forgotten early nineteenth
century poet Piare Sahib and his numerous disciples who occupy
much of the third period, that the real concern of *Chashma-e Hayat* is
with more recent times. This retrospective temporal foreshortening is
not associated, as in *Ab-e Hayat*, with the desire to celebrate a now
vanished past. It is rather to show – against the background of the
broad atemporal sweep of genres introduced in the opening pages –
the vitality of the urban tradition of Punjabi poetry with which
Kushta and his mostly Muslim forerunners and contemporaries were
particularly associated, instead of the Sufis from rural and often
remoter areas who now far eclipse them in reputation. As *Chashma-e
Hayat* proceeds to its increasingly hurried conclusion, the sketchy and
partial accounts of the poets of preceding eras emerge as having been
little more than a prologue to the arguments advanced in its crabbed
final pages (*CH* 183–6) for an enhanced recognition of the claims of
Punjabi, especially Punjabi poetry in the Persian script favoured by
Muslim writers. Mir Karamatullah's final footnote disparages the use
of Urdu for poetry designed for a mass Punjabi audience by citing his
own pioneering role as a composer of temperance hymns (*tamparansi
bhajan*) in Punjabi.

107

While in keeping with the Kushta agenda of confirming the place of his sort of Punjabi in the modern polysystem in its emphasis on a linguistic rather a critical or a more ambitiously ideological agenda, *Chashma-e Hayat* is little more than a palely mechanical attempt to adapt something of the *Ab-e Hayat* model so as to give Punjabi a modern literary history of its own, done too quickly to do the job properly. Kushta perhaps recognized the inadequacy of this short Urdu text appended to a Punjabi book to match the agenda of his own poetry, even to supplement the brief example of researched Punjabi literary history prefaced to his *Hir*, from whose second edition of 1915 *Chashma-e Hayat* was dropped into a subsequent obscurity from which it was unable to exert further influence. Although parts of it reappear in Kushta's later works, briefly described in the final section below, the relevance of *Chashma-e Hayat* to the argument of the present paper is less for its own sake than as an illuminating contrast to the contemporary achievement of a Sikh author which is next considered.

## Engineered reconstruction: Budh Singh

If the marginality of the Sikh presence to the Punjabi literary enterprise is a striking characteristic of the Muslim materials surveyed in the preceding section, the importance of parts of the Punjabi Muslim literary and cultural presence to the Sikh reformist project and its associated programme of cultural redefinition is hardly to be underplayed. The closer definition of religious and cultural identity demanded by the Singh Sabha reformers went beyond an explicit readjustment of primary linguistic allegiance to the modern standard Punjabi in Gurmukhi script whose creation was one of the reformers' greatest successes (Shackle 1988).

It also required a shift of cultural allegiance away from the orientation of the old Gurmukhi schools (Leitner 1991: 33–7), in whose syllabus the prominence of such very popular classics as the Braj Bhasha *Hanuman Natak* (1623) by Hirdai Ram became suspect on linguistic as well as theological grounds. The new focus of Sikh cultural allegiance was to be the neo-Sikh literature which from around the turn of the century was being created with increasing artistic success in the new standard Punjabi by such gifted and prolific writers as Vir Singh.

All these closely linked parts of the reformist project had important implications for the understanding of literary history – or, rather, what was called for was a literary historical underpinning for the proclaimed new cultural allegiance which would not be in palpable tension with the new religious identity. The strongly Muslim cultural orientation of Kushta's sort of Punjabi literary history was hardly suitable to help achieve this important agenda, whose groundwork was substantially laid in a series of pioneering works produced in the first decades of the twentieth century by Bava Budh Singh.

Budh Singh was a rather unlikely candidate for the post of first Sikh historian of Punjabi literature, since his training was hardly that of a litterateur at all and his background and career could hardly have been more unlike that of his almost exact contemporary Kushta. Budh Singh (Khanna 1983: 11–22) was born in Lahore in 1878 into a family of Bhalla Khatris directly descended from Guru Amar Das, and holders of a jagir under Ranjit Singh. After initial studies of Urdu and Persian with the local mullah, he matriculated from the Lahore Mission High School in 1894, followed two years later by an FA Degree from the Mission College. It was from this early period that his interests in Sikh scripture and Punjabi poetry were first awakened by extra-curricular attendance at other circles in the city.

But his career was determined by the subsequent study of engineering at Roorki college. After his graduation in 1902, he was appointed to the Punjab Public Works Department, where he pursued a successful career, ultimately reaching the rank of Superintendent Engineer. Budh Singh thus belonged to the very small number of turn of the century Sikh professionals (Oberoi 1994: 365). The alignment with modernity evident from his professional position is graphically demonstrated in the photographs attached as frontispieces to his works, in which a propelling pencil neatly projects from the breast pocket of his well pressed suit. Modernity clung to him, indeed, even in the manner of his premature death in 1931, caused when his car crashed outside Lahore on his way back from a late summer vacation in Dalhousie.

In his spare time Budh Singh was an immensely productive researcher and writer, who was passionately committed to the cause of Punjabi and Punjabi literature. The thirteen books now traceable which were published in the last two decades of his life, usually at his own expense, included essays and several full-length plays, besides collections of translated and original verse. Budh Singh is however now chiefly remembered for the three books he produced on Punjabi poetry, to which he gave the poetic titles *Hans Chog* (Soul-Swan Peck, 1915), *Koil Ku* (Cuckoo Coo, 1916), and *Bambiha Bol* (Songbird Sing, 1925).[6]

Although *Hans Chog* was published slightly after *Chashma-e Hayat*, it makes no explicit reference to that sketch. Its preface sets out Budh Singh's agenda, to do what he can to address the shameful status of Punjabi. The characteristically folksy style of this humble 'engineer's Punjabi' is of course itself consistent with the book's strategy:

> This breast has become pierced and bleeding from the sight of the humble state of 'Punjabi' and from suffering neighbours' taunts and ridicule ... The writer is no poet or scholar, just a simpleton who loves the Punjabi language and who has written what he feels in a quite unpolished language. The worth and rank of Punjabi are not to be judged by this essay. Instead, enjoy reading the verses of the old poets in this book and see what a status this language had once attained (*HC* 1–2).

The emphasis upon language is sustained in Budh Singh's ample introduction (*HC* 3–32), which draws directly upon the most recent colonial scholarship in the form of Grierson's recently published *Linguistic Survey of India* to establish the full place of Punjabi among the languages of India. He then turns to Punjabi literature, beginning with the impediments to its growth caused by the cultivation first of Persian, then of Urdu after the British conquest, before dealing with its history, which is divided into three periods: the old period, beginning with Shaikh Farid and the Sikh Gurus; the middle period beginning with Bullhe Shah and Varis Shah and continuing through Sikh rule to the British imposition of Urdu, when only the Sikhs stood up for Punjabi, giving some hope for new developments in the present period. A final brief sketch of genres emphasizes the modern need for the cultivation of prose writing. The main text of *Hans Chog* or 'The Punjabi Flower Garden' (*panjabi phulvari*) is finally introduced, with a plea for special reverence in approaching the works of the Sikh Gurus and Sufis which it contains:

> Sit down in the assembly and listen quietly, engrossed in the contemplation of their thoughts filled with spirituality which fly to the highest peaks of heaven and of the graceful beauties of their poetry. It is forbidden to cheer and clap here. Take off your boots and shoes before entering this court of the spiritual knowledge of holy personages. This is no lecture hall (*HC* 32).

Once inside the main text, the personalized image of the holy founders of Punjabi literature is elaborately sustained:

110

Look, the head of this court is a holy man of aged appearance, whose long white beard gives a glorious appearance to his face which is filled with immortal light. Behind him stands a man standing holding a flywhisk and in front of him another playing a prelude on the six-stringed rebab in a *rag* which would bring the dead to life. Ecstatic with love as he listens to the notes of the *rag*, the great saint sometimes nods his head, sometimes recites some verses of very sweet and delightful *bani*, whose sound casts all the courtiers into delight-filled rapture as they listen to it. Do you know who this holy man is? It is Sri Guru Nanak Dev ji. Right next to him sits an aged Muslim fakir with a turban on his head and clad in a long tunic. The presence of a crowd of disciples around him shows that he too must be a person of authority or a spiritual leader. Because he is next to the Guru, the old man talks to him quietly, sometimes smiling and nodding his head as if agreeing with his utterances. This holy man is Shaikh Farid ji (*HC* 34).

The book itself then falls into the familiar pattern of sequential notices of individual authors with samples of their poetry, beginning with Guru Nanak (*HC* 37–65) and Shaikh Farid, identified as Guru Nanak's contemporary Shaikh Brahm (*HC* 61–8). Since Budh Singh's clear purpose is to emphasize the common Punjabi heritage, there are no further subdivisions in the following chronological presentation down to the late eighteenth century of the later Gurus and their followers and of Sufis and other religious writers. In spite of its superficially similar form, it should be noted that Budh Singh's treatment is substantially different in inspiration from that of Azad and the humbler *Chashma-e Hayat*, both derived in substantial measure from rich oral tradition. Budh Singh works from written sources, including both deductions from the poetic originals and reference to secondary sources like the *janamsakhi* evidence cited in the discussion of Nanak and Farid. In this sense, his is the first 'researched' history of Punjabi literature, whose pioneering status needs to underlined.

The evocative imagery used by Budh Singh to introduce his bold attempt to cover the most sacred territory of Sikhism at the same time as mapping a broader picture of Punjabi literature was not entirely successful in disarming all criticism. The objection that this demeaned the status of the Sikh Gurus was voiced, among others, by this reviewer in *The Khalsa Advocate*:

However, we deprecate the idea of putting Guru Nanak, etc. with other poets because their Bani was a revealed one (*KK* 193).

Still associated today with one view of Sikh religious identity, this privileged ring-fencing of the scripture from all possibility of being considered in terms of the same aesthetic criteria as may be applicable to secular literature indicates a intrinsic major difficulty in the translation of Hali's project for the reform of Urdu poetry into a programme for the reconstruction of Sikh Punjabi cultural identity. Whereas the sharp linguistic divide between Arabic and Urdu allowed Hali to idealize the ancient literature of Islam, the Sikh reconstructive project inevitably involved the inclusion of the scripture in whose language Punjabi is so significant an element. In his foreword to the second edition of *Hans Chog*, Budh Singh defended his position robustly:

> Some learned friends of the old way of thinking were critical of the first edition, saying it was wrong to place the Gurus in the same tradition as other poets, since poetry is a human creation and *gurbani* is the Eternal Word (*dhur di bani*). This is a serious charge from a Sikh perspective, but if we reflect for a moment it loses its force. *Hans Chog* is an account of Punjabi poets and poetry. What is poetry? That is carefully described in the introduction to *Koil Ku*. The Divine Word (*dev bani*) can flow through poetry, and it is written in that introduction that the Vedas were the most ancient poetry of the Punjab. Similarly, it is because the *bani* of the Gurus is in poetry that it sanctifies the pages of *Hans Chog* and cleanses the hearts and mind of those readers who were indeed perhaps about to read the *Guru Granth Sahib*. Writing an account of the Gurus in *Hans Chog* cannot diminish the status of the Holy Guru, whose sun still shines (*HC* i–ii).

If the rhetoric of this passage is not thought quite to answer the substance of the criticism, it may be salutary to reflect on the great difficulty experienced by literary critics far more sophisticated than Budh Singh in wrestling with issues of just this type – in Kantian terms, with rival understandings of the Sublime and the Beautiful (Zima 1999: 174–88).

In *Koil Ku*, Budh Singh proceeded more securely to the second part of his agenda, which deals with the theologically less controversial *qissa* poets. This volume again begins with an extended introduction, devoted to 'Poetry' (*KK* 1–73). This owes a great deal to Hali, whose ideals of natural poetry were of course peculiarly well suited to the development of poetry – supposedly drawn directly from 'nature' – in the new Sikh Punjabi literary language. Hali is repeatedly cited throughout, along with passing references to Azad and to English sources. The wholesale adoption of Hali's agenda in turn requires a consistent condemnation of the nineteenth century Persianization of Punjabi, viewed at best as a temporary aberration from the purity of style found in older poets which is held up as a model for modern writers. Quoting highly Persianized passages by the two nineteenth century *qissa* poets Ghulam Rasul and Fazl Shah, Budh Singh thus remarks:

> These verses are stuffed full of Persian images, and the custom started by these masters has continued down to the present. Even the poetry of today simply clings to the example of Fazl Shah. Those same Persian images which infuriated Azad and Hali and to which they said 'Enough!' have today found a home in Punjabi poetry ... But they are after all quite alien, and hardly pleasing to the Punjabi ear (*KK* 53).

The main part of *Koil Ku* consists of rather extended treatments of the principal early *qissa* poets. Several of these, notably the lengthy notice of Varis Shah (*KK* 118–66), testify to Budh Singh's powers of original research and appreciation. There is no substantial introduction in the third and largest volume of the trilogy, *Bambiha Bol*, which includes pieces on further *qissa* poets and other authors. These are divided chronologically into a 'Mughal section' (*muglai vand*) and a 'Khalsa section' (*khalsai vand*). The curtailment of the treatment before the start of the British period is a telling difference from the presentation in *Chashma-e Hayat*, where the point was to emphasize the continuity of a tradition – if only through relentless enumeration of long lists of minor poets – in order to argue for its claims to an enhanced present recognition. Budh Singh's purpose, by contrast, is the more ambitious one of forging a myth of past cultural achievement which will allow a quite new literature to flower, and like all myths this requires that there should be no temporal continuity between what magically happened *in illo tempore* (Eliade 1989: 91–2) and what is to happen in this world now.

While Budh Singh's other works may be more briefly reviewed,[7] it is appropriate to give some indication of their general relevance to the reformist cultural agenda. In later life, Budh Singh turned increasingly to the writing of dramas, which he saw as his special contribution to the development of Punjabi literature. Like many plays being written in Indian languages at the time, these owe more to a perceived need to match up to the Shakespearean profile of the English literary canon than to any living local theatrical tradition. For all the apparent authenticity of their elaborate stage directions, these unacted five-act dramas are more interesting as ideological statements than artistically successful creations. The dramatic theory to which Budh Singh worked is set out in some detail in a characteristically methodical afterword (Budh Singh 1928a: 161–83) to his play *Mundari Chhal* (The Ring Trick). While citing the *Encyclopaedia Britannica* and other English sources, this essay too is generated from the usual translation pattern governing the flow of ideas at that time by again drawing principally upon an Urdu source (Ilahi and Umar 1924), itself a mostly unoriginal compilation from English books.

The plot of *Mundari Chhal* is drawn from the legendary corpus associated with Raja Rasalu. While largely neglected in the *qissa* poetry, the Rasalu cycle came to be seen as core material of 'the matter of the Punjab' as the result of its prominence in the Punjabi folk treatments collected by the great nineteenth century British folklorists R.C. Temple and C. Swynnerton. Budh Singh was himself extremely interested in proving the historical existence of Rasalu, and published a book-length study, *Raja Rasalu* (Budh Singh 1931). In a rather remarkable exercise of back-translation from Orientalist text to Westernizing vernacular, this includes a complete Gurmukhi transliteration of Temple's romanized recordings of Punjabi oral texts and a Punjabi translation of the English prose versions in which Swynnerton had chosen to reproduce his versions.

Budh Singh's poetry is similar in character to his dramas. His complete verse translation of Bhartrihari (Budh Singh 1919–21),[8] bears testimony to the expert knowledge of Punjabi metres which he had gained from his long and wide familiarity with the older literature, and it invites comparison with Vir Singh's rather better known version of the *Nitishataka* (Vir Singh 1916). Both presumably done with the aid of Hindi versions (e.g. Bhartrihari 1880) rather than straight from the original Sanskrit, they equally underline the importance of reinterpretations of classical Indian material – especially prestigious texts as free of explicitly Hindu content as Bhartrihari – to the development of modern Punjabi literature at a time when the conflict between Indian nationalism and a Sikh ethno-nationalism had yet to emerge.

Budh Singh's own poetry (Budh Singh 1928b) was published in a slim volume entitled *Pritam Chhoh* (Love's Touch). It is not very remarkable, being very much in the vein of the first phase of modern Sikh Punjabi poetry (Matringe 1995: 189–90) in its Wordsworthian combination of spiritual aspiration, closeness to nature and concern with social issues. It is, in other words, a perfect if pallid exemplification of the Halian agenda so energetically set out in the introduction to *Koil Ku*. Interesting as Budh Singh's varied oeuvre may be, it is after all hardly to be compared with the size and artistic success of Vir Singh's huge mythopoeic project of neo-Sikh re-inscription through commentary, novel and poetry (Shackle 1998).

## Conclusion: Sikhs, Muslims and Punjabi literary history

After Budh Singh's death in 1931, his son arranged for the posthumous publication of one more book of literary history (Budh Singh 1932), called *Prem Kahani* (The Story of Love). Although largely a repetition, with some additions, of material included in the earlier trilogy (including the introduction to *Koil Ku*), this large volume was produced in the Persian script, in a striking act of reaching out across religious and cultural boundaries to enthuse a parallel audience of fellow-travellers for Punjabi.

Although *Prem Kahani* does not seem to have received much attention from later Muslim critics, the pre-Partition period provides a number of such remarkable instances of close cross-communal cooperation and communication. Kushta, who had himself composed a poem for the occasion of Budh Singh's daughter's marriage in 1927 (Kushta 1964: 217–8), amalgamated something of Budh Singh's style with material from *Chashma-e Hayat* in his account of Punjabi literature (Kushta 1939) which was published in Gurmukhi under the title *Panjab de Hire* (Jewels of the Punjab) by Dhani Ram Chatrik, one of the few Hindu activists in the cause of Punjabi literature (Narula 1985). The same secularist possibilities of the 1930s encouraged the beginnings of more professionally academic approaches to Punjabi literary history, most notably in the publication in English of doctorates by Mohan Singh (Mohan Singh 1933) – himself also the author of a potted guide to Urdu literature (Mohan Singh n.d.) – and by Lajwanti Rama Krishna, whose study of the Punjabi Sufi poets (Rama Krishna 1938) repeatedly footnotes references to Budh Singh's volumes. Later developments have led to separate traditions of

Punjabi literary history in Pakistan, where Kushta produced a greatly expanded final *tazkira* of Punjabi writers (Kushta 1960), and in India, where the most recent histories written in English by writers best known for their creative output in Punjabi continue an intimate if no longer a very conspicuously fructifying dialogue between literary practice and literary history (Sekhon and Duggal 1992, Sekhon 1996).

These English histories of Punjabi literature and their Punjabi counterparts all continue to bear the impress of Budh Singh's original synthesis. The early protagonists of Hindi who felt the need to reconstruct a Hindu literary and cultural identity necessarily worked exclude the Muslim heritage so powerfully vested in Urdu (Dalmia 1997). But the Sikh cultural framework continues to require a dual reliance of Punjabi literary history upon Sufi poetry as well as Sikh scripture long after the disappearance of a living Muslim presence from an Indian Punjab.

Without those safely distant guarantees, a separate Punjabi linguistic heritage is made vulnerable by the pre-modern tendency to exploit the opportunities provided by the inherent closeness and mutual intelligibility of neighbouring and closely related Indo-Aryan languages, rather than to emphasize their differences, as has become the rule in modern times. So the mixed language of even, say, Nanak has always allowed the possibility of the assimilation of the older Sikh tradition into the grandly all-embracing narrative of standard Hindi literary history (e.g. Shukla 1933: 80–3).

Budh Singh's discussion of the Lahore Sufi Shah Husain (*HC* 112) refers to the story (Santokh Singh 1929: 2116–7) of how Guru Arjan when compiling the *Adi Granth* refused to include Shah Husain's verses in the *bhagatbani*. Macauliffe presents this version:

Shah Husain's turn came next. The following was his composition:

Be silent, *O my friend*, be silent;
There is no necessity, O my friend, for speaking;
My friend, there is no necessity for speaking.
Within and without us is the one Lord;
    to whom else shall we address ourselves?
The one Beloved pervadeth every heart;
    there is nowhere a second.
Saith the humble faqir Husain,
    I am a sacrifice unto the true Guru.

116

This was rejected by Guru Arjan on the ground that he did not consider it the duty of holy men to conceal the message which God had commissioned them to give to the world

(*Macauliffe* 1909: 3, 62–3)

Transposing this story into the context of Punjabi literary history, its moral is that Sufis must not be allowed to remain silent. Just as Mardana the Muslim Mirasi who was the Guru's *kammi* once voiced the *rag* to the Guru's *bani*, so still do Sikh literary historians need their Muslims to sing a separate harmony.

# Notes

1  With a view to the convenience of likely readers of this volume, references relating to Urdu have been purposely confined to secondary sources in English.
2  Azad omits all mention of pre-eighteenth century poets, and passes briefly over those assigned to the first and second periods (26pp. and 21 pp. in Azad n.d.). All the great masters of the later eighteenth century are assigned to the third period (95 pp.), described at similar length to the lesser poets of the fourth period (96 pp.), with those of the fifth period getting twice the coverage (177 pp., including 54 pp. for Zauq alone).
3  Strikingly exemplified by the number of imitations it inspired, later including a complete Punjabi translation by Shihab ud Din (Shackle and Majeed 1997: 45–6).
4  There is however a passing reference to Guru Nanak elsewhere in the poem (Muhammad Bakhsh 1983: 443, verse 15).
5  Besides the full Persian alphabet, Kushta's *Divan* also has separate entries for the aspirated letters *bh, ph,* etc. Doubts as to the exact contents of the first edition (Hamdard 1985: 182–91) are hardly relevant to the brief discussion here, which is based on the third edition.
6  References are to the second editions of *Hans Chog* (Budh Singh 1921) and *Koil Ku* (Budh Singh 1927), hereafter *HC* and *KK*.
7  Their contents are summarized in Khanna 1983: 23–34, a published PhD in whose later chapters each category is usefully gone through and methodically assessed.
8  The British Library has a presentation copy (Panj D 787) labelled by the author in beautifully neat engineer's lettering.

## Chapter Seven

# The Mirror and the Sikh: The Transformation of Ondaatje's Kip

*Nikky-Guninder Kaur Singh*

Michael Ondaatje's *The English Patient* (EP) is a novel published in 1992 by a Sri Lankan of Dutch descent. Readers look into the novel but see an Asian, a Sikh looking at the West. Kip offers reflections for western readers. In his Punjabi accent, he makes them examine their attitudes towards the Other. He embodies the famous Rushdie statement: 'the empire writes back to the Centre' (Ashcroft 1989: 171).

Besides his concern with problems of socio-political identity, Ondaatje raises basic issues of personal identity. Citing Flaubert without quotation marks, he writes that the 'novel is a mirror walking down a road' (EP 91), and indeed, the reader runs into mirrors everywhere in the novel. At times, the mirror is consciously avoided, as it is by Kip and Hana at the beginning of the narrative – 'She has removed all mirrors and stacked them away in an empty room' (EP 23). Their removal becomes all the more conspicuous.

At other times, the mirror is acutely wanted, as in the case of the charred English patient who 'had wanted to see himself' (EP 100). However, the mirror in Ondaatje's work also discloses an Other: it reflects not only the subjects who avoid seeing themselves or wish to see themselves, but also those whose subjectivity is sapped. For example, it was the mirror tacked up high in a fellow European's tent in the desert which showed Almasy – the 'English Patient' who is in fact a Hungarian – the small dog-like lump on the bed, which in fact is a small Arab girl tied up both literally and imaginatively by the Orientalist. And it expresses yet a fourth angle in the book, that of an outsider, one who possesses the power to pierce into the very depths of a person. Cryptically, Ondaatje says:

A man not of your own blood can break upon your emotions more than someone of your own blood. As if falling into the arms of a stranger you discover the mirror of your choice (EP 90).

A stranger with whom there are no familial or cultural ties can act as a mirror in showing what is truly within; by encountering what is distant, different, and 'foreign,' we discover what is closest to us. In all its varied nuances, Ondaatje's mirror is reminiscent of the pan of water presented by Prajapati to Indra and Virochana in their voyage to self-discovery in the *Chandogya Upanishad*. Just like Indra and Virochana who set out to gain knowledge of their Self by examining their reflections in the water, readers begin to identify with the inner feelings of the characters in the novel, and with the exploration of time and space around them.

Both literal and figurative mirrors abound in Ondaatje's text. In this essay, I wish to focus on the phenomenological role of the mirror in the maturation of the Sikh protagonist, Kirpal Singh. When we first meet him, he is an emissary of the British, wearing his turban but their uniform and defusing bombs for them in Italy after the second world war amidst charred bodies, shattered psyches, splintered works of art, and shelled architecture. By the end of the novel, he is a doctor, peacefully sitting at home in a square patch of garden with his wife and two children. One who simply mirrored his colonial superiors and was afraid to look at himself in the mirror, now has 'a wrinkle at the edge of his eyes behind his spectacles' (the last words of the book). He is an integrated person, 'older' both physically and psychologically.

What is intriguing is that the more authentic Kirpal becomes as a human being, the more deeply rooted he becomes in his own faith. His religious sensitivity and political consciousness are parallel phenomena. This correspondence between socio-political harmony and psychological-spiritual harmony has been a crucial theme since the very origins of the Sikh faith. Guru Nanak and his successors promoted orthopraxis over orthodoxy, and their theology and spirituality are intertwined with politics. In order to attain inner peace, the external circumstances have to be peaceful as well. In their aspiration for spiritual liberation, the Sikh Gurus protested against political hegemony, social hierarchy, and patriarchal subjugation. Ondaatje's Kirpal Singh reiterates the message of the Sikh Gurus that a peaceful socio-political context is crucial to spiritual wellbeing. When we encounter him in Italy, although the war is over and colonialism will soon be over, there are severe psychological battles that have to be fought. Kirpal's transformation appears to embody the famous words of Gustavo Gutierrez:

> Peace is not the simple absence of violence and bloodshed ...
> Peace is linked with justice and the creation of a society in which persons will not be objects but can be subjects, creating their own history rather than being pawns in someone else's hands.
>
> (*Brown* 1967: 4)

Kip is an outstanding contribution to our society at large, and to the world of Sikhism in particular. It is so seldom that postcolonial literature has Sikh protagonists, and those who do appear are planting bombs, not defusing them. Unfortunately, however, Kip has become yet another example of the paradigm of neglect that Sikhs have been subjected to. Even the most avid readers and critics of Michael Ondaatje have ignored the essential personality of his Sikh sapper. There have been excellent studies on various aspects of the novel, but somehow Kip has not quite captured the imagination and sentiments of Ondaatje scholars. Often he is relegated to the end: 'The last hero is the Sikh sapper ...' At times, he appears as a homologue to other characters: 'like Caravaggio, he is in love with Italian painting, but his passion is bombs' (Lernout 1992). Or, he is seen as an interesting antithesis: 'the ambivalence of the white man with a black skin and the black man with a white sensibility' (Ganapathy-Dore 1993: 100). Either way, Kip is studied in subordination to or in conjunction with the English patient and/or the Italian thief. He is overlooked as an independent subject, and it is surprising that there has not even been a thorough study of his relationship with Kipling's Kim, a subject worthy of further scholarly investigation.[1] But the brown Kip just has not attracted Western readership, and one wonders whether there is a curious continuation of Eurocentrism at work.

In my study I will explore how Kip transforms from a colonial to a postcolonial Sikh. When and why does he change from reflecting his colonial masters to reflecting on his own image? How do the Canadian Hana, the Hungarian Almasy and the Italian Caravaggio serve as reflectors in showing him his self? What we discover is that Kip's development from a colonial false consciousness to an authentic postcolonial Self mirrors the development of the ego in Lacan. Since the socio-political development of Ondaatje's protagonist is a personal and pschychological one, my analysis will therefore draw upon postcolonial criticism and Lacanian psychoanalysis.

## Afraid of mirrors: the colonial lack of self

Throughout the first part of the narrative, Ondaatje focuses on Kirpal's exterior, and all his external pursuits. This phase is analogous to Lacan's Pre-Mirror Stage, one in which the infant has not yet gone through the specular activity – 'an ontological structure of the human world' (Lacan 1997: 2). In this early phase (prior to six months) the infant is unable to grasp the relation between the tactile body here and the visual body there; a schism between the 'I' who sees and the 'I' who is seen remains. The child may look into a mirror at his face or hands, but there is no recognition of his total self – indeed, there is no 'flutter of jubilant activity'.

Ondaatje's Kip avoids even the sight of mirrors. We see him, but it is as though the author were showing us Kip in his infant state through Lord Suffolk's binoculars or even through the telescope of his own rifle. His name is 'Kip', diminished by his British employers. We get to see Kip's dark complexion and hear his accent, how he confuses his Vs and Ws. We learn about his habits, how he is always washing his hands, eating without the use of cutlery, brushing his teeth outdoors. Even his manner of addressing distant associates as family members comes out distinctly when he refers to the 'English' patient as 'Uncle'. As to Kip's subjectivity, his essential self is recognized neither by Kip nor by the reader.

Religion in this phase is an outward matter, and there is no relation between Kip and his reality, or in Lacanian terms, between his *Innenwelt* and the *Umwelt*. We are first introduced to Kirpal Singh on a dark and stormy night through the eyes of Hana. It is Kip's turban which is immediately noticed by Hana. The flashes of lightning provide Hana a 'quick glimpse of his turban and the bright wet guns' (EP: 64). Five yards of muslin (or thereabouts), the turban is a covering for the *kes* or the uncut hair – observed by Sikhs as one of their five Ks. Long hair is accepted as a part of natural growth, representing strength and vitality. In the Sikh world, heads are not shaved as a mark of resignation or renunciation, nor is hair left matted like eastern ascetics or our western dreadlocks. It is combed, tidily knotted up and kept in place with a small semi-circular comb, and covered with the turban denoting neatness and order.

Kirpal Singh's long hair is mentioned many times in the novel. 'He will sit up and flip his hair forward, and begin to rub the length of it with a towel (EP 217). Or he puts his head back, spreading 'his hair like grain in a fan-shaped straw basket' so that the sun can dry it.

During the nights, Hana 'lets his hair free' and she witnesses 'the gnats of electricity in his hair in the darkness of the tent' (EP 218). Each time Ondaatje's description of the sapper's long hair is imbued with sensuousness and beauty. Kip's long hair does not provide us with an entry into his personal religious and emotional world, but it imparts a multivalency of meanings for Hana and the reader. With his hair undone, the masculine body of the soldier becomes for Hana an Indian goddess holding 'wheat and ribbons'. The 'gnats of electricity' in his hair are analogous to the lightbulbs attached to the wings of the warrior angel in the damaged Church of San Giovanni. The peace, security, and vitality that come with the lighting up of the bulbs on the angel in the Church parallel Hana's emotions as she lies besides Kip in his dark tent with his hair charged with electricity. Ondaatje traces the emergence of Hana's sexuality through Kip's long hair, and braids it with the sacred. The image of electric energy surrounding the hair confirms this connection in the mind of the reader.

Hana also notices the *kara* or the steel bracelet worn around Kip's wrist, 'the bangle that clinks sometimes when he drinks a cup of tea in front of her' (EP 74). The *kara* is a symbol of strength and courage, worn by all Sikh men and women. Its simplicity and circularity are a reminder of the Infinite One, without beginning or end. In this case, however, the *kara* does not lead to any significant disclosure, for Hana only hears it clink as it hits against the porcelain.

Besides the Khalsa format, Kip exemplifies the Sikh institutions of *seva* and *langar*, as well as the popular Sikh precepts of *kirat karni* and *vand chhakna*. The highest ideal in Sikh ethics is *seva*, voluntary manual labour in the service of the community which may take various forms. Beginning with Guru Nanak, it has become an essential part of Sikh life through which Sikh believers cultivate humility, overcome ego, and purify their body and mind. By working faithfully as a sapper, Kirpal Singh performs continual *seva*, being fully dedicated to serving others as he searches for caches of explosives everywhere.

The practice of *langar* is a central practice of Sikhism, and testifies to the social equality and familyhood of all people. Ondaatje's Kip fully participates in this important Sikh institution in the distant Italian landscape. He may not be rolling out dough in the Villa San Girolamo, but daily he brings herbs and onions for his villa mates – eating his simple meals with them, without any gender or racial barriers. He also takes turns in preparing dinners for them, but he remains a vegetarian. Caravaggio, who is fond of meat, finds Kip's meals puritanical, but he does not criticize Kip's 'purist meals' as he calls them, he only sneaks off a piece of dried meat from the cupboard and puts it into his pocket (EP 266). Kip does not take any alcohol either, and when his companions have wine, he joins them with his beaker of water.

While retaining his own traditions, the Sikh sapper creates a wholeness, a family atmosphere, in the zone fragmented by war. He possesses the cheerful attitude much prized in the Sikh way of life: *hasandia khelandia painandia khavandia vice hovai mukati* 'amidst joyous fun, play, wearing fineries, and eating, liberation is achieved' (AG 522). Life is to be embraced at every moment, not shunned. Even though the period following the war is most traumatic, and Kip is involved intensely in his investigations, he conveys an aura of joy, for 'he is always humming or whistling' (EP 74). Even without meeting or seeing Kip, the 'English' patient lying in bed upstairs in the villa recognizes the newcomer by his happy tunes. 'Who is whistling? he asks one night, having not met or even seen the newcomer. Always singing to himself as he lies upon the parapet looking up at a shift of clouds' (EP 74). Temporally and spatially it is a shifting landscape. In their decentred world, nothing is solid. The psyches of the protagonists are dark like clouds, and the blackness of the 'English' patient symbolizes the ailing humanity. Yet the Sikh sapper must have some meaning resonant within him, to which he constantly whistles, and sings.

The way in which he seeks comfort and solace in the various Italian frescoes and statues, further underscores the Sikh point of view that the sacred is not confined to any particular religion or region. As Guru Gobind Singh said in the *Jap*:

> Primal and expansive Being,
>   unborn, primal, and absolute
> Confined to no country or garb
>   to no form, shape or attachment
> The embodiment of love
>   extends to all lands, to every nook and cranny.[2]

All temples and shelters belong to the One, who extends everywhere. The entire cosmos is regarded as the home of the Infinite Reality. Far from his native Punjab, then, Kip reaches out to make himself at home in the precincts of the abandoned Italian churches. He makes no distinction between the sacred space of the Sikhs and Catholics. Like a child he wishes to fall asleep in the arms and laps of figures in paint and stone. He seeks companionship with angelic figures, a connection with Biblical faces. He desires the Queen of Sheba's face and 'leaned forward to rest on the skin of her frail neck' (EP 70). Elsewhere there is a brilliant depiction of his intimacy with the Virgin Mother: 'The colour of his turban echoes that of the lace collar at the neck of Mary' (EP 280). With his verbal camera, Ondaatje leads our eyes to see Kip's turbanned head resting serenely on the Virgin's shoulder.

Such scenes betray a lonely brown Kip in a 'white' country. Dislocated from his home in the Punjab, he pursues the 'familiar' in the dark Queen of Sheba's skin, in the faces on frescoes darkened by centuries of oil and candle-smoke, in the many maternal images. However, Kip searches for the external: the arms, the skin, the complexion, the texture, the features. Even when the Sikh soldier and the Christian Mary are brought together, it is through a harmony of colour. While the author and reader can register this harmony, Kip is unaware of it. He is not experiencing the transcendent link between them.

Kip's predicament is the same as that of Adelle Quested in *A Passage to India*. But Forster's Adelle is aware of her situation and describes it with immense insight and self-awareness. She knows exactly what will happen to her if she continues to confine herself to the society of the colonial elite – 'She would see India always as a frieze, never as a spirit' (Forster 1924: 47). In his present condition, Kip only witnesses the sacred art of Italy as a frieze. He is searching for the transcendent, but the transcendent eludes him. The fact is that Kip searches for the spirit through the telescope of his rifle. Ondaatje gives many instances of the Sikh sapper wanting to know and recognize the foreign faces in Italian religious images but always through the medium of his rifle. During the Marine Festival of the Virgin Mary, 'he raises his rifle and picked up her face in the gun sight' (EP 79). Later, he studies her face through the telescope of the rifle: 'A face which in the darkness looked more like someone he knew. A sister. Someday a daughter' (EP 80). His telescopic lens is like Lord Suffolk's binoculars which sharply scan all surfaces. In fact, its attachment to the rifle makes it all the more frightening. How can he search for 'brothers' and 'sisters' and 'daughters' through such a monstrous weapon? Each time Kip aims the rifle, one feels discomfort and distaste. Even the way in which Kip tries to learn about his subjects is alienating and scientific. Handing the gun to the padre, he asks, 'Who is he? At three o'clock northwest?' (EP 78), treating the face of Isaiah as an enemy to be shot at. His military training has blinded Kip. The faces that he searches for are effaced by him, and their images are dehumanized by his military techniques. Kip's telescopic sight denotes distance and hostility. Though his intent to create affinity across generations and continents may be sincere, Kip's 'western' equipment and methods are not conducive to his goal.

The process of growing up in a colonial India, working in a sterile England, going through the War, has ripped Kip asunder from his real self. His is a very dualized mode of existence, one in which all his energies are extended to looking for explosives in the external world. Kip trusts nothing. He is constantly investigating his terrain, suspicious of explosives planted in the smallest objects, so that he cannot even trust 'the little circle of elastic on the sleeve of the girl's frock that gripped her arm' (EP 105). The Sikh view that 'this world is the home of the True One, and within it dwells the True One – *ihu jagu sachai ki hai kothri, sachai ka vichi vasu*' (AG 463) is reversed in the case of our Sikh sapper. Kip is a construct of the destructive forces of human greed which have infiltrated and contaminated our world, the Home of the Divine. And so, instead of faith and trust, suspicion becomes the ground of Kip's being; instead of the transcendent, it is the enemy who becomes Kip's ultimate concern; instead of growing into a person, he becomes a 'radar,' a sharply intelligent, walking, working, eating, humming radar.

It is ironic that his keen eyes provide Kip with no insight into human affairs. Ondaatje tells us enigmatically that the smart Kip who succeeds brilliantly in British exams is a failure when it comes to basic human experience. 'He may look intently at eyes but not register what colour they are, the way food already in his throat or stomach is just texture more than taste of specific objects' (EP 219). Kip's scientifically honed talents and his hypernatural senses prove to be an anaesthetic for him – paralysing him and preventing him from registering the colour of Hana's eyes or enjoying the food he eats. The sapper's style of existence is a contrast from the one posited in his religion. The Western-trained Kip forsakes the heightened aesthetic experience which is upheld in Sikh scripture: *rasia hovai musaka ka taba phulu pachhanai* – 'only by relishing the fragrance is the flower comprehended' (AG 725 M1). 'Savouring' is the ideal offered by the Sikh Gurus. But Kip's training has taught him to eat, not savour. He is a victim of the modern war machine which numbs his senses and sensibilities. Sadly, there is no 'jubilant activity' that would parallel the child's in Lacan's Mirror Stage theory.

Indeed it is very curious that Kip who is so meticulous about his attire should refuse to look into mirrors. He is the only character in the novel who in Italy remains in uniform after the war. There is a vivid depiction of him emerging out of his tent – uniformed, his buckles shining immaculately, and 'his turban symmetrically layered' (EP 75). But there is some deep fear in this outwardly fearless sapper which prevents him looking at himself. 'He himself has no mirrors. He wraps his turban outside in his garden, looking about at the moss on trees' (EP 219).

Psychoanalytically speaking, Kip has not yet reached the Mirror Stage. Drawing on the work of Wallon, Lacan locates this phase from eight to eighteen months of the child's development. He explains:

> We have only to understand the mirror stage *as an identification*, in the full sense that anlysis gives to the term: namely the transformation that takes place in the subject when he assumes an image – whose predestination to this phase-effect is sufficiently indicated by the use, in analytic theory, of the ancient term *imago*.
>
> (*Lacan* 1977: 2)

Unfortunately, Kip does not yet have an image of himself. Over the years he has been too busy imitating his imperial masters – attending their schools, learning their language, wearing their uniforms, and following their codes. In order to serve them, he has dislocated himself from his family and culture. He cannot identify himself at this stage. He cannot look into his inner self; indeed, he cannot look into the mirror. What is there to come face to face with? Perhaps Kip believes that there is nothing in him that deserves any consideration. Why else would he opt to tie his turban looking at the moss on the trees rather than at himself in a mirror?

His colonial upbringing has so degraded him that he thinks he is not worthy of reflection. In Lahore his body was dehumanized – scribbled with coded results by army officers and doctors in yellow chalk. In fact, he has more in common with bombs than with people – the scribbles on his body are like the yellow scribbles on the side of bombs (EP 199–201). Later we come across 'his body draped around the body of the Esau bomb ... his thighs braced the metal casing, much the same way he had seen soldiers holding women in the corner of NAAFI dance floors' (EP 210). How could his body, a companion of bombs and a partner of metallic casings, ever feel or imagine enough to hold the transcendent, or even behold himself? He may

126

have heard the popular Sikh verse *jo brahmande soi pinde* 'whatever lies Beyond, that in the body here can be found' (AG 695),[3] but probably could make no sense of it. In England he was ignored in the various barracks, and became so used to his invisibility that he 'came to prefer it' (EP 196). What could have been left for him to see in a mirror anyway? There is no 'image' to reflect. Burdened by colonialism, Kip is busy carrying the white man's burden all the way from India to England to Italy. But inside, there is a lack of selfhood. Kip may look, speak, and act like a Sikh, but he is out of touch with himself.

## Looking into mirrors: the Italian landscape

The time that Kip spends in the Villa strengthens and revitalizes him. We could read it as the beginning of the 'mirroring' process. He lives with Hana, the 'English' patient, and Caravaggio in the Villa San Girolamo which is both exposed and enclosed – many of its war-shelled walls and doors open into landscape. The paintings of gardens with trees and bowers on its walls and ceilings merge with the wild gardens outdoors. 'There seemed little demarcation between house and landscape, between building and the burned and shelled remnants of the earth' (EP 43).

The Villa was once a convent, an all-female space. It has also been an army hospital. Its construction goes back to 1483, but Ondaatje now reconstructs it in 1945 as a mirror for an important set of historical figures. As discovered by the topographically brilliant 'English' patient, it was built in 1483 for Poliziano, the translator of Homer. The room of the reposing 'English' patient was once a meeting place for Poliziano and his guests, Pico della Mirandola, Lorenzo, and the young Michelangelo, who 'held in each hand the new world and the old world' (EP 57). These men were at the threshold of the middle ages and the modern world with its scientific and geographical inventions and discoveries. In 1498 Vasco da Gama would drop anchor at Calicut and initiate the European plunder of India by bringing back with him to Lisbon three shipfuls of Indian spices, silk, ivory, and sandalwood. The Dutch, French, and British would follow his example, and India would become their empire.

The four ghosts of the late fifteenth century seem to return to the villa in 1945. Like Poliziano, the 'English' patient is an image of the owner, for it is in 'his' room that the four gather together. We find other historical allusions as well. Like Poliziano, the 'English' patient

127

is a 'brilliant, awful man,' and his passionate love for Catherine, who tragically dies very young, is a replay of Poliziano's great attraction for Simonetta Vespucci who died of consumption at the age of twenty-three. Poliziano had a friend called Pico della Mirandola, and Hana incidentally admits that her nickname as a kid was Pico (EP 57). Parapsychologically or paratextually – however we may want to read Ondaatje – Kip is Michelangelo reborn. The emphasis on his youth and his meticulous search for the faces on the Sistine Chapel identify the Sikh sapper with the renaissance artist.

History repeats itself, and our four characters, though silent at first, begin to converse with one another. Interestingly, they each have their own separate entry, an entry which symbolizes their different personal and psychological state of mind when they arrive. All of them find shelter in the villa, and shut off from the rest of the world, the four begin to talk to one another. The fragmented architecture of the villa expresses their selves, and its open-cum-closeness, the secrets they begin to share with each other. The war breaks their walls too, and just as the rooms of the villa open up to the sky and gardens, their secrets and emotions reach out to one another. As the days pass, their wounds begin to heal until the horrors of Hiroshima and Nagasaki. Poliziano, Pico, Michelangelo, and Lorenzo would also sit in Poliziano's room with a bust of Plato and argue all night until the time of Savonarola's cry from the streets . . . 'Now came the bonfires – the burning of wigs, books, animal hides, maps' (EP 57).

Although Hitler is not mentioned directly in the novel, the parallel with the zealot Savonarola burning books is evident. The flashback to 1483 reflects the historical richness of the Villa and its surroundings. Our protagonists are walking the same corridors as those great historical figures who brought about the mergence of the classical and the western civilizations. But whereas the former four created a magnificent fusion of cultures, the latter quartet wander through the rooms witnessing its destruction, its charred remains even being embodied in the 'English' patient. And in their individual ways, they too like their predecessors, try to restore and rebuild a post-war world. Almasy brings his book of Herodotus to which he adds many of his new adventures and explorations; pages he loved from other books are also cut and glued in it including segments from the Old Testament – 'so they are all cradled within the text of Herodotus' (EP 16). At some point 'he had passed his book to the sapper, and the sapper had said we have a Holy Book too' (EP 294). What Ondaatje does here cannot merely be categorized as 'supplementarity' or 'intertextuality' as advanced by some literary critics (Scobie 1994: 92–106). He has two men of the Book across cultures and continents share a profound human experience that goes beyond words, bringing together the Greek-Hebrew and Punjabi texts, bringing together western and eastern civilizations, the pagan Herodotus, the Jewish Prophets, and the Sikh Gurus. The arrival of the Sikh from the Punjab adds a new dimension into the twentieth century humanism of the Villa. The exclusively Italian group that met in Poliziano's room has now become very international with the Hungarian count as the 'English patient,' the Canadian nurse from the new world, another rather shadowy Canadian figure with the Italian name of Caravaggio, and the north Indian sapper.

According to Almasy, the two of them get on so well because they are nowhere men: 'Kip and I are both international bastards – born in one place and choosing to live elsewhere. Fighting to get back to or get away from our homelands all our lives' (EP 176). Whereas the older man has gone through the Mirror Stage and understands their common situation of colonial dislocation, Kip, as Almasy states, 'doesn't recognize that yet' (EP 177). Totally seduced by the Empire, Kip is unaware of the harm it has done him, and instead, seems to bask in the presence of his 'English' father figures.

The bond between the 'English' patient and the Sikh sapper ultimately becomes a fusion of the two men. The 'I' who sees and the 'I' who is seen become linked at a fundamental level, for the 'English' patient begins to perceive the Sikh sapper as his own youth, a part of his past, a segment of his life. In one of his conversations with the Canadian Caravaggio, he describes in detail the painting of David and Goliath done by the famous Italian Caravaggio, and admits, 'I think when I see him at the foot of my bed that Kip is my David' (EP 116). Though paralysed and physically powerless, the 'English' patient commands a lot of authority, and while he reposes in his bed 'like a king', Hana, Kip, and Caravaggio serve him hand and foot. The paralysed patriarch lying still on his bed feels close to the energetic Sikh sapper. Perhaps Kip is the man who has been able to break upon the emotions of the 'English' patient. He may not have been of his Hungarian blood, yet the Punjabi succeeds 'more than someone of his own blood' in showing Almasy himself. Ondaatje here could also be alluding to the different 'families' of David and Goliath, viz., Israel and the Philistines. But in Almasy's version of Caravaggio's painting, the opposing factions blend into the singular person of the painter; rather than a murderer of the strong Goliath, David becomes a part of his own self. Standing at the foot of his bed, Kip unfolds layers and layers of the old man's history; simultaneously he is the image of a son – the next generation – in whom the 'English' patient invests his future.

The late fifteenth century Villa was a turning point in history, and so it is in 1945. As Kip's relationship evolves with his three Villa residents, so does his passage into himself. He begins to recognize himself. As he remembers his past, his dismembered self begins to heal. There are many scenes in which he reminisces about his brother, his maid, his sacred place of worship. Through developing these delicate and intricate patterns, Ondaatje displays Kip's psychological progression.

With 'sunlight in his eyes' Kip turns to Hana and recalls the many 'battles of opinion' he has had with his anti-colonialist brother. As the words of his brother now begin to echo in Kip, sunlight also enters his eyes. Metaphorically Ondaatje prepares us for Kip's awakening from the false consciousness which has blinded him from childhood.

While lying with Hana, he also remembers his South Indian maid. Like Rudyard Kipling's Kim, Ondaatje's Kip is brought up by a poor and distant woman, an 'intimate stranger'. All comfort and peace during childhood, Kip remembered, had come from his South Indian ayah with whom he had played, never from the mother he loved or from his brother or father. In a touching scene Kip recalls how the ayah eased him into sleep 'with her hand on his small thin back'. His closeness with Hana opens up the deep psychological vacuum created by the absence of his mother and his immediate family. Lacan's formulation of *manque-à-être* (a want-to-be or lack in being) helps us understand Kip's emotional handicap, his lack of identity and selfhood. According to Lacan, the gap or lack (*manque*) is formed by the separation between the infant's fantasy and the mother's reality, and that original want gives rise to desire as an incessant series of displacements (Muller 1985: 248–9). Kip's attraction towards his imperial masters is a misappropriation of his primal desire for his mother, his father, and his brother. The neglect and abandonment suffered from those at home are shifted into admiration and attachment for those far from home.

So intense is Kip's adoration for 'outsiders' like Lord Suffolk and their scientific gifts, that he even forgets the one person who gave him solace and comfort as a child. Now in his relationship with '(an)/(m)other' stranger, he remembers his ayah. But this stranger, unlike his British officers, is more of an equal. Both are about the same age, both have suffered, both have sympathy for each other, and both are drawn to each other physically and emotionally. And both have avoided mirrors. As Kip tenderly touches Hana's back, he journeys back to his past, to the servant's quarters when he was nine years old. The ayah had lost her mother, and was weeping profusely. The little boy stood behind her hunched-over body (as described at the end of the chapter entitled 'The Holy Forest'), 'he began to scratch her through the sari, then pulled it aside and scratched her skin – as Hana now received this tender art, his nails against the million cells of her skin, in his tent, in 1945, where their continents met in a hill town'. This is the only time he recalls returning the love he received from her. All kinds of dualities, past and present, east and west, platonic and sexual, joy and guilt, body and mind, give and take, converge as Kip and Hana lie together in his tent in the precincts of the Villa San Girolamo. Even though the regimented Kip is still not able to relinquish his army habit of sleeping in the tent, his polarized and shattered person is becoming whole. As Kip begins to touch Hana, he begins to get in touch with his missing self.

Memory and imagination superimpose as Kip and Hana travel together during those verbal nights to the central shrine of the Sikhs, their Golden Temple in Amritsar. Ondaatje presents a most beautiful and sensuous experience of the Sikh shrine which no artist, photographer, or scholar has been able to capture as effectively. We see the structure of the shrine inlaid with gold and marble lifted by the shimmering waters surrounding it – what a pity that the Hollywood version omitted this! As we walk barefooted beside the pool with Kip and Hana, we too smell pomegranates and oranges from the temple garden, while hearing the scriptural recitations. It is altogether a holistic feeling which lifts up the fallen psyche. The harmony of the sights and sounds and smells and touch fills up all fissures and cracks, strengthening the individual. Though thousands of miles away, by envisioning his very special space in this intense way, the disintegrated senses of Kip begin to reassemble. Unlike the external harmony between the colour of his turban and the Virgin's collar, this is an inner link, colouring his arteries with spiritual energy which he can pass on to his companion Hana, and to the reader as well.

What the desert did for Almasy, the Golden Temple does for Kip (and Hana). Miles and miles of sheer sheets of sand appear a contrast to a golden and marble structure set in the middle of a pool. Yet, as places that provide absolute openness breaking all barriers of race and nation, and as places which inspire inner retreat, producing peace and poetry recitations, the desert and the Golden Temple are very alike: 'Men had always been the reciters of poetry in the desert' (EP 240), and 'The desert was the place they had chosen to come to, to be their best selves, to be unconscious of ancestry' (EP 246), or 'There is God only in the desert, he wanted to acknowledge that now. Outside of this there was just trade and power, money and war. Financial and military despots shaped the world' (EP 250).

Great religious figures like Moses, John the Baptist, Christ, the Desert Fathers, and the Prophet Muhammad were all attracted to the desert. It was in that open and limitless space and silence of the shimmering sand that they carried on their communication with the Divine. Ondaatje's early twentieth century explorers in the desert also acknowledge the presence of the Divine in their midst. Whereas the world outside is sunk in economic and political wars with everyone fighting to shape and fashion matter and materials after their own name and profession, people in the desert renounce all their artificial hierarchies and possessions, and become a part of the infinite space. It is the desert that makes them truly human, 'their best selves'.

Similarly, 'the temple is a haven in the flux of life, accessible to all. It is the ship that crossed the ocean of ignorance' (EP 271). The openness and inclusivity of the desert are architecturally articulated in the Sikh shrine completed by Guru Arjan. Its four doors reach out to embrace all castes and races. Beginning with Guru Nanak, the Sikh Gurus stressed the equality of all humans. They rejected the fourfold division of Hindu society. When one enters the Sikh shrine, one is to become unconscious of social divisions and hierarchies. Like the desert, the shrine is also a retreat, a haven from the hustle and bustle of outward commotion. Resting serenely in the middle of a pool it is a place of equanimity and freedom. It does not drown in chaotic ignorance but remains gently afloat on the shimmering waters. Ondaatje uses the image of a ship. Accessible to all, the shrine is a 'ship' which carries us from darkness to light. Guru Arjan's construction of the first Sikh building – with its four doors –became the architectural paradigm for all gurdwaras, literally, doors to the Divine. As an opening to the innermost self of the person, the Harimandir leads Kip and Hana towards the transcendent.

The Golden Temple, the Desert, and the Villa San Girolamo are resonances of each other. The desert has no walls, the walls of the villa are broken open, Guru Arjan consciously had the four walls of the first Sikh shrine broken by four doorways. By entering these spaces we rid ourselves of our narrow walls of prejudice, hatred, and greed. While Kip begins to remember the temple of Amritsar welcoming the different faiths and classes and people eating together, Hana becomes filled with the hope of visiting it. 'She herself would be allowed to place money or a flower onto the sheet spread upon the floor and then joining the great permanent singing' (EP 272). Both Kip and Hana approached the Villa from a different and separate entry, but they move together into the Golden Temple. The split personalities are uniting. There is a dynamic momentum and rhythm as they move beyond. There are no racial barriers and there are no gender barriers and there are no temporal barriers as past and future coalesce in Kip and Hana's journey to the Golden Temple. In fact, even the rigid walls between the subject and the object dissolve as 'Kip watches her as she washes her feet, covers her head.'

Kip's revisiting of the Punjab through his memories of his brother, his maid, and his sacred space is a vital juncture in his transformation. In spite of the fact that the tragic Jallianwala Bagh massacre, in which hundreds of innocent men, women, and children were killed on order by General Dyer in 1919, has not surfaced in his memory of Amritsar, we do find that Kip grows and evolves over the months leading up to 6 August 1945. Were it not for his imaginary journey with Hana in the garden of the Villa San Girolamo, his postcolonial epiphany and his return home would not have had the same effect. And those who miss out on his gradual psychological and spiritual progression misjudge Kip's role. Critics who have found Kip's final act of 'moral heroism' to be that of a 'moral adolescent' (Scobie 1994: 93–5) have failed to read through Ondaatje's carefully planned and compelling narrative. The finale is not abrupt and clumsily handled. The Sikh acts as passionately as he does not because he is an adolescent, but because he has matured through the post-war months with his comrades in the Villa San Girolamo.

## Breaking mirrors: Kip's nationalism

And then Kip hears about Hiroshima and Nagasaki through the earphones 'tight against his brain'. He had always regarded Europe and America as the paradigm of sophistication and refinement. Until now he had tried to mirror the best of the West, but the news of the savage attack on Japanese civilians by Western civilization shocks him. He wants only to shatter those mirrors he had held up so high.

133

As soon as he hears the news, Kip emerges from the tent with a gun, ready to shoot his enemy, the 'English' patient. The always courteous and balanced fellow who 'believes in a civilized world. He's a civilized man' (EP 122), is all set to fire out the colonizer's presence from his life. The aggressive act is a meaningful response, revealing Kip's newfound ego. Feeling insulted and violated – perhaps for the first time in his life – Kip seeks to insult and kill the perpetrator. More than 'like a steel ball moving in an arcade game' as Ondaatje describes him, the reader sees him explode like a bomb himself – blasting 'plaster dust in the air around them'. Gone is the civility, gone is the formality, gone are all the polished manners and polished buckles that he was taught as a kid in the British public schools. Instead, he slams doors and shouts. Witnessing the brutal attack by his revered Western nations shocks Kip into exorcizing the conduct that was bred in him. He becomes the rustic Punjabi brother that we have come to know through Kip himself.

With his aim of ejecting the world and the mode of representation dictated by the English, he rushes up to the 'English' patient's room. His gun aimed at his 'English' enemy, Kip hurls all that was pent-up in him:

> I sat at the foot of this bed and listened to you, Uncle. These last months. When I was a kid I did that, the same thing ... I grew up with traditions from your country. Your fragile white island that with customs and manners and books and prefects and reason somehow converted the rest of the world. You stood for precise behaviour. I knew if I lifted a teacup with the wrong finger I'd be banished (EP 283).

At last Kip is awakened from his stupor induced by Western colonialism. Kip realizes how the British and then the Americans converted the Indians through their 'missionary rules.' He was seduced as a child by the grand customs and manners and medals of the Western culture prevailing in India. The best of the West was nothing but a trap to ensnare the innocent natives into playing their games, for their sake, according to their rules. Kip's oblivion and ignorance of Western manipulation dissolve into thin air like plaster dust.

Kip even begins to accept and endorse his own sibling's point of view:

> My brother told me. Never turn your back on Europe. The deal makers. The contract makers. The map drawers. Never trust

Europeans. Never shake hands with them. But we, oh, we were easily impressed – by speeches and medals and your ceremonies (EP 284–5).

His adoration shifts from distant figures like Lord Suffolk and the 'English' patient, and comes closer home, to his brother. The brother begins to make more sense than all the sensible figures that he had admired through the course of his life. He can even see through the Western custom of shaking hands. The seemingly friendly ritual is rooted in the egotistical notion of the 'I'. The extension of the hand is an extension of power, greed, territory; it is nothing but a gesture for making deals and contracts. This extension of the self over others would be so different from his own Sikh greeting 'Sat Sri Akal,' where both hands are folded together and each party salutes the Timeless Truth. The two hands gently join together, they do not invade other people's space as does the handshake; and whereas the Sikh greeting brings in the Divine, the rather negative one-handed Western contact rules out the sacred. But Kip is now able to identify the enemy behind the friendly gestures: 'Night could fall between them, fog could fall, and the young man's dark brown eyes would reach the new revealed enemy' (EP 284).

The disclosures from the deed of Western destruction keep darting at Kip. He becomes totally disillusioned with his profession. The years he had spent preparing to get enlisted in the British army, then working for his officers in England and Europe, diligently defusing bombs to help the West, all come to a naught. 'What have I been doing all these years? Cutting away, defusing, limbs of evil. For what? For *this* to happen?' (EP 285). He cannot fathom how he could have been in a service that would be so destructive, and the ironic tragedy of it startles him. Before the day is over, he begins to strip off all the professional paraphernalia from his life. He strips his tent of all military objects and bomb disposal equipment. He even strips all insignia off his uniform. The next morning he gets rid of his tent, and as its 'canvas walls collapse like a sail' the reader thinks of Katherine's parachute and knows that Kip's employment in the army is all over – a mere shroud like the parachute around Katherine's corpse.

In this nationalist phase, Kip cleaves to his own. Instead of the West, Asia becomes Kip's Mirror in which he looks for his identity. He rejects the divide and rule policy of the Western imperialists, and begins to see Japan as a part of his own Asian continent. He feels oneness with all the brown and yellow races. 'If he closes his eyes he sees the streets of Asia full of fire' (EP 284).

Kip is terrified and responds with the shock of a post-nuclear sensibility. He only hears the news through his earphones but he accurately envisions the details of the victims of Hiroshima and Nagasaki that we are all familiar with. The recurring metaphor of fire in the novel blazes through all of Asia for Kip, and he can feel the burning and scorching. He cannot even light a lamp lest it ignite everything around him. Deeply feeling the tremor of Western wisdom, the Sikh fully empathizes with the victims of Hiroshima and Nagasaki. Weeping profusely, he is unable to swallow anything. Kip knows for sure that the Allies would never have dropped the bomb on Germany or Italy, and even Germany did not destroy Naples: 'They would never have dropped such a bomb on a white nation' (EP 286). The postcolonial Kip is awakened to White supremacy and White brotherhood. His trust and kinship with the white Lord Suffolk or his belief in 'the burned man and the meadows of civilization he tended' are totally shattered. He doesn't care about any differences between the English or the American or the French – they are for Kip all White and all alike. 'When you start bombing the brown races of the world, you're an Englishman' (EP 286). Now with the awful discovery, Kip bonds with people closer to his own complexion and to his own continent.

The explosion of Hiroshima and Nagasaki shatter Kip's construction as a loyal subject by the imperialists, and he begins to reinterpret and redefine himself. He brings out the photograph of his family, which was somewhere hidden in his tent, and looks at it. As he unwinds his ancestral affiliation and uncovers his communal memory, he realizes that 'his name is Kirpal Singh and he does not know what he is doing here' (EP 287). It is a moment of self-definition. He is not a fractured entity, a Kip or Kipper grease or a Mr. Kipling cake; he is Kirpal Singh, reconnected with his family and with his Sikh community.

Ondaatje hauntingly captures the essence of Kirpal Singh who has just rediscovered himself and recaptured his identity. 'He stands under the trees in the August heat . . . standing on the edge of a great valley of Europe' (EP 287). The intensity of the heat is due to both the season and the nuclear explosion. Kip is looking down at Florence, the birthplace of renaissance, the heart of Western art and culture. But now as he stands on the top, he can have a full view of this 'great valley of Europe'. He can see it all. The magic is gone. He is no more in awe of the West. All those mirror-images and mirages have disappeared.

At this moment Kip is unturbaned, bare-footed, wearing only a *kurta* and carrying nothing in his hands. The parallel with Aziz at the end of *A Passage to India* is striking. The Doctor who would invariably be dressed in western three-piece suits eventually rejects the colonialists' style and returns to his traditional Islamic attire. Exorcized of his army uniform, Kip too wears his native *kurta*, a loose and light shirt. He is so casual that he is not even wearing his turban or shoes. Later he will even remove his *kurta*. Native Indian nationalism pinches just as much as the shoes of his colonial uniform. Kip's body is now freed from the tight and stifling uniform, and his hands from the weight and burden of weapons. Without the oppressive imperial codes and equipment, Kip's body becomes 'alive', making him receptive to his inner feelings and thoughts.

The very next morning, he leaves the Villa without formal goodbyes – Singh (no longer Kip) just 'touched' Hana's arm. Kip is on his motorbike. Without trying to take control of the machine, he lets it roll away. He slides through quickly, recognizing 'only the Black Madonna shrines'. Having awoken from his colonial slumber, Kip begins to reject and shun the White Madonna figures. The very places where he had found comfort now appear threatening to him. He erects artificial walls of prejudice and hate, and wanders around 'like somebody unable to enter the intimacy of a home'.

This exclusionary mode is against Kirpal Singh's character. In a temporary fit of rage, he wears blinkers and goes full speed. Riding his Triumph, he spits on the goggles as though (to use Fanon's words) he were 'vomiting up the white man's values'. When he turns around the curve, which is also a turning point in his life, Kirpal Singh slides with his motorbike down the centre of the bridge. With verses ringing from the Apocalypse and a halo of 'blue sparks from the scratching metal around his arms and face', he falls into the river. This is his total crash, the death of his former colonial self and that of his brief nationalist rage too. As his bare head emerges out of the water, and he gasps in all the air above the river, the reader feels he has been reborn. Kirpal Singh's emotional crisis is over. His rebirth intimates Guru Nanak's experience in the River Bein where he disappeared and emerged after three days with a new message for humanity.

## Seeing through mirrors: at home with himself

'There is no Hindu; there is no Muslim.' With these words which, for Sikhs, contain a foundational statement of their faith, Guru Nanak urged his society to go beyond the external differences to the basic

137

core of humanity. Thirteen years after his fall in the river in Italy, we meet our Sikh protagonist simply sitting with his family in a garden. He is Kirpal Singh, spatially situated in the square patch of grass at home – not the gardens of Italy or the gardens on the walls of the Villa San Girolamo. Coming home has been coming to the self, connecting back with himself. The square patch is a safe and secure place, holding his cultural roots and his sense of location, here and now. The postcolonial quest to establish control over the past and give it form has been accomplished in Kirpal Singh's case. He waged a battle of mind with colonialism by re-educating himself. He left engineering and became a doctor as his family had always wanted him to do. He has returned to his ancestral womb, and with his wife and two children, Kirpal is spiritually reconciled. The children provide him with continuity. Through his son and daughter, Kirpal Singh recreates and continues his person and legacy. Rather than the turban or the *kara*, we see the father, husband and doctor.

Gone is his nationalist phase as well. Instead of a *kurta*, the stereotypical dress for an Indian nationalist, he wears shirt and trousers and a lab coat. Unlike Aziz in *A Passage to India*, who completely gave up his western form of dress, Kirpal Singh does not seem to reject it. And the reader wonders why there is no mention of the division between India and Pakistan. Isn't he on the soil which was ripped asunder just a few years earlier? Indeed Kirpal has come to see that religion and nationalism which are often tied together are actually opposites. Hindus and Sikhs and Muslims had their bloody split in the Punjab and in the Bengal in 1947 not because they were Hindus and Sikhs and Muslims, but because of the imperial policy of their colonial masters who provoked and fomented ethnic rivalries amongst their subjects. If religion were the problem, why would there be a bloody division soon after between West Pakistan and East Pakistan which were both Muslim territories? And why would even Sikhs kill fellow Sikhs? No matter how the discourse is masked, the source for these 'religious' conflicts is something quite other. Tagore, who was an ardent champion of religion but a vehement critic of nationalism, wrote:

> The hungry self of the Nation shall burst in a violence of fury
>     from its own shameless feeding
> For it has made the world its food,
> And licking it, crunching it, and swallowing it in big morsels,
>     It swells and swells . . .
>
> (*Tagore* 1977: 80–1)

138

Centuries earlier, Guru Nanak had also clarified that it is not religion but greed which divides the human family. Commenting on the atrocities of Babur's invasion of India, Guru Nanak says: *jaru vandi devai bhai – –* 'it is wealth which splits brother from brother' (AG 417). Because of his greed for wealth and power, and his failure to move westward, the Muslim Babur destroyed the Muslim Ibrahim Lodi and established the Mughal empire in India. For the cause of Empire, a Muslim is destroyed by a Muslim.

Yet, in the name of 'religion' individual desires and demands are fabricated into a dangerous rhetoric for arousing exclusivism and communalism. *The English Patient* leaves out the nationalist struggles: the brutal tragedy of 1947 is bypassed from Kirpal's past; the brutal tragedy of 1984 from his future. But the destructiveness of nationalism is powerfully symbolized in Madox's suicide in the church of his home town. This supreme expression of despair was brought on by the words of the priest corrupted by nationalism. While the priest was blessing the government and the men about to enter the war, Madox pulled out the 'desert pistol' and shot himself. What ensued was 'Desert Silence. Planeless Silence' (EP 242). After going through the religious experience in the desert where they were all united – Hungarians, English, Germans, Arabs – Madox could not accept the sermon on the mountainous mapping of boundaries and nations. The planeless silence is an ironic prelude to the single plane in an empty sky carrying the Bomb. Religion has been betrayed. The sacred is forsaken. The technological supremacy of the colonial powers does not make the world a better place; it only bombs and destroys.

Madox returns home and kills himself. Kip returns home but is not destroyed. Instead of despair, there is hope. The memories of Hana are lodged deeply in his person, and he often has the urge to call her up. The novel ends with the sentence: 'Her shoulder touches the edge of a cupboard and a glass dislodges. Kirpal's left hand swoops down and catches the dropped fork an inch from the floor and gently passes it into the fingers of his daughter, a wrinkle at the edge of his eyes behind his spectacles' (EP 302).

We are not sure where each is exactly located. Is he in his dining room? At his kitchen table? Hana in her kitchen? Her dining room? Her pantry? What we are certainly left with is the image of the 'home'. Ondaatje's final imaginative vision for us is this home, the home extending from the Punjab to Canada. So too have leaders like Mahatma Gandhi and Martin Luther King also used the 'house' as a popular image for our world community:

We have inherited a large house, a great 'world house' in which we have to live together – black and white, Easterner and Westerner, Gentile and Jew, Catholic and Protestant, Moslem and Hindu – a family unduly separated in ideas, culture, and interest, who, because we can never again live apart, must learn somehow to live with each other in peace.

(*King* 1968: 167)

From what I gather, Kirpal's response to King's 'undue' separation would be colonialism and nationalism.

In spite of their geographical barriers the Punjabi Sikh and the Canadian nurse live in a close range and cannot survive excluding the other. The fact is that they belong to a post-war world, and a postcolonial world and can never live apart from each other. The local home has been transformed into a global one. Kip and Hana are not strangers but friends – at one time they were even lovers. They mutually understand each other, for, as the glass dislodges in Canada, Kirpal Singh picks it up at his home in the Punjab before it breaks and shatters on the floor. A circle is drawn. A rhythmical pattern of peace and harmony emerges on the global scene. Our postcolonial world, with its falling glass and fork – symbolic of its dangers, uncertainties, and intransigences – can in fact lead to new ventures and new relationships. Kip and Hana are residents of our international and plural society, one in which we need to live together, understand one another, value one another. In this final union, Kirpal Singh wears spectacles, not his grey goggles. He can see clearly without illusions about England or the Western civilization. He is no longer afraid to see himself. He is his own authentic person, reconnected with himself, his history, his culture, and his land. There is complete harmony 'between the organism and its reality – or, as they say, between the *Innenwelt* and the *Umwelt*.' This was the function of Lacan's Mirror Stage, and Kip has developed far beyond it. The Harimandir is he for the infinite light is housed in him. With full self-awareness Kirpal Singh can now reconnect and relate with his Canadian friend and her New World. Together they can open up a whole new world of exciting possibilities.

The body is the mansion, it is the home and temple of the Divine
  In it is housed the infinite light;
Says Nanak, the enlightened are invited to the mansion
  the Divine Unifier brings about the union (AG 1256).

140

# Notes

1 While Kipling's Kim is a white in a brown landscape, Ondaatje's Kip is a brown figure in a white landscape. Technologically both Kip and Kim are very talented and both are attracted to Lama-like figures.
2 The translations from the Sikh sacred texts are my own. Some are from *The Name of My Beloved* (HarperCollins, 1995).
3 Throughout the Guru Granth we find many verses with a variety of nuances coming together to underscore the spiritual ingredient of our body.

## Chapter Eight

# The Limits of 'Conventional Wisdom': Understanding Sikh Ethno-nationalism

## Gurharpal Singh

The interest and fascination which Sikh ethno-nationalism has aroused among scholars in the 1980s and 1990s have not been reflected in any sustained engagement with the theory of nationalism and its application to either the Sikhs or India. Many of the publications that emerged after Operation Bluestar (1984) neglected to discuss the conditions which made Sikh ethno-nationalism such a potent force (Pettigrew 1995; Mahmood 1996). Where the emphasis of scholarship has been on Indian nationalism as the critical agent in precipitating the 'Punjab problem' (Brass 1991; Juergensmeyer 1988; Veer 1996), the main lines of enquiry have concentrated on the decline of Nehruvian values, secularism, and the rise of the Bharatiya Janata Party (BJP) and its programme of *Hindutva*. The intervention of poststructuralists in the debate (Oberoi 1987; 1994) has not added to clarity. At one level they have been quite successful in deconstructing the content of Sikh identity. At another, however, such deconstructions have left unanswered central questions about the nature of Indian nationalism and how it relates, structures and defines the ethno-nationalism of minorities on the borders of the Indian Union.

In order to understand the dynamic of Sikh ethno-nationalism it is necessary to situate it in the context of ethno-national movements on India's border states. To a large extent these movements have been misunderstood because of how ethnicity has been defined or, rather, not defined since 1947. This reluctance to do so is based on a set of common assumptions that constitute what can be called 'conventional wisdom' – the traditional reading of politics of identity in India. This chapter evaluates the limits of that conventional wisdom by drawing

142

attention to its ahistorical nature, to the role of the state, and to the persistence of strong ethno-nationalist movements in the peripheral regions. In contrast to this traditional understanding, it is suggested that India should be considered as a form of an ethnic democracy in which hegemonic control is exercised over ethnic minorities, particularly in the peripheral regions. A view of India as an ethnic democracy helps us to better appreciate the sense of turmoil in the border regions – as well as a sharper focus on current internal restructuring with ethnic democracy (the rise of the BJP and *Hindutva*) – the real limits of nation and state-building.

## Ethnicity

Discussion of ethnicity in India normally evokes a strong partisanship which is rarely evident elsewhere. Whereas other societies have ethnic divisions, similar divisions in India are often defined as non-ethnic. Language and definition are power; and in contemporary India this power is jealously guarded (Banton 1998). Indeed, one observer has noted the tendency of leading academics to avoid the term ethnicity in favour of identities and other signifiers (Manor 1996). He himself uses it with quotation marks. This ambiguity, as we shall see below, is part and parcel of the conventional wisdom about ethnicity and politics in India.

Most definitions of ethnicity combine some elements of objective and subjective factors (Brass 1991: 18–9). Whereas objective factors are often distinguishing characteristics, such as language, religion, colour, tribe, caste, dress or diet, subjective factors pertain to collective action associated with these characteristics. Thus an ethnic group is 'sometimes defined as one that perceives a common identity based on characteristics acquired at either birth (colour for example) or through cultural experience (language, religion, caste, sense of regional identity etc.)' (Jeffrey 1986: 3). Ethnic groups are almost like complete societies with elements of 'division of labour and reproduction' (Brass 1991: 19). As such they either are, or could be said to resemble, a nation – and 'where an "ethnic group" ends and a "nation" begins is one of the smouldering questions of the twentieth century' (Jeffrey 1986: 5).

The mere existence of objective difference does not necessarily make a particular group ethnic, however. Ethnicity may be imposed – by another group – latent, uncontested or suppressed. In addition to objective factors three other elements are necessary: 'the sense of unique group origins, the knowledge of unique group history and belief in its destiny and a sense of collective solidarity' (Smith 1981: 68). Taken together these elements give an ethnic group a sense of distinctiveness, individuality, and collective solidarity – in short, a consciousness of being as well as being recognized as such by others.

Manor (1996) has mapped out the main 'ethnic' categories in Indian politics. According to him these are really permeable 'identities' based around religion, language, tribe, and the Aryan/ Dravidian divide. Religion is the key identity that dominates, and is identified with Hinduism (82 per cent of the population), Muslims (12 per cent), and Sikhs (2 per cent). Linguistically, there are nine major languages each spoken by over 25 million people and several minor ones like Punjabi and Kashmiri. Tribal identities include those outside or on the margins of Hindu society, now referred to as Scheduled Tribes, and recognized tribal populations in the Himalayas and the north-eastern states who are often considered racially distinct. Lastly, there are the overarching identities of Aryan and Dravidian which were significant in the past but are no longer powerful symbols of mobilization.

For Manor these identities are rarely primordial, cumulative or homogenizing: they encourage heterogeneity and fluidity which are further accentuated by caste identities, religious sectarianism, and the existence of clans and familial loyalties, as well as modern associations such as party, class, the region and locality. This pattern of crosscutting, overlapping and intersecting cleavages ensures that

> ... Indians tend not to fix on any of these identities fiercely and permanently. ... They tend instead to shift their preoccupation, readily and often, from one identity to another, in response to changing circumstances. As a result tensions do not become concentrated along a single fault-line in society, and do not produce prolonged and intractable conflicts – 'ethnic' or otherwise – that might tear democratic institutions apart.
>
> (Manor 1996: 463)

The 'efficient secret' of the Indian experience, in Manor's assessment, therefore is that ethnic fault lines are blurred, indeterminate and, most of the time, quite insignificant to the wider operation of the polity. Those Jeremiahs who have been predicting the break-up of the Indian Union since its creation along ethnic lines have been proved disappointingly wrong.

## Conventional wisdom

The arguments advanced by Manor restate what might aptly be termed as conventional wisdom: that is, the traditional, familiar, formal way of addressing the issue. Conventional wisdom is rooted in a particular reading of Indian politics and society, of problematizing (or vaporizing) ethnicity, and emphasizing India's heterogeneity, diversity and complexity. Often conventional wisdom is articulated in metaphors and cliches such as 'unity-in-diversity', 'nation-in-the-making'; sometimes it is even elevated to the level of civilizational uniqueness, an exceptional societal virtue that has enabled the Indian state to escape the pernicious consequences of ethnic and nationalist conflicts that have bedeviled twentieth-century Europe (Parekh 1995). The main ingredient defining civilizational uniqueness, however, is Hinduism, a plural religious tradition which abhors centralizing institutions or a single holy text by accepting, tolerating, and even encouraging diversity. Hinduism, according to some observers, provides the basis for the self-regulation of conflicts, underpinning a 'functioning anarchy' and a non-denominational state.[1]

This form of conventional wisdom has been predominant in the nationalist historiography of the independence movement, those American political scientists who have dominated the study of Indian politics, the uncritical readings of the Nehruvian state, and the works of Neo-Gandhians. It has also received a further confirmation from postmodernists who are keen to rejoice in India's diversity, difference and infinite pluralism.[2] Thus conventional wisdom, far from weakening under the pressure of contemporary developments, continues to provide the point of departure for most standard interpretations of the Indian state and society.

Most accounts that fall in the remit of conventional wisdom share four key assumptions:

1 *Ethnic identities are not primordial but constructed, permeable and contingent.* This extreme instrumentalism is supported by the 'deconstruction' of ethnicities, the role of the colonial state often in 'constructing' ethnicities where they did not exist (Kaviraj 1997; Pandey 1990), and the apparent permeability of the most enduring identity: religion. Religious boundaries, it is suggested, are not fixed, constant or quasi-racial. Rather, in India they are vague if not self-consciously defined. Even subcontinental Muslims, it is contended, are 'thin' Muslims, being largely former converts from

145

Hinduism. Similarly, Sikhism has struggled to establish clear boundaries between itself and Hinduism (Manor 1996).

2 *Ethnic groups selectively emphasize particular dimensions of their identity as appropriate.* Ethnic group identities are not constant, solid or unchanging. In practice ethnic groups highlight aspects of their identities – religion, language, tribe – as appropriate (and convenient), constantly shifting the focus of attention (Brass 1974). This flexibility casts doubts not only on the 'primordial' content of ethnicity but also highlights its often selective political articulation to meet particular exigencies. Ethnic groups operating within the framework of democratic rule, like other interest groups, are compelled to make strategic as well as tactical choices – choices which regularly undermine their own rhetoric of self-identification.

3 *Ethnic groups lack cohesion.* Conventional wisdom is dismissive of ethnic group solidarity. As Manor has pointed out, collective action by ethnic groups is prone to disarticulation because of the cross-cutting cleavages of caste, language, religion, tribe, party and class. Because of such barriers, it is difficult to sustain ethnic mobilization, especially if the ethnic group cannot enforce collective solidarity (for example, through coercion).

4 *The Indian state is secular and seeks to foster political integration alongside a multicultural society.* Conventional wisdom shares common assumptions about the state. These include: an explicit commitment to secularism; an ability to stand aloof from the main cultural force in Indian society (Hinduism); and the pursuit of political integration alongside the development of a multicultural society (Brass 1991: ch.5). In brief, the state is not the embodiment of an ethnic will but is a non-ethnic actor that has nurtured and developed Indian democracy.

Much of conventional wisdom locates the causes of India's contemporary ethnic conflicts in political perversion: that is, the decline of Nehruvian values identified in the post-Nehruvian processes of centralization, deinstitutionalization, and political decay (Kohli 1991). Some elements, in particular Neo-Gandhians and postmodernists, have also critiqued the modernizing zeal of the Nehruvian state in creating false antinomies between secularism and religion, of introducing a Eurocentric state tradition to a largely segmentary society (Baxi and Parekh 1995). But this school of thought stops short of interrogating the cultural basis of the state's legitimacy and instead decries its supposed desecularizing mission under Nehru – a mission that disturbed the traditional equipoise of Indian society.

## The limits of conventional wisdom: it is ahistorical

In the last two decades conventional wisdom has been severely tested as India has witnessed violent insurgencies in the peripheral regions and the rise of the BJP. The assumptions sustaining it have been increasingly exposed while its explanatory value has diminished to a point where for some it no longer provides a satisfactory framework for those contesting the legitimacy of Indian statehood or seeking to redefine it in terms of *Hindutva*. That conventional wisdom is an ideological construct can be further highlighted by its ahistorical character, its assumptions about the state, and its inability to explain the tenacity of ethno-nationalist movements in the peripheral regions.

The most obvious problem with conventional wisdom is that it is ahistorical. It selects, rarefies, historicizes and ignores the foundational event of the modern Indian state: the partition (Jalal 1996). Of course it can be argued, as Parekh has done, that the project of Jinnah and the Muslim League to create Pakistan was unashamedly Eurocentric, an alien intrusion into a civilizational society in which the Congress was leading a 'non-nationalist' nationalism (Parekh 1995). But such a defence is untenable for two reasons: scholarship has demonstrated that Pakistan was a contingent factor for achieving political equality (Jalal 1985), and it ascribes to ideas and elites an autonomous role in the development of nationalism which was evidently not the case.[3] What the Indian nationalism of the Congress represented was a combination of the elite secularism of individuals like Nehru with the populism of Gandhi and his appeal to a subaltern culture dense with Hindu religious symbolism. This union placed Muslims in a awkward predicament: their acceptance as modern Indians required a denial of Islam, a forgoing of their claim to equal citizenship based on identity. 'Muslim separatism', it followed, 'was not the expression of a primordial identity but the necessary Muslim response to a modernity that offered them only a partial identity of being the minor term, the other, of Indian nationalism' (Mitchell and Abu-Lughod 1993: 80).

Apart from the partition, which created an overwhelmingly Hindu India, the question arises as to what the content of civilizational society was. For Vanaik (Vanaik 1997), the concept of India's

147

civilizational unity and cultural essence was largely developed to fulfil the needs of an emerging Indian political elite at the end of the nineteenth and early twentieth centuries. Far from being devoid of religious essence the idea was founded on the 'catholicity of Brahmanical Hinduism'. In so doing, an 'indissoluble connection' was established between Hinduism and Indian civilization – a connection which was popularized by M.K. Gandhi as a form of cultural nationalism of inclusion only by the denial of existing identities of non-Hindus. Behind the central tenets of civilizational essence lurk difficult questions about Hinduism's pluralism, tolerance and passivity. Embree for one has called for a critical appraisal of nineteenth century German hermeneutics which celebrated the idea of Hindu tolerance embedded in the assertion that there are many levels of truth. 'What follows from this assertion,' he notes, 'is not toleration; rather, all truths, all social practices, can be encapsulated within the society as long as there is willingness to accept the premises on which encapsulation is based' (Embree 1990: 30). Encapsulation of course can facilitate accommodation, cooption and, eventually assimilation, but not political equality for movements that assert their exclusivity or externality against the Hindu universe. And where the state defines such religious tolerance (à la secularism) as a form of variegated truth – as in India after 1947 – the preconditions for encapsulation can said to have been created.

## The limits of conventional wisdom: the state

The assumptions underpinning the nature of the state within conventional wisdom can be sustained only because the latter is ahistorical. But increasingly a radical assessment of the Indian state has begun to question whether the political pluralism it is renowned for maintaining applies 'only to cultural groups that remain broadly in the Hindu fold but discriminates against non-Hindu minorities' (Brass 1994: 69). A major preoccupation of this assessment has focused on the assumption of state secularism, its intersection with the majoritarian political discourse, and as a negative elite strategy of Nehruvian rule. For T. N. Madan, one of the leading exponents of this school of thought, the Indian state's secularism is an essentially 'negative' strategy.

At best, Indian secularism has been an inadequately defined

'attitude . . . of good will towards all religions'

(sarvadharma sadbhava)

in a narrower formulation it has been a negative or defensive policy of religious neutrality (*dharma nirpakshta*) on the part of the state. In either formulation, the Indian state achieves the opposite of its stated intentions; it trivializes religious differences as well as the notion of the unity of religions. And it really fails to provide guidance for viable political action, for it is not a rooted, full-blooded, and well thought out *Weltanschauung*; it is only a stratagem (Madan 1987: 750).

This negative strategy had no particular agenda for the secularization of Indian society. It offered asymmetrical accommodation (encapsulation) in the form of state neutrality. But while the state's official policy was to treat all religious communities equally, 'one would be more equal than others – namely the majority Hindu Community' (Upadhyaya 1992: 817). This outcome was implicit in the demographic majoritarianism built into the new state; it was also inevitable in the model of Indian 'secularism' advocated by Gandhi and adapted by Nehru.

For some revisionists, Hinduism in the post-1947 period functioned as a meta-Indian ethnicity in which Nehruvianism, was at best, a 'defensive strategy against communal conflict rather than a charter for secularization of Indian society' (Upadhyaya 1992: 828). This strategy accommodated Hindu religious interests because in the early 1950s Nehru initiated a pattern in which the 'Indian state would respond positively to religious pressures, particularly those emanating from Hindu groups, but would keep a distance from communal parties and platforms' (Upadhyaya 1992: 828).

The paradox of state without ethnicity becomes further untenable when we examine the logic of Indian nation and state-building since 1947. The partition ensured that the Indian nation and state-building project was founded on failure; the determination to succeed thereafter provided a natural coincidence of interest between elite secularism and Hinduism, the main cultural force in Indian society. Such was this unholy marriage of convenience that legitimate political challenges were regularly disarticulated as 'communal', 'religious', and 'sectarian'. This dominant discourse was normally presented in binary opposites such as secularism versus communalism, national unity versus separatism, 'authentic' religion versus fundamentalism, mainstream versus regionalism, and integration versus disintegration. While the Nehruvian state spoke the language of modernity, it simultaneously tolerated the equation of Hinduism with national culture, its elevation to a form of 'civic religion' (Embree 1990: 89).

Indeed, the assertion of civilizational essence founded in Hinduism was seen as *the defining* characteristic of the nation. In one memorable instance the Government of India insisted:

> The Indian people do not accept the proposition that India is a multinational society. *The Indian people constitute one nation.* India has experienced through her civilization over the ages, her strong underlying unity in the midst of diversity of language, religion etc. The affirmation of India's nationhood after a long and historic confrontation with imperialism does not brook any challenge.
>
> (*Government of India* 1984: 17, emphasis added)

Even if we accept the arguments of those scholars working within conventional wisdom that the above statement is an aberration, a deviation from actual practice, the issue arises of consistent *a priori* insistence on 'underlying unity' alongside the idea of multiculturalism, pluralism or difference. The reality of 'underlying civilizational unity', however, is actually encoded with Hindu myths, symbols and imagery and has little to do with issues of stateness (Sen 1997). As Kothari reminds us, the concept of a centrally ruled polity emerged only with the latter Mogul tradition and was perfected by colonialism (*The Sunday Tribune*, 15 August 1997). The recognition of India as a genuine plural society, on the other hand, 'does not need an underlying unity, or any commitment to a single truth, to hold people together. It needs mechanisms to make integration possible without denying those characteristics that define the essential life of its component groups' (Embree 1990: 65–5).

To suggest, as Kaviraj (1991) has done, that the Nehruvian state waged an unrelenting struggle against Hinduism in seeking to erase the 'language of belonging' is to seriously misinterpret the project of nation-building after 1947 in which Hinduism functioned as a meta-ethnicity of the new nation. Thus the challenge of linguistic reorganization of the states in the 1950s could be addressed because no fundamental issues about the ethnic character of the state were at stake. This dualism was also possible because, as Gellner has noted, 'Hindus "speak the same language" even when they do not speak the same language' (Gellner 1983: 109, note 1). In other words, the process of Indian nation and state-building has not typically been along linguistic fault lines as elsewhere: instead it has followed the contours of meta-ethnicity (Hinduism) in which there is inclusive, accommodating and encapsulating pluralism. As we shall see below, these fault lines become unbridgeable zones when we examine the process in India's peripheral regions.

## The limits of conventional wisdom: ethno-nationalist movements in the peripheral regions

One of the central weaknesses of conventional wisdom is its inability to explain the persistence of ethno-nationalist movements in the peripheral regions. In the last seventeen years these movements, and the efforts to manage them, have cost tens of thousands of lives and have tied down almost half of India's security forces (Thandi 1996). Some of these movements, which date from the pre-1947 period, have been able to maintain their opposition not only because of the 'external factor' (a euphemism for support from India's surrounding states) but mainly as a result of their ethno-nationalist resources – distinctiveness, history, collectivity, and a sense of destiny.

Scholars working within the assumptions of conventional wisdom have questioned the solidarity of peripheral ethno-nationalist movements by extending the argument of cross-cutting cleavages (Hewitt 1995). Apart from the obvious fact that most global ethno-nationalist movements are affected to some degree by cross-cutting loyalties, what tends to be overlooked in the Indian case is that these cleavages, especially in the peripheral regions, are cumulative. Thus Sikhs (religion) are overwhelmingly attached to one language (Punjabi) and are preponderantly from one caste (Jat) grouping. Likewise, in Kashmir the congruence between language and religion is unproblematic. In the north-eastern states, distinctive identities of caste, tribe and language (and sometimes religion, as for example in the case of the Nagas) are mainly reinforced rather than cross-cut.

Similarly the attempts to explain the rise of these ethno-nationalist movements in terms of political perversion cannot sustain critical examination. The main political science explanation put forward for these movements is the acute manifestation of the centralizing tendencies unleashed by the post-Nehruvian leadership. Whereas objective tendencies within Indian politics over the last three decades have been towards regionalism, pluralism and decentralization, the response of the national leadership to these pressures, it is suggested, has been to centralize power in New Delhi.

But there are four basic limitations of the centralization thesis. First, it does not satisfactorily explain why centralization drives

151

should have *disproportionately* adverse consequences for India's religious minorities, especially a minority like the Sikhs who were deliberately integrated into the state's coercive apparatus. Second, the differences in the centralization drives of the Nehruvian and post-Nehruvian leadership were one of degree rather than kind. A less sympathetic reading of the Nehruvian era, particularly in the peripheral regions, would reveal a high degree of 'bossism', constitutional subversions, and conscious efforts to achieve the cultural and political assimilation of minorities (Pettigrew 1975). Third, decentralization as a strategy for containing these ethno-nationalist movements would, paradoxically, in the short term, require further centralization lest the forces that have supported separatism make decentralization untenable.[4] Fourth, and related to the last point, underpinning ethno-nationalist demands are parallel claims to political sovereignty which would be (and have been) difficult to accommodate within the framework of the Indian union. If anything the demands of these movements are for separate statehood and confederalism rather than neo-federalism (Bombwall 1986).

Largely because of their shortcomings, political perversion accounts are commonly supplemented by auxiliary explanations. Peripheral ethno-nationalist movements therefore may be the product of economic 'underdevelopment' or 'overdevelopment' (Dasgupta 1997); of an ethno-nationalist intelligentsia's malevolent design on the Indian Union by 'constructing' identities (Varshney 1991); of Machiavellian machinations within Congress (Brass 1991); of emerging regional bourgeoisies seeking to undermine the threat from the landless and the proletariat (Sathyamurthy 1985); of hostile intent by India's neighbours (GOI 1984); of inadequate political institutionalization (Kohli 1991); and of a perceived threat to the orthodoxy of the ethnic group in question (Brass 1991). But though all these explanations have major empirical limitations, their principal shortcomings are twofold: the failure to explain the self-evident irrationality of ethno-nationalist movements in the Indian Union which have cost so many lives, and the persistent need of a self-proclaimed, self-confident nation-state to regularly define *itself* against them.

Such irrationality can be better appreciated in terms of what Connor has called the psychological bond of a nation 'that joins a people, in the subconscious conviction of its members, from all its non-members in a most vital way' (Connor 1993: 187). Indeed, it is the ethno-national bond, 'the emotional depth of national identity' (Connor 1993: 386), that has been the mainspring of resistance in the peripheral regions. This is not to suggest however that ethno-nationalism in the peripheral regions is anchored in a form of primordialism which is immutable, unchanging and constant. Ethno-nationalism and nationalism, as Gellner reminds us, are primarily modern phenomena and, in the Indian case, nation and state building provided ideal conditions for the emergence of ethno-nationalist movements in the peripheral regions. Some of these movements have always contested their accession to the Indian Union, maintaining that they were either coerced or deceived into joining the new state. More significantly, they have all the characteristics of 'low culture' and a 'powerless intelligentsia' pitted against confident power holders who had privileged access to the majoritarian 'high culture' of Hinduism which defines the quintessence of 'civilizational unity'. The dialectic between these two phenomena over the last fifty years has engendered, on the one hand, a confident 'high culture' nationalism that has attempted to deform, disarticulate and delegitimize ethno-nationalist movements as the 'communal' byproducts of colonialism through its control of ideological resources and the process of state-building, while on the other hand, the resistance to this overwhelming process has been from negative, defensive and timid ethno-nationalisms based in traditional social institutions without access to the scarce resources of the state.

To sum up: in its totality, conventional wisdom reasserts the view of India as unique, exceptional, a universe unto itself where the logic of comparative analysis is inapplicable. At the same time built into this uniqueness is the dominant paradigm of the Nehruvian state as a benchmark against which the post-Nehruvian state is evaluated, conveniently omitting the foundational failure of the partition. As conventional wisdom has proved to be inadequate in understanding ethno-nationalist movements in the peripheral regions, an alternative interpretation of the Indian state and its relationship with ethnicity is required.

## India as an ethnic democracy and hegemonic control

The recognition that Hinduism as a meta-ethnicity has been an essential component of Indian nation and state-building calls for a radical revision of the experience of Indian democracy since 1947. It clearly does not conform to secularized majoritarianism (where the state encourages acculturation and assimilation but allows ethnic groups to maintain ethnicity in the private sphere, as for example in the USA). If anything, as Upadhyaya has demonstrated in a pioneering article, Indian democracy subordinated secularism to the 'nationalism of the Hindu majority' (Upadhyaya 1992: 816). This process was further possible because the political structures of the new state included the Westminster model with its first-past-the-post system of elections which underpinned ethnic majoritarianism. The 'institutionalization' of one-party dominance under Congress went hand in hand with an essentially unitary structure with the supremacy of the elite all-India administrative service. Within the shell of Westminster-style democracy Hinduism established a hegemonic position, as *primus inter pares* − a position from which it was able to promote the religious assimilation of minorities (for example, Buddhists, Jains and Sikhs), establish linguistic and ritual pre-eminence, and undermine the political challenge from minorities.

Nor does the Indian experience resemble ethnically accommodative consociationalism, where ethnicity, along with individual rights, is recognized as the basis for the organization of the state which acts as an arbiter between ethic groups, as for example in Belgium. For one, the structures of majoritarianism excluded elements of proportionality and autonomy central to consociationalism; for another, the partition of India was a partition *against* consociationalism and for the construction of a majoritarian and a unitary state (Talbot and Singh 1999). Lijphart's effort to understand the 'puzzle of Indian democracy' in the form of a 'consociational interpretation' (Lijphart 1996) misunderstands religious 'encapsulation' as autonomy, tactical political accommodation within the Congress as elite power-sharing, and linguistic pluralism within meta-Hindu areas as developed federalism. In an ideal consociational system minority rights are entrenched, guaranteed and backed by a minority veto. In India the minority veto has been practically non-existent for most religious minorities (e.g. Sikhs, Jains and Buddhists) and, in the case of Muslims, has been frequently undermined by 'compensatory' concessions to the Hindu community.[5] The visual metaphor for Indian consociationalism therefore is not one of balanced scales, of ethnic groups counterweighing each other within the state, both proportionally and politically, but of a puppet on a string where ethnic groups, especially religiously based ones, respond, often reluctantly, to the puppet master (the state).

In contrast to majoritarianism and consociationalism, India would appear to resemble a third variant; namely, an 'ethnic democracy'

154

(Peled 1992; Yiftachel 1992). According to Smooha, the leading
theorist of the concept, ethnic democracies combine 'the extension of
political and civil rights to individuals and collective rights to
minorities with institutionalized dominance over the state by one of
the ethnic groups' (Smooha 1990: 391). Whereas in some ethnic
democracies the process of 'institutionalization' is formal and explicit,
in others it is informal and implicit. In India the 'institutionalization
of dominance' would appear to derive from unspoken assumptions
about state secularism and 'civilizational essence', the historic
ascendancy of the Congress in fashioning the post-1947 state in its
image, and the existence of Hindu majoritarianism. Thus though the
minorities have been granted individual and, in some cases, collective
rights, the recognition of these rights has been based on a tactical
accommodation with hegemonic Hinduism.[6]

Although ethnic democracies share most features of liberal
democracies for the inclusive ethnic group, their relationship with
excluded, peripheral and marginal ethnic groups is more problematic.
At the other end of the continuum, ethnic democracies might exercise
'coercive rule' in which the 'superior power of one segment [dominant
ethnic group] is mobilized to enforce stability by constraining the
political action and opportunities of another segment or segments
[subordinated ethnic group]' (Lustick 1979: 328). In between these
two extremes an ethnic democracy might attempt to move towards a
liberal democracy or practise brute majoritarianism, thereby circum-
scribing the rights of marginal groups. In such a context the main
ethnic group 'can effectively dominate another through its political,
economic and ideological resources and can extract what it requires
from the subordinated' (O'Leary and Arthur 1990: 9). This form of
rule has been termed 'hegemonic control' because 'it makes an overtly
violent ethnic contest for state power either "unthinkable" or
"unworkable" on the part of the subordinated communities' (O'Leary
and Arthur 1990: 8). Hegemonic control can coexist within the formal
shell of liberal democracies and is characterized by the use of coercive
and cooptive rule to undermine ethnic challenges to state power.[7]

The recognition of a Hindu non-Hindu distinction would suggest
that in India an ethnic democracy co-exists alongside hegemonic
control over non-Hindu minorities. Where non-Hindu minorities
have constituted a majority in the federating unit, the operation of
hegemonic control has been exercised through the Hindu minority
(and other supporters and ethnic groups); the use of residual powers
by the union government; the use of administrative structures ('the

155

official regime'); and the coercive power of the Indian state. Hegemonic control in India therefore is not only based on majoritarianism common to situations of binary ethnic group conflict. Rather, it operates within a framework of *de facto* ethnic democracy which extends constitutional rights to minorities but mitigates their *de jure* application through the excessive application of residual controls and placation of dominant ethnic sentiment. Where ethnic groups have contested, often violently, the nature of hegemonic control, the Indian state has readily resorted to violent control and has made such contests 'unthinkable' by the ideological, economic and political resources at its disposal, and 'unworkable' by its coercive practice.

## Ethnic democracy, hegemonic control and peripheral ethno-nationalist movements

A view of India as an ethnic democracy in which hegemonic control is exercised over ethnic minorities necessarily requires a reassessment of the post-1947 period. Applied to the peripheral regions it calls for re-evaluation of India's secularism, the ethno-nationalist movements and the strategies used by the Indian state to manage them. Such a reassessment would require a careful examination of how ethno-nationalist demands have been processed in terms of the consistent pattern of 'regional accords' which have been followed by non-implementation and, ultimately, revocation. It would question the role of political institutions (for example, the Congress) and administrative structures in underpinning hegemonic control by facilitating co-option, accommodation, encapsulation and ethnic negation. It would assess the language used to delegitimize ethno-nationalist movements and justify nation and state-building. It would reflect on the extent and the regularity of violence used to maintain control – coercive and non-coercive. It would contrast the operation of civil liberties and the processing of comparable regional demands within India's ethnic core with the peripheral regions. It would question the social and economic policies that have encouraged assimilation through settler populations which have transformed indigenous majorities into irrelevant minorities. It would examine, alongside hegemonic control, the creation of internal zones (tribal areas), redrawing of state boundaries, and the creation of special tribal rights as a way of managing and eliminating ethnic conflict.

156

Punjab, Kashmir, the north-eastern states and India's Muslims provide analytically appropriate cases for the study of hegemonic control within the Indian Union since 1947 as well as illustrating the thesis that India is an ethnic democracy. All these elements are

> aggrieved sections of [Indian society] with a long list of grievances against the centre, deeply resentful of the latter's encroachment of their political autonomy and democratic civil rights. In different ways and to varying degrees, they have desisted from taking part in the orthodox nationalist discourse.
>
> (*Sathyamurthy* 1996: 15)

Before 1947, these regions were mostly outside the dominating influence of the Congress and were controlled by regional parties which did not share the former's vision of post-colonial India. At independence some of these regions were coerced into the Indian Union or became the battleground of ethnic cleansing associated with partition. Since 1947, these regions have been the sites of Indian nation and state-building failure, maintaining a degree of resistance to these processes which has consumed an inordinate amount of the Indian state's scarce resources, exposed it to international opprobrium, and made counterinsurgency the preoccupation of its armed forces. These states or union territories, moreover, are populated by non-Hindu ethnic group majorities (Kashmir, Punjab, Nagaland, Mizoram, Arunachal Pradesh, Meghalaya), or others who feel deep resentment against Hindu Bengali mainland settlers who have turned the 'sons of the soil' into an insignificant minority (Tripura and Manipur), or others again who have witnessed a revival of regional ethnic identity pre-dating the conversion to Hinduism (Assam). Finally, these territories are also distinctive in that they form the external borders of the Indian state – borders which have been the site of several wars which have sacralized the territory of the Union within the inner core of Indian nationalism.

Lastly, although the operation of hegemonic control in the peripheral regions is only likely to give us indirect insight into the character of India's ethnic democracy, the challenge of the BJP in seeking to redefine it more exclusively demonstrates the increasing irrelevance of Nehruvian 'pseudo-secularism' as an elite strategy. Yet the BJP's project of *Hindutva* is not markedly different from encapsulated secularism: what distinguishes it, however, is the rhetoric, the assertiveness, the homogenizing drive around particular Hindu icons, and the belligerent tone towards the minorities, both in the peripheral and non-peripheral regions. This project may create difficulties for Hinduism as a meta-ethnicity; equally, Hinduism may only be in the process of being restructured in line with contemporary developments to articulate the new 'language of belonging' which the Nehruvian elite derided, marginalized and ostracized. Whichever direction it follows, the exercise of hegemonic control over the Muslims within the ethnic core suggests that we need to distinguish more clearly between meta-ethnic conflicts (those between Hindus and Muslims, Hindus and Sikhs, and Hindus and Christians) and those that occur within the plural pantheon of Hinduism. Or to put it in other words: it seems *obvious* to highlight the continuity between the Indian Army's operation in the Golden Temple in 1984 and the demolition of the Babri Masjid Mosque in 1992.

## Conclusion

This chapter has argued that there is a serious need to rethink the implications of conventional wisdom on ethnicity and ethnic conflict in India. Conventional wisdom is distinctive only insofar as it represents a remarkable unanimity in asserting the plurality, diversity, secularism (of the state) and, above all, the underlying unity of India. Fifty years after independence, such falsehoods have been cruelly exposed by the thousands who have died in challenging the state's legitimacy in maintaining these beliefs. They have also been shattered by the destruction of the Babri Masjid Mosque in Ayodyha in 1992 which, according to one leading commentator (Brass 1994: xiv), provides the future trajectory of the Indian state. Against this background therefore it is appropriate and, indeed, necessary to interrogate the assumptions which underpin conventional wisdom and the political consequences that it has produced. It seems valid therefore to argue that the Indian state is not a non-national civilizational state but one which has explicitly laid claims to an exclusive ethnicity rooted in an ancient past. This meta-ethnicity has defined the limits of sub-national pluralism. As the challenge to these limits has come mainly in the peripheral regions with non-Hindu majorities, these regions have been the sites of bitter struggles between ethno-nationalist movements and Indian nation and state-building. The dynamics of Sikh ethno-nationalism are to be discovered in this dialectical relationship. The Nehruvian state managed the underlying tensions between a multi-national society and ethnic democracy by majoritarianism, the ideological rhetoric of multiculturalism, and hegemonic control; the post-Nehruvian state is in the process of restructuring ethnic democracy which may result in a more overtly assimilationist state or a resized Indian Union, like the Russian Federation, without the quarrelsome and costly peripheral nationalities.

# Notes

1 This form of self-regulating 'structural functionalism' seems to be implicit in popular views of Indian society. As Rushdie writes: 'India regularly confounds its critics by its resilience, its survival in spite of everything. I don't believe in the Balkanization of India ... It's my guess that the old functioning anarchy will, somehow or other, keep on functioning, for another forty years, and no doubt another forty years after that. But don't ask me how' (Rushdie 1991: 33).

2 For historians see the works of B. Chandra, B.R. Nanda, B. Parsad and A. Tripathi; for political scientists see M. Weiner, P.R. Brass, Susan and Lloyd Rudolph, and A. Kohli; for Nehruvians, D. Gupta; and for Neo-Gandhians, B. Parekh and A. Nandy; for postmodernists, see the works of A. Appadurai and N. Dirks.

3 Parekh's insistence that 'the confusion and mischief caused by Jinnah's introduction of the nationalist language into Indian politics (eventually) broke up the country' (Parekh 1995: 39), echoes Kedourie's (1960) idealist argument that nationalism is the result of a world-historical intellectual error.

4 For those focusing on the centralization thesis the paradox of decentralizing a highly centralized state structure as a remedy to ethnic conflicts has hardly been addressed. From the experience of the former Soviet Union and Eastern European Communist states, it can perhaps be argued that centralization rather than decentralization is necessary to keep state structures intact.

5 The Shah Bano case was followed by concessions to Hindu militants by Rajiv Gandhi. This set off the chain of events that led to the demolition of the Babri Masjid in 1992.

6 This is clearly the case with Scheduled Castes and Scheduled Tribes and such accommodation dates from the time of Gandhi. After 1947 some minorities, for example the Sikhs, had their collective rights revoked and were made subject to Hindu Personal Law. Article 25 of the constitution moreover defined the Sikhs as a sect of Hinduism.

7 The terms hegemony and hegemonic control are used distinctly. This distinction is necessary to grasp the difference between India's ethnic core and the peripheral regions. Our operational use of hegemony therefore conforms to the common Gramscian reading as a 'sphere of cultural and ideological influence of pure consent' (Forgac 1988: 423). More particularly it refers to the ideas of dominant elites ('hegemonic beliefs')

159

within the ethnic core about boundaries, nationhood, and self-determination movements. Hegemonic control, on the other hand, refers to the peripheral regions and implies the use of coercion and consent, as well as the manipulation of consciousness, to exclude certain possibilities. When hegemonic control breaks down, it is replaced by overt coercion and domination ('violent control'). Hegemonic control therefore is unlike the concept of 'control' as overt domination by ordinary means (Lustick 1979). In the Indian case hegemonic control is certainly more appropriate as in the peripheral regions formal democratic structures have provided the front for nation and state-building.

Chapter Nine

# Imagining Punjab: Narratives of Nationhood and Homeland among the Sikh Diaspora

*Darshan S. Tatla*

O why don't you rescue mother India
  And get rid of the foreign yoke
What a shameless life to live as slaves
  Arise as time calls for martyrs

Punjab our land and country is in agony
  Calling on all its well wishers
Our homeland is tangled in many woes
  Arise and share in its grief

The stark contrast of the two couplets above, one from the Ghadar movement in 1913–14 and the other from the Khalistan campaign of the 1980s,[1] is perhaps an appropriate introduction to the main theme of this chapter. How has the idea of Punjab as a Sikh homeland become 'naturalized' among the Sikh diaspora? How has the incipient Indian nationalism of early Sikh migrants been replaced by the Punjab as an imagined homeland? Any study aiming to charter such radical transformation in an ethnic community's outlook towards its land of origins will be an arduous task. This chapter has a more limited objective of presenting related literature which bears on this issue, and suggests some possible conditions and events which might have contributed to the construction of Punjab's image as a Sikh homeland among the Sikh diaspora.

## Competing imaginings: India and Punjab

Despite much official propaganda, eloquent arguments, and reworking of historical events, the idea of India as a bounded territorial
nation-state is a recent innovation (Khilnani 1997). A product of the
collective imagining of a select Hindu elite during the era of British
rule in India, it has been contested by regional elites, equally
convinced of a claim for their province as a nation-in-the-making. In
the post-1947 period, the Akali Dal, a major Sikh organization, has
successively engaged in several battles of accommodation and
confrontation with the Government of India aimed at securing some
measure of autonomy for the community's cultural, religious and
political future.[2] The Akalis had advocated the idea of a Sikh
homeland as the Pakistan demand came on the horizon in the 1940s.
While the British were aware of the Sikhs' special place in the Punjab,
the post-colonial nationalist leaders, faced with the task of integrating
diverse languages, cultures, and peoples into a viable state, dismissed
the Akalis' claims as anti-national or a camouflage for a Sikh
homeland. Indeed, constitutional, ideological and coercive measures
were used to undermine the intellectual case for a Sikh homeland. The
Indian state's increasing centralization with its submission to the
majority community's cultural, political and linguistic concerns, has
led to many ethnic conflicts in peripheral states.

In the Punjab, arguably, this has meant the central government
taking measures varying from violent control to power-sharing while
maintaining a hegemonic control of over Sikh community's
institutions and political ambitions, as is suggested in the preceding
chapter of this volume. In the latest contest, the Akalis had led a
major campaign for Punjab autonomy in 1981, resulting in the
deployment of the Indian army in the Golden Temple complex in
June 1984. The Sikh diaspora has become increasingly involved in
such developments in Punjab, and in the aftermath of the 1984
débâcle, has advanced the cause of a Sikh homeland.

The Sikh diaspora is now scattered across the globe, from the Far
East to Western countries. This chapter's focus is on three countries,
namely Britain, Canada and the United States, which are the home of
about a million Sikhs, almost three-quarters of the total overseas Sikh
population.[3] It draws on an extensive diaspora literature consisting of
vernacular Punjabi press, creative writings, popular songs, and
numerous booklets and propaganda materials by political groups
and associations. The chapter is organized in three parts. The first

162

section outlines some general remarks about the Sikh diaspora and its social setting while offering some speculation on its beliefs about territory, space and time. In the second section, the murmurings of the homeland in the 1970s are recorded. This is followed by an analysis of the anguished cries for a Sikh state expressed in the wake of the tragedy of June 1984.

## The diaspora's many homelands: pre-1947 narratives

A reconstruction of the mental world of the pre-1947 Sikh diaspora is a hazardous undertaking which is made more difficult by the lack of sources. With only fragmentary secondary literature to hand, in the absence of extensive personal histories, oral records, letters and memorabilia, one has to tread carefully. Fortunately the extant Ghadar sources, although the outcome of rather special circumstances, do nevertheless throw some light on the ideas of space, landscape, region and country among the Sikh diaspora.

The idea of a homeland did not exercise the minds of late nineteenth and early twentieth century emigrants from colonial Punjab. If a crucial link to a territory forms an essential part of emigrants' collective identity, they did not satisfy this criterion of being a diaspora. Can they be classified as part of the Indian diaspora? Only in a limited sense in that they had some notion of being an Indian, certainly so for administrative purposes of carrying identification papers (e.g. passports) which pointed to their status. Thus, for early Sikh emigrants of the nineteenth century, the homeland was a vague idea expressed through multiple Punjabi expressions e.g. *vatan, des, mulk;* it did not embody any sacred space, nor was their collective identity tied to territorial aspects of Punjab.

Instead, the location of their ex-homes imparted regional affiliations, and social hierarchy provided a nomenclature to the social groups. They defined themselves as Doabias, Malwais, or Majhails – inhabitants of the three subregions of the Punjab – and at most as Punjabis. Being Indians would have exhausted their social imagination. Thus in the Far East, gurdwara committee members dominated from a particular area, e.g. Malwa. In their daily life interaction was limited to fellows Sikhs, or in some cases with Muslims. The shared religious tradition of Sikhism transcended such social categories such as caste. In establishing a gurdwara, distinction shifted to that between *amritdharis* and *sahajdharis*. By the early decades of twentieth century, the Chief Khalsa Diwan and Singh Sabha activists were also influencing overseas Sikhs' behaviour. Religion was thus an important aspect of the diaspora Sikh identity and its salience increased over time.

In terms of political mapping, Punjabi emigrants' loyalty towards the British empire was underwritten by economic gains and recruitment into armed forces. Except for a few dissenters, local complaints were not converted into political campaigns. This was to change however with the new rush towards Pacific states at the turn of the twentieth century. By the first decade, many thousands of Sikhs who were stranded in the Far East had reached the Pacific states, where they faced racial discrimination previously not experienced. Since many Sikh migrants were of military background, these ex-soldiers viewed the British raj as guarantor of their rights even in overseas situations. They made fervent appeals to British officials in Punjab, and when they failed to get attention, their anger was then directed at British rule in India. As the campaign progressed, a new organization, the Ghadar party, called for an armed revolution, inspiring several hundred Sikhs to sail for India. But the revolution failed. The Ghadarite Sikhs' imagined India was free from foreign rule, a socialist republic, with social and economic equality and without religious divide, an idealism unconstrained by messy realities of India's multinational peoples, religions and cultures, with ill-defined borders and boundaries. The imagination of Ghadarite Sikhs was fired by a fierce Hindu nationalist, Hardayal, who was entertained at India House, London.

For the pre-1947 period, the diverse voices of Punjabi emigrants thus found no coherence in terms of their collective identity. Their universe admitted a range of associations, nomenclature and self-definitions. More crucially there was between Punjab and India no particular preference or tension. The notion of being a Punjabi or an Indian carried none of the modernist connotations of homeland or citizenship. Furthermore, no major event impressed upon them the need to differentiate this ambiguous and comfortable duality. If their Punjabi or Sikh identity was weaker or ambiguous, there was no notion of overarching Indian identity either. Thus, on the day India attained freedom, the Stockton and Vancouver gurdwaras held a gathering for thanksgiving and arranged flowers for Nehru's sister. This goodwill towards India was sustained until new events in the partitioned Punjab under post-colonial state of India started making dents in this ambiguous relationship.

# Muted voices for the homeland: 1947–1983

It is evident from even a cursory reading of literature that ideas of an independent homeland hardly stirred in the overseas Sikhs' imagination till 1984. A few disparate Sikhs who cultivated this idea had neither resources nor the sympathy of common Sikhs. In Britain, apart from Davindar Singh Parmar, an early exponent of independent Punjab, the few Sikhs who were involved in the 'save the turbans' campaign in the late 1960s veered towards this issue. The case had arisen as a clean-shaven Sikh bus driver returned, after illness, to his duty with a turban on his head. He was promptly dismissed by Wolverhampton Transport Authority for having violated the customary code of drivers' dress. Although a similar case in Manchester had been resolved by allowing the wearing of a turban, the Wolverhampton Transport Authority refused to follow suit. The case gained wider publicity, with protest marches by local Sikhs and petitions from Punjab. While Sikhs in Delhi organized a rally at the British High Commission, the Akali chief minister of Punjab raised the issue with the Indian prime minister. Sikh activists also appealed to the Indian High Commissioner on their behalf, who visited Wolverhampton but declined to intervene. According to Charan Singh Panchi, an activist at the time, 'despite repeated appeals to the Indian High Commission in Britain, we gained little sympathy.' The Indian High Commissioner's reluctance to intervene in this 'delicate matter' was sound, but it led to bitter heartsearching among some of the community leaders involved. Davindar Singh Parmar argued that a Sikh ambassador would have been more sympathetic to their cause while Panchi joined the newly formed Sikh Homeland Front, a breakaway group from the Akali Dal (UK). The case was eventually resolved as a Sikh threatened suicide by immolating himself. In view of such 'external factors', the Transport Authority thus decided 'under duress' to allow turbans for its Sikh drivers.

However, this decision hardly 'normalized' the turban as part of Sikh dress in Britain or North America. The issue kept cropping up in schools, the construction industry, railways, hospitals and the security forces. Almost every case required special pleading. Then in the 1980s, when a Sikh pupil in the West Midlands was refused admission to a school because of his turban, the argument shifted to claims that the Sikhs were an ethnic group. Such cases in Britain as well as in North America, and their attendant mobilization, along with shifting arguments, were unpleasant reminders to community leaders regarding the Sikhs' lack of 'national status'. The propagation of Sikhism as a 'world religion' alongside Sikhs' emerging self-image as a confident world national community sat uncomfortably with increasing cases of racial discrimination and daily humiliation.

Meanwhile ordinary Sikhs contributed funds to India during the Indo-Pakistan hostilities of 1965, and also gave generously in 1971 when due to India's intervention, Bangladesh was created as a new nation. But the arrival in 1971 of Dr Jagjit Singh Chohan, an ex-minister in a short-lived government of Akali dissidents, saw an alignment of a small group of like-minded Sikhs. Chohan placed a half-page advertisement in *The New York Times* of 12 October 1971, making several claims about Punjab as a Sikh homeland:

> At the time of partition of the Indian subcontinent in 1947 it was agreed that the Sikhs shall have an area in which they will have complete freedom to shape their lives according to their beliefs. On the basis of the assurances received, the Sikhs agreed to throw their lot with India, hoping for the fulfilment of their dream of an independent, sovereign Sikh homeland, the Punjab.

But Chohan won little sympathy from ordinary Sikhs. The Khalsa Diwan Society (KDS) Vancouver and a Leeds gurdwara in Britain were the first to pass strictures against him in December 1971. Other gurdwaras followed, censuring Chohan's anti-Indian activities. Dr A. K. S. Aujala, an Akali Dal leader, warned against 'traitors', clearly implying the activities of Chohan and his associates, by placing a full-page advertisement in the Punjabi media. The Indian authorities, to show their displeasure at ideas of Sikh separatism and perhaps to strengthen the hand of moderate Akalis in Britain, arrested Chohan's supporter Giani Bakhshish Singh during a visit to Punjab in 1972. Detained for a year without trial, he was released only after the intervention by the British government. Thus frustrated, proponents of a Sikh Homeland took to the Punjabi media. Charan Singh Panchi warned:

> Sikhs have to realise that there is no future in India dominated by Hindus. The honour and prestige of the community cannot be maintained without state power. The sooner we realise this challenge the better it will be for us to set our objective of establishing a sovereign Sikh state in the Punjab. We cannot keep ourselves in bondage forever.
>
> (*Des Pardes*, 12 December 1971)

This characterization of India as a Hindu state did not please many Akalis, communists or ordinary Sikhs, who denied Panchi entry into major gurdwaras. In 1977 Chohan proposed that Punjab should be renamed as a Sikh Homeland. Later, in November 1979, he raised the issue of radio transmissions from the Golden Temple. In this cause, some religious-minded Sikhs joined him, setting up an International Golden Temple Corporation and holding several meetings at the Shepherds Bush gurdwara during 1979–82. Besides extending an invitation to Sant Jarnail Singh Bhindranwale to visit Britain – which did not take place – the Corporation arranged a 'World Sikh Festival' in July 1982 and a seminar on 'Sikhs are a nation'.

In North America Sikh leaders were also being alerted to 'major' issues above the 'petty politics' of gurdwara committees. Ganga Singh Dhillon, an American Sikh, had meetings with Pakistan officials during the late 1970s and early 1980s, and talked of seeking a Vatican-like status for Nankana Sahib, the birthplace of Guru Nanak which had been left in Pakistan following the partition. Dhillon also addressed the Sikh Educational Conference in Chandigarh stressing the idea of 'Sikhs as a nation'. This resulted in a long debate as to whether Sikhs constituted a nation. The noted Sikh historian Khushwant Singh responded:

> ... in your articles you make a large number of assertions which are totally at a variance with my reading of Sikh history ... the demand (for Khalistan) is manifestly mischievous and goes against the interests of the Sikhs ... We have the interests of the Khalsa at heart as much you and your supporters in the States and Canada. For you this may be an academic exercise; for us it is hard reality.
>
> (*Khushwant Singh* 1992: 41–2)

The Canadian Sikhs were also confronted with issues of collective representation and some turban cases requiring mobilization. Stakes for official representation became higher as under the policy of multiculturalism initiated by the Canadian government a consultation process encouraged the formation of an umbrella organization for each major immigrant group (Dusenbery 1981). For East Indian immigrants, it supported the formation of NACOI (National Association of Canadians of Origins in India). While NACOI claimed it represented Sikhs along with other Indians, the newly formed Akali Dal of North America asked the federal government to recognize Sikhs as a distinct ethnic group, arguing:

We do hope that this brief would better state our position as *Canadian Sikhs* (emphasis in original) and the government will not fall into error in dealing with questions whenever the question of so-called 'East-Indians' or 'origins in India', comes up. Even our 'origins' go further than 'India', since our people are composed of the Indo-Scythian stock that had settled in northern India since the first century AD.[4]

The process of using Sikh symbols to differentiate the Sikh community had gathered pace. The Khalsa Diwan Society's 1981 annual report depicted the Ghadarites and other Indian freedom fighters together. In 1982, it carried pictures of Canadian Sikh volunteers who joined the *Dharam Yudh Morcha* in the Punjab. In 1982, a British Columbia gurdwara hoisted the Indian flag along side the Sikh flag on Indian independence day. This matter was referred to the Akal Takht, Amritsar, where the *Jathedar* instructed the gurdwara not to fly the Indian flag (*Indo-Canadian Times*, 21 September, 8 October 1982).

Surjan Singh, also based in Vancouver, led a small group who supported the idea of Sikh independence. Besides filing an application to the United Nations for an 'Observer Status' in October 1981, which was promptly rejected, he set up a 'Republic of Khalistan' office on 26 January 1982 with a 'Consul-General' who issued 'Khalistani passports' and 'Khalsa currency notes' (*Indo-Canadian Times*, 4 September 1981). Chohan offered support to bolster this Canadian campaign, but gained little sympathy from common Sikhs. During the Baisakhi festival procession in April 1982, these Khalistani activists were beaten up and allowed to join only after they took down their placards.

These developments would have been of little consequences if events in the Punjab had moved to neutralize the question of a Sikh homeland. But in April 1978 a clash occurred in Amritsar between a group of orthodox Sikhs and the heretical sect of Nirankaris in which thirteen people were killed. This provoked much anger among overseas Sikh associations. A Committee for British Columbia Sikhs was formed, which accused the Indian government of supporting the heretical sect, and condemned, 'atrocities committed against the devout Sikhs by the Nirankari Mandal ... in Amritsar, Kanpur and Delhi' (*Indo-Canadian Times*, 2 February 1979). This event led to a partial rapport between Sikh Homeland protagonists and other community leaders. But despite a commendatory letter from Sant

Bhindranwale to Chohan 'appreciating his services to the Panth' (*Des Pardes*, 14 January 1983), the latter was unable to address Sikh audiences within any major gurdwara.

Further calls for support came from the Punjab. In September 1981, the Akali Dal launched its campaign for Punjab autonomy, the *Dharma Yudh Morcha*. This campaign was vigorously supported by the Sikhs diaspora. Aware of the diaspora's considerable resources, Harchand Singh Longowal, President of the Akali Dal in the Punjab, sent a general letter to overseas Sikhs. Major gurdwaras responded with resolutions of support and financial contributions. The Khalsa Diwan Society, Vancouver, led others by passing a comprehensive resolution on 18 October 1981:

> The KDS Vancouver, BC, demands from the government of India to stop discriminatory policies against the Sikhs. Like other nations, justice should be done to the Sikhs by accepting its reasonable demands ... The KDS Vancouver, fully supports the Special Resolution 'The Sikhs ARE A NATION' (emphasis in original) passed during March 1981 by the general body of Shiromani Gurdwara Parbandhak Committee, Amritsar, Punjab, India. The KDS Vancouver further declares its full support to Shiromani Gurdwara Parbandhak Committee to represent the Sikhs' case at the UN.[5]

Similarly, the Akali Singh Sikh Society of Vancouver wrote a strong letter to the Indian and Canadian authorities, asking them to accept the status of 'Sikhs as a nation'. A *Dharam Yudh Morcha* Action Committee was formed from twenty-one societies across Canada on 23 July 1983. American and British Sikhs also provided moral and financial aid.

## Cries for a homeland: post-1984 narratives

As the support for the Punjab campaign became more organized both in Punjab and among the Sikh diaspora, the government of India responded with the army assault on the Golden Temple which led to several hundred deaths of pilgrims and militants as well as inflicting irreparable damage to Akal Takht, one of the holiest shrines in the complex of sacred buildings. The dishonour and hurt felt led to a spontaneous response among the Sikh diaspora, with protest and anger directed against the government of India, and an outcry for independence. Among the diaspora this 'critical event' brushed away traditional political associations. Akali leaders were indignantly removed from gurdwara committees to be replaced in many cases by much ostracized Khalistanis of the 1970s. Protest marches and funds flowed to Amritsar. A new sense of vulnerability, fear and helplessness gripped the Sikh diaspora amidst calls for revenge, retribution and a break from Indian tyranny. The community leaders were to learn a painful transition from a self-confident community with haughty discourse, to the self-defensive strategies of a vulnerable minority.

The corpus of writings which appeared in the post-1984 period is quite large and includes two poetry books on the Akal Takht. Among these narratives of 'writing the homeland', there is also a proliferation of popular songs, general writings of protest, and political leaflets. This literature, though much contested, nevertheless illustrates the diasporic imagination about its place of origins. It marks a radical shift of previous nostalgic expressions of Punjab to assertive evocations of its new identity as a 'threatened homeland'. This literature can be conveniently studied under several separate categories.

## 1 Anguished voices

The army entry into the Golden Temple, an act of desecration of the holiest centre of the Sikh faith, tainted many Sikhs' imagination of India as their country, and resulted in snapping emotional ties with its polity. The moral outrage of Sikh sensitivity can be gauged by the denunciations of India:

> Let us burn our Indian passports, we no longer belong to India ... We are now just American Sikhs.
>
> (*Des Pardes*, June–July 1984)

A similar sentiment was echoed by a British Sikh:

> I always said I was first Indian, second Sikh. For all these years, I've kept my Indian passport, but now I feel like burning it.
>
> (*The Times*, 6 July 1984)

The poetry probably best conveys Sikhs' anger about the tragedy. The sight of the devastated Akal Takhat, a tragic outcome of the army action, was seen as a graphic illustration of India's callous behaviour

170

and betrayal of Sikhs' place in India. Sher Singh Kanwal, an American Sikh, expressed his anguished feelings thus:

It's not just the Akal Takhat
But an immortal throne that you destroyed
It's my heart you wounded
God's demolished house will ensure
India perishes in the dust

(*Des Pardes*, April 1985)

Another poem by Anant Kanpuri from New York, echoing an early peasants' popular song, interpreted the enfolding tragedy thus:

Take care of thy turban, O Sikh
Oppression has surpassed all limits
Burning all that you cared for
Beautiful flowers, indeed the whole yard
Charred is your beautiful Punjab

(*Indo-Canadian Times*, 31 August 1984)

The army action in the Golden Temple was followed by several years of unrest when thousands of Sikh youths took to armed rebellion and retribution. The government of India enacted draconian laws giving unprecedented powers to the security forces. Ajit Rahi from Australia decried the security forces' excesses on Sikh militants thus:

By a canal bridge,
After deliberate killing
An encounter is announced
How far is the day
When these horrendous deeds will rebound?
How pitiful the hope
To link the state's survival
To eliminating us all

(*Des Pardes*, 7 February 1986)

## 2 Calls for mobilization against 'Hindu imperialism'

While poetic expressions narrated the tragedy, more urgent appeals were made for mobilization by new political associations. A second category of literature portrays the post-1984 Indian state as 'Hindu imperialism'. In the immediate aftermath of June 1984 period, with a profound sense of humiliation, an unprecedented mobilization took place among the Sikh diaspora. In Britain the International Sikh Youth Federation (ISYF), the Babbar Khalsa and the Council of Khalistan emerged, while in Canada and America, in addition to these two organisations, the World Sikh Organisation was also formed. In the USA, a Council of Khalistan was led by G.S. Aulakh, who became a prominent lobbyist at the Capitol Hill. New leaders appealed for restoration of the 'community's honour' and they got an enthusiastic response from common Sikhs with funds and major protest marches against Indian officials and consulates.

In numerous leaflets published by these organizations, the new leaders called for struggle for an independent Sikh state free from 'Hindu imperialism'. The ISYF leaders warned about the dangerous period for the Khalsa Panth:

> The Sikh nation's culture, religious traditions, identity and integrity are being crushed. India's Hindu government is using all its power including the army, the police commandos, armoury and tanks to annihilate the Sikh nation.

The worst intentions of Indian government, routinely described as 'Hindu imperialism', were underlined by selective facts and powerful rhetoric:

> The army invasion of the Golden Temple, humiliating demolition of the Akal Takhat, burning down of the Sikh Reference Library, priceless manuscripts of the Gurus, hand-written copies of the Guru Granth Sahib, and sacred letters of our Gurus ... These were atrocities committed by the Hindu imperialism. .... cannot be overlooked despite lies spread by the government.
>
> (*Indo-Canadian Times*, 17 November 1985)

In making repeated references to how Sikhs have been betrayed by the ungrateful Hindus since 1947, a dualism of Hindu versus Sikh was offered, with the Hindu personifying the Other. This new discourse is replete with references to the glorious Sikh past in particular to its tradition of martyrdom. In numerous speeches and pamphlets, the new leaders called for liberation from tyranny of India:

> Our martyrs ... fought for the community and sacrificed everything for the sake of our nation ... Yet thanks to the courage and sacrifices of our brave martyrs, the Sikh nation

stands upright and firm in the face of Indian tyranny ... Our war of independence goes unabated.

(*Awaz-e-Qanm*, 25 April 1991)

## 3 Imagining Punjab as a Sikh homeland

The army action had another profound impact: it forced many Sikhs to re-think their relationship with Punjab and India. Besides a considerable flow of moral and financial support to various militant groups, a ferocious debate ensued on the collective fate of the community among the Sikh diaspora. New community leaders forcefully argued for an independent Punjab as a secure Sikh homeland. Ganga Singh Dhillon constructed this case as follows:

> We are not looking just for a piece of land. We are looking for a territory where Sikhs can protect their women and children. Where a Sikh can become a master of his own destiny. Where our religious shrines are not allowed to be run over by army tanks. You can call it an independent Punjab, a sovereign state or Khalistan. What we are asking for is a homeland for the Sikh nation.
>
> (*Dhillon* 1985)

Blending history with mythology, Kirpal Singh Sihra, a Kenyan Sikh settled in Britain, elaborated further:

> God gave the Sikhs their land, a rich and fertile land blessed with much sun and irrigation, the land of five rivers, the Punjab ... Maharajah Ranjit Singh gave the Sikhs their state, later handed in trust, first to the British then to the Hindu raj. But the Sikhs never surrendered their ultimate sovereignty to any power other than their own. Today after forty years of abuse of their trust, the Sikhs are ready to create again their independent, sovereign state.
>
> (*Sihra* 1985a: 55)

He also set out an analysis of contemporary India:

> It is abundantly clear ... India of today is a superficial state imposed from above by the transfer of power from the British

173

Raj ... Several nationalities of India ... should be able to form
their own sovereign states of Maharashtra, Tamil Nadu, Assam,
Sikkim, Nagaland, Mizoland, Kerala, Jammu and Kashmir and
come together in a new economic union ... The reorganization
of India on the basis of regional ethnic nationalities ... has
become imperative ... to end the perpetual conflicts with the
underground movements that have constantly engaged the
police and the army ... since 1947 at great economic cost and
loss of life.

(Sihra 1985b: 10)

This seemingly smooth case for independent Punjab saw opposition
from within the community. Sikh communists argued for a broad class
war in India rather than a narrow nationalist struggle for Punjab
which they dubbed 'fascism'. Another communist group led by
Hardial Bains (Bains 1985), while denouncing Sikh separatism,
blamed India's Congress and other leaders for fanning Hindu
fundamentalism. Such arguments were not limited to only to writing.
During 1984–5, physical clashes took place between Sikh activists and
leftists. Ujjal Dosanjh, later to become a minister in the British
Columbia government, argued:

Khalistan is not our demand, all religious and political
grievances are soluble within the context of one united India.
The attempts to promote a division of India or violence
associated with those attempts are not condoned by the
overwhelming but silent majority of the people residing abroad
... We have not only the integrity, communal harmony and
unity of India at stake but also the credibility and respect of our
community in Canada and other parts of the world.

(The Vancouver Sun, 22 August 1984; Indo-Canadian Times, 31 August,
21 September 1984)

Dosanjh's stand was rebutted by many. A reader argued, 'if Ghadar
leaders could wage a war for India from San Francisco seventy years
ago, why aren't we now justified in demanding Sikh independence?' A
Canadian Sikh, S.S. Dharam, building on fears generated by the crisis,
elaborated on the community's predicament by visualizing three
alternatives: to accept the status quo, 'which will ensure a certain
death for the community', to campaign for the Anandpur Sahib
Resolution, which would only lead to being 'entrapped by the
government's false promises', or to campaign for an independent

homeland. This last alternative, he suggested, was the 'most realistic option'. He also noted how 1984 had ushered a new consciousness for a secure homeland:

> The concept of Sikh Homeland which appeared to exist only in imagination has now taken a turn for reality.
>
> (*Dharam* 1986: 90)

Maluk Singh Chuhan, a British Sikh, besides castigating the mild tone of the 'controversial' Anandpur resolution, argued the Sikhs' right for self-determination:

> It [the Anandpur resolution] describes Sikhs as a religious minority and protection of religious rights are demanded for the sake of national unity. Sikhs in India are one of the nations of India ... The question that Sikhs constitute one of its nations is not negotiable ... It is internationally known principle that all nations have a right of self-determination, be they Palestinians, Basques, Jews, Kurds, Welsh or others.
>
> (*Chuhan* 1984)

A more liberal version of Sikh nationalism came from student intellectuals. In a 1995 leaflet, the Khalistan Society of London School of Economics called upon all Punjabis, not just Sikhs, to join in the struggle for 'freedom, prosperity, justice, equality, liberty and human rights'. It reminded them that an 'independent Punjab' will ensure equality for all religious minorities based on a truly 'secular and democratic political system'.

This contest over Punjab can also be discerned through creative writings and popular songs. Ravinder Ravi, a Canadian Punjabi poet, challenged leftist writers to oppose India's tyranny in Punjab:

> From Palestine to Irish struggles
> Pens that rolled copious tears,
> Why has the ink suddenly dried?
> The land of Punjab is shackled,
> Terror is loose, our motherland cries
> Where are my red-faced (leftist) sons?
> Where are my angry and rebellious ones?
>
> (*Des Pardes*, 18 January 1985)

Leftist writers, on the other hand, dreamed of a Punjab shared by Sikhs, Hindus and Muslims living in harmony. They squarely blamed Sikh militants and the government of India for the tragedy in equal measure. In a Canadian anthology of Punjabi poetry, dedicated to revolutionary communists, 'fighting for Punjab's common people' and 'against state repression and fascism', its editors Sadhu and Sukhpal summed up their sentiments:

> The state's repression, its laws
> And religious extremism
> Are like two foxes
> Roaming in the same jungle.

Another poet, Amarjit Chandan, offered a vision of Punjab of universal fraternity, calling Sikh militants prisoners of the past:

> You are a prisoner of history
> We won't say to you anything
> We will leave you to repent it all

> We will ask Shah Husain and Daman to share our vision
> We will hear Guru Arjan's words from Ghulam Ali
> Let Suba Lakshmi recite Nanak's words
> Hear Farid's lyrics from Samund Singh's voice
>
> *(Punjabi Darpan,* 25 March 1988)

This romantic vision was contested by other Sikh poets equally assuring justice for all irrespective of race, creed and caste in an independent Punjab. A further theme emerged of Punjab as a mythical land of powers and sublime beauty. Thus Bawa wrote:

> I should write thy name
> Borrowing shades from moonlight
> I should name thee
> Among the glittering stars
> Punjab, bled and unloved
> Thou art my soul, my sustenance
>
> *(Bawa* 1993)

Another poet, Kanwal alludes to the Punjab as 'our safe sanctuary', where emigrating birds —meaning the Sikh diaspora – will eventually return to its 'nest'. Creative writers' imaginations were supplemented by popular songs recorded by traditional bards *(dhadis)*. In these records, love for Punjab as a homeland is clearly marked, while sympathy with its suffering population is echoed in many passages. In a typical song, such sentiments are shared:

176

The Punjab – to seek answers from Delhi
Why have you created havoc?
Why have you set a beautiful home on fire?

In another song an appeal is made to join in the 'national liberation':

O arise my brothers-soldiers
Share the responsibility
While the nation is in peril
Do not shirk from duty
And the time is ripe too.

A few popular songs narrate 'India's repression' on Punjabi population, in some cases much exaggerated and imagined, while others describe tales of harrowing brutality. A few songs celebrated the 'heroic' defence put up by Sikh militants within the Golden Temple while others venerate new martyrs. Still others seek a commitment to liberate Punjab:

Till we breathe our last
We promise to fight for Khalistan
Until we gain independence
The burden lies heavily on our hearts[6]

## Alternative narratives of Sikh identity

While Khalistani protagonists sought to consolidate Sikh ethnicity by attaching a territorial aspect to it, the crisis also provided space for those advocating a spiritual dimension too. For them Sikh identity did not require a territorial dimension or a Sikh homeland. These were not the panaceas for the preservation of Sikh values or the Sikh heritage. There was a less disastrous alternative. Gurutej Singh Khalsa, an American-convert to Sikh faith, claimed that:

True spiritual education is needed. This religion belongs to no one nationality. It is not to be confined to a homeland, for the nature of the Khalsa is a sovereign, spiritual nation which knows no physical boundaries.

(*Khalsa* 1985: 84)

This emphasis on spiritual aspect of Sikhism, its universal human values for personal emancipation, found wider appeal among sects such as Namdharis, and perhaps a section of Ramgarhias. This non-Jat constituency refrained from the militants' rhetoric of Khalistan, preferring a reconciliatory attitude towards India. Although there were no public writings on this theme, perhaps they feared that a Jat-dominated Khalistan would be far worse than contemporary India. Thus, emphasis on baptism was stressed leading to increasing number of Sikhs undergoing *amrit*, among them many new leaders who were mostly clean-shaven. There was also a greater awareness about the faith, as an activist managed to see some optimism through the tragedy:

> Sikhs who had deviated from basic Sikh principles started learning them again, they took on the Sikh attire, the *Gurbani*, and an understanding of history. They started teaching Punjabi to their children.
>
> (*Harbans Singh Saraon, World Sikh News*, 19 February 1988)

There was also a concern to present the more honourable face of the community. The Sikh Welfare Foundation of North America made this appeal:

> It is time to organize to improve our image, welfare and self-dignity. We should work to shatter the myth India has created that Sikhs are terrorists; become an ambassador; study Sikhism and history; create an understanding among ourselves, and among our communities and citizens of the country we live in.
>
> (*World Sikh News*, 19 February 1988)

More rudimentary goals also became part of collective endeavour. The Foundation asked all Sikhs to 'ensure (that) Sikh children receive the best education and achieve scholastic merits.'

## Contest in the international arena

The critical event of June 1984, besides forcing a keen and acrimonious debate and contest over the meaning of nation and homeland, also led to a more significant battle in the international arena. Letters and memoranda to senators, parliamentarians and international organisations were written by community activists, generating a new learning process. This literature should be contrasted with publications emanating from Indian official and unofficial sources.[7] To take up the official sources first, the government of India issued a *White Paper* in July 1984, a month after the June tragedy, attacking the role of overseas Sikhs:

> The ideological underpinning for the demand for a separate Sikh state was provided by certain members of the Sikh community in foreign countries.
>
> (*White Paper* 1984: 1–2)

Completely ignoring the unpopularity of Sikh Homeland campaign before June 1984, the *White Paper* nevertheless charged stated:

> The essence of the problem in Punjab was not the demands put forward by the Akali Dal in 1981 but the maturing of a secessionist and anti-national movement with the active support of a small number of groups operating from abroad.
>
> (*White Paper* 1984: 3)

Perceiving overseas Sikhs' protests and involvement in the Punjab after the June 1984 tragedy, the government immediately announced a series of coercive measures to penalize activists and instil fear among common Sikhs. Besides concluding an extradition treaty with Canada, measures such as surveillance, freezing of funds and pressure on the Punjabi media were put in place. Sikh activists could hardly match the resources of Indian embassies and their briefings and propaganda. Overwhelmed by the official campaign, an American Sikh observed:

> Indian intelligence seeks to damage our movement for Khalistan ... by falsely characterizing our struggle as a 'terrorist movement'.
>
> (*India Abroad*, 7 December 1990)

India's obvious success in portraying Khalistani Sikhs as terrorists alerted many non-political groups who objected to such wholesale slandering. The National Sikh Centre reacted against 'false propaganda about Sikhs as terrorists' (*World Sikh News*, August 1986). A Canadian Sikh objected to the disinformation techniques used by the Indian media with reference to a pamphlet called *Facets of a Proxy War* whose five glossy sections branded Sikhs as terrorists, through connections, activities, revelations, links and human rights violations (*World Sikh News*, 16 April 1993). Nor was India's interference confined to politics alone. The setting up of a Sikh Studies chair at the University of British Columbia became embroiled in Indo-Canadian diplomacy, and was saved only as prominent academics rallied around the issue. Even a scholarly work on Sikh nationalism in Sweden brought a protest from Indian authorities (Ahmed 1996: vii).

While the Indian authorities projected the Sikh activists' campaign as mere international terrorism, the latter highlighted the Indian state terrorism perpetuated on the Punjab. Sikh activists sought a parallel with other ethnic groups seeking freedom, citing cases of Jews, Palestinians, Ukrainians, Kurds, Armenians, Kashmiris, Nagas, Tamils and many others across the world. At the United Nations Sikh activists joined the theatre for ethnic diasporas seeking independence.

The responses by the host states to Sikh lobbying and to pressure from the Indian government varied considerably. The Canadian government, after the Air India plane disaster in 1985, hastily concluded an extradition treaty with India, and agreed to boycott major Sikh organizations. In Britain the extradition treaty was concluded only after prolonged pressure from India. Prompted by Sikh and Kashmiri delegates, many opposition members of parliament objected and sought safeguards for Sikh and Kashmiri citizens. Roger Godsiff was one of those who voiced their concerns:

> How can the government argue that there are sufficient safeguards, that under the treaty, the person being extradited would not be prejudiced ... or be punished detailed, or restricted on grounds of political opinion, when the Indian army is daily carrying out a war ... and when under the Indian constitution, it is an act of treason to advocate secession by any part of the union from the state of India?
>
> (*Hansard* 229, 22 July 1993)

Both in Britain and Canada, Sikh activists solicited members of parliament to link foreign aid with India's record of human rights. In the USA, India was reprimanded almost every year for its human rights record in Punjab and Kashmir through a debate in the Congress and this led to small cut in its aid programme for some years. For Sikh lobbyists, it was matter of triumph to raise the Sikh issue in parliaments and in the US Congress. It proved, they asserted, how Punjab was an international issue.

Sikh spokesmen have projected Sikhs as a national minority and hence argued for the community's right for self-determination as a national one, citing UN covenants and international statues in support of their claim. Representation at the UN and lobbying various state officials has made community leaders aware of an acceptable language of diplomacy, wherein calls for self-determination for national minorities are considered legitimate. Such 'learning through lobbying', has led the World Sikh Organization and the Council of Khalistan leaders to proclaim the Sikhs' right for self-determination through many resolutions:

> The UN Charter recognizes every nation's right of self-determination. On the basis of this recognition of the fundamental human rights of liberty and freedom by the world body, Sikhs living in occupied Khalistan have the right of self-determination in their homeland. We, the American Sikhs support their just and legitimate demand for self-determination.
>
> (*Sacramento Resolution*, 28 July 1991)

International public space has also provided opportunities for symbolic battles. Thus the unfurling of a Sikh flag at the UN Congress of Ethnic Groups was a matter of 'pride' for Sikh representatives, while the Indian delegation filed a protest and walked out. Sikh lobbyists' attempts to gain an non-government observer status at the UN, although rejected several times, saw a major diplomatic contest with Indian officials. Similarly, being a member of the UNPO can be seen in this context of gaining justification and respectability. When the UNPO granted membership to the Khalistan Council for a brief period, Dr G.S. Aulakh declared it as a 'major milestone for Sikh independence' while 'proudly' announcing that the 'Sikh flag' was hoisted at the Hague among other non-represented nations and peoples of the world (*World Sikh News*, 29 January 1991).

Contests between Sikh activists and Indian officials have also taken place in law courts, at human rights organizations, and various other venues. Numerous cases of Sikh refugees in need of representation and financial help have been taken up by Sikh activists, who have also established liaison with Amnesty International and other human rights organizations regarding many cases of 'disappearing Sikhs'. India's record of human rights has attracted condemnation by many parliamentarians and senators, as well from international human organizations. Thus unclaimed bodies in Amritsar, cases of abducted Sikhs such as Mr Khalra, have provoked keen concern in the corridors of Washington, London and Ottawa. The setting up of National Human Rights Commission in India was, in part, intended to diminish Sikh and Kashmiri lobbyists' success in raising such cases of torture and repression on many international platforms.

## Conclusion

In this brief survey of literature relating to the Sikh diaspora's conception of a 'homeland' and its 'ethnic status', two tentative conclusions can be drawn. The first concerns the nature of discourse on the homeland in the past hundred years or so. For the pre-1947 period, it transpires that the Sikh diaspora did not entertain an idea of territorial identity. It seems Punjab and India were no more than mere reference points, mere overlapping geographical entities without there being any strong emotional attachments to either. For the post-1947 period, with increasing number of Sikhs abroad, and with ever-increasing communication channels, the Punjab and Indian events started impinging upon their minds and as a consequence their reference points widened, and Punjab increasingly became part of their collective identity. Being a Punjabi also meant being an Indian, the two were neither in competition nor in contradiction. From the 1970s, the Sikhs' conception of Punjab as part of their collective identity started to constrain an easy mix of provincial identity against an overarching Indian identity. However until the 1980s, the idea of nationhood was not a dominant theme nor a part of the Sikh diaspora's debate or vocabulary.

The cataclysmic agent for major shift towards Punjab as an imagined homeland was June 1984. This 'critical event' has made the major differentiation between Punjab and India, transformed from a mere geographical spaces into two specific regions. In the post-1984 period, invoking 'Sikhs as a nation' and their right for an independent 'homeland' has become routine among the Sikh diaspora.

How have such 'meta-commentaries' (Oberoi 1987) become part of popular rhetoric? One approach would be to dismiss such expressions, as 'emotional outbursts' of diaspora Sikhs who are 'romantics, fools or knaves', and who live in a 'make-believe world of their own' (Chopra 1985: 337), hatching conspiracies inspired by foreign agencies. A more useful approach, however, would be to view such assertions as arising from new ethnic consciousness of a diaspora community, the overseas Sikhs' vulnerability and fear for their collective future. The 'critical event' has instilled such a feeling across Sikh overseas communities scattered over several countries, and governed by different polities, but linked by their common origins, shared cultural and religious traditions.

As a result of the events of 1984 in the Punjab, it seems that overseas Sikh communities have undergone a psychological transformation.

The post-1984 discourse indicates a shift from relatively confident communities to a defensive and an introspective 'victim diaspora' (Cohen 1997). The cry for a state has thus become a necessity in terms of community's self-respect, collective dignity, and a desire 'not to be dictated by others.' With the revolution in global communications, the fears of the Sikh diaspora across the world have become widely shared concerns. Thus news of a Sikh visitor's arrest in Punjab, the plight of Sikhs in jails, or news of the prosecution of Sikhs in the Middle East, find wide publicity across the diaspora. Isolated cases of discrimination against Sikhs are now discussed in Singapore, Southall, Stockton and Vancouver. This inter-linking has contributed to a sharpened sense of community's common and endangered fate. Thus, the WSO announced:

> The issues facing the Sikhs in India are too serious to be left to the emotional outbursts of a few individuals. Sikhs must develop approaches on a sophisticated level, beyond individual whims and work TOGETHER, to develop strong organizations. It thus becomes the utmost responsibility of the politically conscious Sikh wherever he or she may be – in order to foster full commitment and discipline for its effective workings.
>
> (*World Sikh News*, 19 February 1988)

The Sikh diaspora's claim on the Punjab as a homeland is certainly a new innovation, perhaps symptomatic of an insecure diaspora. The imagined Punjab is not even a geographical identity. Some Sikhs are nostalgic for the greater Punjab of Sikh rule, while others see a non-partitioned Punjab as an ideal. For others, the idea of Sikh homeland does not correspond to any existing boundaries, but is a spiritual space encompassing the historic shrines of the Sikh Gurus. We know even less of how second and third generation Sikhs born and schooled in western countries feel or perceive about Punjab. Indeed, concrete ideas about the geography of Sikh homeland and its implications are quite vague. Nevertheless, the cry for such a homeland does excite passions. It certainly concurs with Connor's observation that, 'passionate feelings for one's homeland are not constrained by inconvenient historical facts' (Connor 1986:18). Certainly theories lag behind the intensity of attachments which cut across borders and nations. As Said and Simmons put it:

> As emerging actors in the international system, they (ethnic groups and the emerging new ethnic groups) are indications that

our perceptions of international relations and the causes of war and peace lag behind the consciousness of the men and nations we study. The ethnic nation cannot compete with the state in nuclear warheads and warships but it continues to exercise formidable influence over the primary authority patterns of men. It is from this exercise of power that revolutions are born.

(*Said and Simmons* 1976: 14)

Perhaps a few general remarks on this territorial identity are in order. There has been a dramatic shift in this discourse on the Sikh homeland, essentially as a reaction to a state's violation of a community's most sacred and venerated shrine. The language of inter-community debate has generally been Punjabi, but the international platform required justifications and arguments in English. With this, a new set of formulations acceptable to international organisations and host states are in evidence. While debate over Punjabi words like *qaum* and *vatan* and phrases such as *raj karega Khalsa* are still evolving with shades of meanings, the English words 'nation' and 'homeland' are clearly understood on international platforms.

Thus repeated assertions of Sikhs as a nation and its right for self-determination seem to provide an honourable resolution to uncertainty of the diaspora setting. However, the idea of Punjab as a Sikh homeland and campaign for Sikh independence, despite its popular rhetoric, remains highly contested. Moreover, new events and situations are likely to influence this contested domain. The election of an Akali-BJP government in the Punjab in 1997, after years of turmoil and killings by the state as well as militants, has considerably softened the attitude of some of the leading protagonists of an independent homeland. The prominent American Sikh Didar Singh Bains not only closed the *World Sikh News*, an influential weekly for the Khalistani lobby in North America, but further pledged that 'India is Sikh community's mother country,' while the Punjab government made him a 'state guest' during the tercentenary Khalsa celebrations in April 1999. Many Sikhs have again joined annual celebrations of get-togethers organized by Indian embassies abroad. As coercive measures are gradually being replaced by accommodation policies, perhaps the Indian state could create an environment whereby the cry for Punjab as an exclusive Sikh homeland will lose its fatal appeal.

To conclude, the Sikh diaspora, through its location and its involvement in Punjab affairs, has helped in providing an ideological framework, widening Sikh consciousness of their place in the world, bringing a considerable shift in collective loyalty, and redefining Sikh ethnicity in terms of an ethno-national bond. Such shifts in group loyalty are immensely difficult to measure. However, it seems from a preliminary reading of relevant literature, a quest for homeland has become part of the Sikh diaspora's identity. The Punjab, with all its varied geography, has emerged, through much contest and debate, as such an imagined homeland for the Sikh diaspora.

# Notes

1 The first couplet is from *Ghadar di goonj*, a collection of songs first published in the *Gadr* weekly from San Francisco in 1913–14. The second passage is from a popular song by Mohan Singh Khiali, a traditional bard from Wolverhampton. Translations of songs, poetry and Punjabi media news are by the author. Punjabi words used in the text are italicized followed by their meaning in English. It should be apparent that some Punjabi words used for collective identity or geography, such as *qaum*, *panth*, *vatan*, *des*, etc., present serious semantic difficulties while rendering them into English.

2 For literature on Sikh politics in the post 1947 period, and especially for events associated with June 1984, see (Singh, 1987) and his subsequent publications.

3 Although this article's focus is quite different, on some points relevant literature and further discussion can be found in Tatla (1999).

4 Letter by Molla Singh, President, Shiromani Akali Dal Association of Canada, to Rt. Hon. John Roberts, Secretary of State, Government of Canada, 23 August 1977.

5 Resolution provided by Surjit Gill, Secretary Kalsha Diwan Society, Vancouver, 1981.

6 These passages are from popular songs recorded in Britain and Canada during the post 1984 period. The following two passages are from songs by Balwant Singh, a Derby-based group. Several Sikh militants killed in encounters have been remembered through songs, such as Brahma, Manochahal, Gurjant, Gora, Beant, Satwant, Sukha, and others. See also Pettigrew (1992) for one such song.

7 *Sikhs in their Homeland* (1984), a government of India sponsored booklet was widely circulated among overseas Sikhs by Indian embassies. See also *White Paper*.

Chapter Ten

# What Has a Whale Got to Do With It? A Tale of Pogroms and Biblical Allegories

*Harjot Oberoi*

> Deep in Time's crevasse
> by the alveolate
> waits, a crystal of breath,
> your irreversible
> witness
>
> (*Celan* 1980)

One of the most innovative anthropologists writing on India today is Veena Das. In introducing a recent collection of essays she writes: 'A part of the self lies buried in every piece one writes' (Das 1995: viii). And although the book is largely concerned with exhuming private and collective memories of communities and nations, paradoxically the memories of the author, her personal self, stays buried in this single sentence. For Das her book has a 'double location' (Das 1995:1). It identifies 'certain critical moments in the history of contemporary India, and these moments are then redescribed within the framework of anthropological knowledge' (Das 1995: 1). In brief the book is explicitly about the secular nation-state in India and anthropological theory and not about the author. And yet we know from Das's cryptic confessional at the beginning of her volume that the text is as much about her (and not merely in terms of self that has produced the text) as it is about the cultural dialectics of modern India and anthropological practices. One would then be justified in amending the semantics of 'double location' and speak of a triptych that would include the locality, discipline, and the author.

In the pursuit of what Richard Rorty felicitously calls foundational truths, social scientists are discouraged from expressing what may be described as the third location, encompassing, their inner life-world, personal dilemmas, private solidarities, and change of heart. There are powerful disciplinary conventions that censor turning personal predicaments into social texts. Despite the avid promotion of positionality by many from within cultural studies, reflexive anthropology, and feminist scholarship, each calling for a complete confessional of one's class, gender, and racial make-up, any connectivity between theory and autobiography, the personal and the academy, remains both elusive and suspect.[1] Even Freud, who was often candid about imbricating his personal experiences and desires with the science of psychoanalysis, in the end advocated a retreat from turning the private into public:

> And here I may be allowed to break off these autobiographical notes. The public has no claim to learn any more of my personal affairs – of my struggles, my disappointments, and my successes. I have in any case been more open and frank in some of my writings (such as *The Interpretation of Dreams* and *The Psychology of Everyday Life*) than people usually are who describe their lives for their contemporaries or for posterity. I have had small thanks for it, and from my experience I cannot recommend anyone to follow my example.
>
> (*Freud* 1953: 73)

Freud's stern warning was taken seriously. In the human sciences there continues to be an uneasiness when it comes to expressing affective concerns or talk of personal crises. For those who seek to address the private domain we have carved out special genres: journals, memoirs, and autobiographies. But when it comes to critical theory as both Roland Barthes and Michel Foucault famously told us: the author is dead.[2] A first-person account was thought to be incapable of illuminating complex theoretical matters. Structuralist theory has for long insisted that individuals do not generate discourses (linguistic, religious, or secular), it is discourses that produce individuals. Similarly, postcolonial critics propose that it is cultural hegemony that scripts our roles. Those who do not pay heed to these propositions are said to suffer from 'diary disease.'[3]

I must confess that as a practising historian I have never before succumbed to this malady. But of late, I have been repeatedly been compelled to reflect on two episodes: one that can be bracketed in the space we call the nation-state, and the other in the geography of the transnational. Both of these cases cannot be easily sorted out either by structuralism or postcolonial theory. In the first of these episodes, I was terrorized for belonging to the Sikh community, a highly visible religious minority in India, and the other also a personal memoir of terror, but this time around ironically for not properly belonging to the Sikh community, or at least in the form of a good/proper/authentic/militant Sikh. In short, I encountered what has elusively come to be described as Hindu and Sikh nationalisms. Of late both these metanarratives have been the subject of considerable discussion and commentary within the academy. My aim in this chapter is to engage with these academic writings based on my subjective experience. Hopefully, this will help in this volume's agenda of seeking 'new perspectives in Sikh Studies.'

## 'Teach the Sikhs a lesson'

In 1947 at the time of India's partition my family, alongside tens of thousands of other Punjabi households, experienced the bitter harvest of a religious and political dispersion: they were forcibly driven out of ancestral lands and homes in what came to be known as Pakistan. They left because we were Sikhs. The new state across the Radcliffe line was to be an Islamic Republic. After crisscrossing many towns and cities the family eventually found sanctuary in Delhi. It was hard to call this new place home. The first decade was filled with nostalgia for Lahore, Rawalpindi, and Jhelum. All Punjabis who came from across the line were called either refugees or displaced persons. These categories recognized the unevenness of India's freedom: while the vast majority of people had become citizens, others started their lives under the shadow of social stigmas. Fortunately, the family had for long been in the business of land-development and construction. Delhi as the capital of a brand new nation-state needed a lot of new buildings for the government: offices for all the bodies that were going to fill in the new federal ministries and bureaucracies. It was in the process of creating space for others that the family discovered a city that soon became home. By the early 1970s family stories were no longer located in exotic localities and neighbourhoods that we of the next generation had never been to. Aunts and uncles coming of age; the building of homes; the great big family weddings; legendary loyalties and feuds; the buying and selling of businesses; births and deaths – all of these now routinely took place in Delhi. Much as this imperial city had once provided a sense of identity for Rajputs, Mughals and British, we too now began to feel as if we had been crafted out of its various pasts. I was surrounded by the capital and it was impossible for me to make sense of my personal biography as apart from its environment. Delhi simply was my native city. My friends, schools, and interests made it the place I most identified with.

In graduate school I became interested in the social history of modern India. During 1984 I spent most of my time in search of Punjabi tracts and newspaper files in order to complete a dissertation on religion and society in mid-nineteenth century Punjab. Having spent months reading up vernacular materials I decided on a change of pace. Occasionally, I would now go to the National Archives to look up British records. To examine Indian society based on the correspondence, notes, and intelligence reports of colonial officials was for me a new experience. By early autumn I had settled into a comfortable pace with my research project. Every morning I looked forward to going down to the city's central district. It took me about twenty minutes to get from my parents' home in Green Park to the pink-sandstone building that housed the Archives.

At 10.15 on the morning of 31 October I was just about to follow my daily routine when I heard our neighbour's son scream in the driveway: 'They have shot her.' He was repeatedly shouting these words with great urgency from his motorbike, to his mother who was standing outside on a small balcony that jutted out of their first-floor home. I had never before seen our neighbour's son so agitated. Clearly, he had been out on an errand and had picked up a rumour of some grisly murder. Shaken by his demeanour and the mysterious pronouns, it took me a few seconds before I could react. And then I asked him what he was talking about. He simply stated: 'The Sikhs have killed Mrs Gandhi.' The next thing I knew he had disappeared in the stairwell above the driveway.

Bewildered by what I just heard, I turned back in to tell my parents what had transpired outside. My father rushed to the radio but there was nothing on the news. We were all in a state of disbelief. To us it seemed implausible that someone had cut through the heavy rings of security that surrounded the prime minister and killed her. But what if this rumor was indeed true? What if those who killed her turned out to be Sikhs? For the past six years political violence in the Punjab had been on the rise and it had been brought to a bloody halt when in June 1984 Mrs Gandhi ordered the Indian army to invade the Golden

Temple, the holiest Sikh shrine. The objective of the army generals was to flush out Sikh radicals who had turned the sacred site into an armed citadel. Outside this violent strike a great ideological struggle had been going on between the Indian state and Sikh radicals. The secular state saw them simply as terrorists, many within the Sikh community viewed them as freedom fighters. Ordinary Sikhs did not have much of a choice in deciding these rubrics: the media and many of the general public were beginning to quarantine them quite independently of how they might have wished to arrange the labels of citizenship and nationhood.

The consensus in our living room that morning was that in case the news was eventually confirmed there would be public grieving, considerable displays of emotion and some of these events could turn ugly. Often in Delhi when some unsettling news circulated or a large union called for a general strike (*bandh*), high school and college students in particular were known to stone public buses and other state owned property. We concluded that it would take a day or so for things to turn normal. The next few hours were best spent at home. I should point out here that our decision to stay put was not at all based on the fact that my father and I, as Sikh males, would be highly visible to the public with our turbans and beards. We simply wanted to avoid being trapped in the midst of an emotive crowd that would not have made any subtle distinctions between Sikhs and Hindus. In hindsight this decision possibly saved our lives. By early afternoon a newscaster on BBC radio announced that Mrs Gandhi had been killed by two of her Sikh bodyguards. Soon after, the same news was repeated by several evening papers in the city, and finally at 6.00 pm, the All India Radio carried an official confirmation on the death of the prime minister. We still had no particular reason to be alarmed.

Unknown to us, barely a thousand metres from our home a massive crowd had gathered outside the All India Institute of Medical Sciences. This is a premier medical facility where for almost the entire day doctors had been struggling to revive Mrs Gandhi's crumpled body. When the doctors finally gave up, the crowds outside had become so large and uncontrollable that they almost managed to prevent the cavalcade of the Sikh president from entering the Institute. The presidential limousine and other cars that carried his entourage were stoned. Next to be targeted were Sikh commuters riding home on Delhi Transport Corporation buses. Sections of the crowd, standing across the entire width of the road, would signal a bus-driver to stop, then they would check to find out if there were any

Sikh male riders. If this was the case, the Sikhs would be singled out, dragged out, dumped to the ground and then assaulted with hockey sticks, bicycle chains, and iron rods.[4] By 9.00 pm the first phase of mayhem came to a close. Perhaps there were not enough Sikh commuters to be found. The crowd now broke into several columns that quickly marched into the residential areas surrounding the Institute. Here they started a long night of pillage, arson, and assault. The primary targets were Sikh businesses and homes. It did not take us long to gather news of what was going on. Based on telephone conversations with friends and extended family, and on an almost hourly update from concerned neighbours (all of them non-Sikhs) we had a vivid account of crowd tactics and terror. By now conscious of our vulnerability, we desperately hoped for Delhi police to intervene.

I was twenty-seven then, and never in my life had I once thought that one night I would have to negotiate my religious identity with an armed crowd intent on doing harm to me. As a student of history I had of course read accounts of Hindu-Muslim riots, and even heard traumatic accounts of partition, but in postcolonial India there had not been even a single instance of pogroms against the Sikhs. In Indian public discourse Sikhs were represented as patriots par excellence. Sikh officers and soldiers had distinguished themselves in two major wars with Pakistan and another one with China. Punjab where the bulk of the Sikh population lived was a granary for the rest of the country. The country was headed by a Sikh president. I had grown up in a milieu where there was simply no contradiction between being Sikh and being Indian. Ironically, it had never occurred to me that I belonged to a religious minority. There was no reason to do so. I had never been discriminated against or targeted because of my ethnicity. My palpable fear that night was made worse by my cultural confusion.

On such a night one barely sleeps. We stayed awake: whispering, waiting, speculating, and above all trying to distinguish sounds. In everyday life it is so easy to name sounds. A distinction between stillness and clatter is basic. But what does a lynching mob sound like? I had no expertise in the cadence of violence and that of my parents was badly rusted. The partition riots of thirty-seven years ago were a hazy memory for them. Having been told of roving bands of armed young men, we expected the stillness of night to be shattered any minute by a multitude of footsteps and cries of anti-Sikh slogans. With the resources we had it was hard to come up with any solid plan to save our lives. There was no way the three of us could have put up any barricades or escaped to another part of the city. To be out on the road in the middle of the night was even more dangerous than being at home. All we could think of was to pretend that no one was at home, extinguish the lights, draw the blinds, retreat into the storage at the far end of the house, and in case the crowds did break in let them walk away with whatever they took a fancy for: clothing, couches, crockery, food, television, stereo, fridge or any other item inside the house (the first reports we had all indicated the mob's penchant for looting household goods). But what if the crowd came right to the deepest recess of the house where we had taken refuge? That first night of the pogroms we were in no mood to speculate about that eventuality. In hindsight all of this sounds so naive, perhaps even dim-witted. But when one has never before been the victim of religious violence it takes time to map out new realities.

When the first light came through the glass doors, at the front of the house, the three of us had been awake for twenty-four hours. The pogroms were to continue for another three days. The grisly violence that had first started on Wednesday night in South Delhi now rapidly spread to other parts of the city: Trilokpuri, Kalyanpuri, Sultanpuri, Mangolpuri, Jankapuri, Gandhi Nagar, Palam Colony, Punjabi Bagh. All these place names find repeated reference in the documents and literature describing the Delhi 'riots'. What these reports and studies also tell us is that a fairly standard ritual of violence had emerged in less than a day. Armed mobs of Hindus travelled from suburb to suburb in city buses either commandeered from the DTC or gleefully driven by the corporation's drivers. In the anonymity of urban living it was not that easy to know where exactly the Sikhs lived. But these mobs had precise instructions on where to go: group leaders gathered the required intelligence from voters' lists, ration-card inventories, and the assistance of local party-functionaries from the Congress (I), who for reasons of electioneering knew the neighbourhoods intimately. Four to five hundred men (sometimes as many as five thousand) would arrive in a locality, proceed to Sikh residences on the block, ransack the homes, where the men inside would either be set alight with kerosene or disembowelled. Soon after the pogroms the late Raj Thapar, a prominent Indian public intellectual, posed the question: 'How do you do it?' And then went on to answer his own Zen *koan* on collective violence:

> Yes. How is it done? You take a stick, wrap some cloth around it, dip it in a mixture of kerosene and some other deadly stuff, and

you hurl it into a life time's work, a shop, a taxi, a mud hut, a scooter. Then you catch the inmates, you chop of their hair and amidst gleeful shouting, you hurl them into a raging fire, one by one. When a wife comes out wailing at the death of her husband, you seize her, you bash her bones with *lathis* and you hurl her in as well. You leave the child because you gloat in the agonised survival of that orphan.

(*Thapar* 1985: 19)

We knew very little of these sorts of details on 1st November. The official media were not much help during those dark days. All we saw on television was Mrs Gandhi's body lying in state at Teen Murti House, various dignitaries coming to pay homage, mourners filing past the bier, and many among those who had gathered outside shouting: *khun ka badla khun se lenge* (We will take blood for blood). Our key source for alternate 'news' continued to be concerned neighbours and friends. Throughout the day what we heard were the following items: a large number of Sikhs had been killed in the city; all of the trains coming in to Delhi railway station from Punjab that morning were full of headless bodies; countless Hindus en route to Delhi had been slaughtered by Sikhs in the Punjab; Sikh extremists had poisoned the sources of water supply in the city; caravans of heavily armed Sikh militants from the Punjab were headed for the capital. Many of these items were conveyed to us by a neighbour who was a high-ranking police official. There was no reason to suspect what he had to tell. He may have embellished some of the details but much of what he said sounded credible to us then. None of us was then well read in the phenomenology of ethnic riots. It was only later that I learned much of what was passed to us as 'news' that day was part of the standard repertoire of rumours that fuel modern urban violence. Rumours are a powerful psychological weapon for aggressors from populations who constitute national majorities. By showing that victims were intent on violence, for instance, the canard of headless bodies being despatched from the Punjab, it made it emotionally comfortable for crowds to transgress and perform acts of violence.[5] In this misreading of terror the victims deserve what they get.

Terrified by what was conveyed to us, much like a Greek tragedy, we culpably awaited our rituals of death. We did take one small step to avert what could soon turn up on our doorstep. Around midday I briefly walked out of the front compound to remove a sign that would have made the mob's task of spotting a Sikh household easier.

Outside many houses in Delhi, out on a fence-post or a wrought-iron gate, hangs a name board. Much like entries in a phone book it makes public the identity of those who live inside. The one that I unhinged on day two of the pogroms simply carried the inscription Sharnagat Singh, my father's name. The Singh in the name signified his loyalty and fundamental commitment to the Sikh faith. Tens of thousands of Sikh men have that as their last name. It would have never occurred to anyone that the semiotics of a Sikh name would one day become ominous and have to be turned invisible. A source of self-identity, however minor, stood breached. What I had gone out to retrieve had suddenly become emblematic of life and death. It possessed an eerie power of turning living beings into objects of violence.

Having stepped out once earlier in the day I was tempted to try it one more time. My innermost wish was to drive around the city, converse with friends, and busy myself with some project beyond the poverty of waiting. By early evening, a clawing sense of claustrophobia and a little less afraid of injury, led me to the terrace of our three-storey home. This was my first glimpse beyond hearsay into what was going on. The twilight sky was lit not by the fading sun but by innumerable fires. It was as if arsonists had come to rule the city. All around me were wafting columns of smoke. I witnessed houses half-burnt standing out like ancient skeletons, taxis badly mangled and turned into shells of raw metal, and the Ring Road, usually one of the busiest in the capital, empty of both traffic and people. Delhi's urban landscape had been refigured in the image of a battle zone. What had been denied Hindu imaginary by history suddenly took on a life of its own. It was disconcerting to have always questioned Sikh absolutist rhetoric and then be faced, quite literally, with subjectivities and categories one had never quite acknowledged: a majoritarian state, Hindu nationalism, religious alterity. To accept these terms and descriptions was to confirm the 'truths' of Sikh militant discourse.

It was no more a question of living with what once Freud usefully described as the narcissism of minor differences. Religious violence produces substantive cultural disfiguring that makes it difficult for diverse populations to conduct their differences in the shadows of history. A semantic unit – the Sikhs – had been unleashed through organized violence that rapidly gathered in a new collectivity and vocabulary, for manipulation and control, for intimidation and violence, imperiously ignoring historical descriptions; innumerable contemporary alignments; substantive internal differences; and the

194

question of individual biographies. I allude here to a diverse population being violently commodified into a religious minority. A commodity that would soon be traded by institutions of the state, ballot seekers, and judicial discourse. Henceforth, I was not going to be read for my own moral ontology. A theological vocabulary and ethnic paranoia that I had always disfavoured was permanently attached to my identity, for I had been commodified as a Sikh and inserted into a new exchange of (human) goods. The traumas of personal identity and usurpious alchemy of modern politics.

By Friday morning we had made it through two days of unstoppable religious violence. At approximately 4.15 in the afternoon of 2 November, I received a message from Professor Satish Saberwal, a former teacher of mine. He proposed that he come that night and drive us all to his home located on the campus of Jawaharlal Nehru University (JNU). I had known Satish for over a decade – he had taught me sociology and by the time I graduated from JNU we had become close friends. The popular news network that we had been tapping into predicted that 3 November was going to be the worst day of 'rioting'. This was the day when Mrs Gandhi's body was to be cremated and the speculation was that as soon as her body was consigned to the pyre Delhi would burn even more brightly. Based on what we had heard up to that point and what I personally witnessed the previous evening, we came to the conclusion that all we could do was to abandon home. Just before midnight, as promised, Satish arrived in an official jeep. Besides him there were two others – a driver and a guard, both personnel from campus security.

The physical arrangements that we worked out for this flight were extraordinary and require some description. My mother sat next to the driver in the front, my father and I lay down flat at the back of the jeep. We covered ourselves with a large number of blankets and quilts. This was most humiliating but the security guard insisted we do this. In case we were stopped en route and a mob looked inside, all they would see was a sari-clad woman and three tall Hindu men. The assumption was that since our bodies were pressed close to the floor of the jeep with a shroud of coverings on top we would go undetected. Satish and the security driver sat opposite to each other on the back seats that ran vertically on each end of the jeep. Just as we got ready to leave my father changed his mind. He simply could not bring himself to leave and there was no way we could make him change his mind. I found all this deeply embarrassing: Satish had risked his life on our behalf and we were unable to decide on what we wanted from him. Eventually my father decided to stay with our Hindu neighbours and the two of us (my mother and myself) departed with Satish. The violence outside had as yet not physically smashed us, yet psychologically it succeeded in splitting our family. Once again we were ejected from home and turned into refugees, albeit postcolonial ones.

The journey to the campus, located on the southern edge of the city, took close to twenty minutes. The only roadblock we passed was one outside the JNU campus. I was back in the midst of old colleagues and friends. Warm memories of youth from years ago came tumbling back. In 1984 the JNU campus was probably one of the most secular enclaves in the country; and my fears began to abate. It was a relief no longer to feel like prey. Satish and I spoke late into the night. Next morning he proposed that, given our mutual interest in history, we both work on a piece for the national papers exploring what had gone wrong. To speak about politics of identity is notoriously difficult. Where does one begin? How does one historicize ethnicity? What precisely were the *origins* of Hindu-Sikh violence? Does one go back to Guru Nanak in the fifteenth century or to the Arya Samaj in the nineteenth? Afraid that we would end up dealing in cliches we decided on an interview format. I reproduce a few extracts from that conversation on the morning of 4 November 1984 (by this time over 3,879 Sikhs had been killed in Delhi alone and over 50,000 were homeless):

> **Harjot**: It is being suggested to me that the rioting, particularly in Delhi, had a discernible pattern both in the targets chosen and the way the rumors which infuriated the civil-population spread. The anonymity of large cities was quickly lost. Sikh houses, businesses, and institutions pinpointed. Similarly, rumours were spread systematically, implicitly inciting immediate reprisals. For instance, without any basis, it was rumoured that trainloads of dead bodies belonging to a particular community were coming in from Punjab. Similarly, anonymous phone calls warned Delhi residents of the water supply having been poisoned. Satish, does this pattern, especially with your first hand experience of Moradabad riots in 1980, suggest any organized effort on the part of certain groups in our society?

> **Satish**: Sure, Harjot, you know it strikes me that we Indians are the world's most experienced people in the matter of communal riots. Today these hit the Sikhs, recently the blows have fallen on Muslims, in Maharashtra the Shiva Sena has attacked South

196

Indians and scheduled castes, and the list could go on. We never know whom this demon is going to strike next. It could be my turn tomorrow. You are quite right about rumours. Shortly after what happened in Moradabad in 1980, my friend Mushirul Hasan and I went there to understand how it built up, and it was the same pattern. Anonymous phone calls about 'poisoned' water supply. There was one rumour, absolutely without basis, that a temple priest in the city outskirts had been killed by Muslims. People believed it, and a Muslim colony was wiped out. Out of such rumours are riots made ...

**Harjot**: Satish, you have been doing some work on the rise of bureaucratic states in Europe, and also in a recent article you indicated the relevance of such study for understanding the political crisis in contemporary India. Could you tell us why similar developments did not occur in the subcontinent?

**Satish**: Yes ... for the last three or four years I have been reading about what happened in Europe during the medieval period. As you know, I am a sociologist and not an historian. So it was necessary for me to work hard to reduce my level of ignorance. And there are three things which I have found to be very striking. One is that there are many ideas, if you like, models, which continue in Europe for a very long time, something like 2000 years. This is to say there is a live tradition which comes down from ancient Greece and Rome. It went into what happened in mediaeval Europe, and prepared the ground for the rise of capitalism there, and their later ability to expand into the Americas, India, Australia and so forth. The second thing that struck me was that the Roman Catholic Church was extremely important in the shaping of modern Europe, especially until the end of the thirteenth century. This is a very large question, and we cannot go into much detail here. But there is a third element which is astonishing. That is, the Roman Catholic Church was able to absorb a good deal of the Greek tradition. With it came the idea of reason, and the importance of reason in human affairs. This influence came in quite early; it went into the New Testament, which is the second part of the Bible. But also it was because of this element that, in the twelfth and the thirteenth centuries, the project of reconciling reason with faith became very important within the Church ...

197

Retrospectively what we largely (though not exclusively) spoke about were metanarratives: national political formations, colonialism and imperialism, communalism, the Roman Catholic Church, the Jesus myth, and the emergence of nation-states in Europe. Together we addressed the collective but not the individual. It has taken me over thirteen years to get to the personal I-witnessing. Then, as Clifford Geertz would have it, this is not simply a matter of jesting and tropes. It can also entail events of considerable personal trauma and dislocation. These as Freud repeatedly made clear are only belatedly recalled and can have a considerable period of latency (Freud 1939: 84). And even when one becomes aware of the scope and magnitude of what one experienced, at a personal level it is far easier to exercise what psychoanalysts call repression, rather than construct narratives about it or seek to incorporate this information into social analysis. It is perhaps for this reason that Madan and Veena Das seek personal forgetfulness.

## What is a Sikh?

It is Hegel who first spoke of how things in history tend to happen twice. Marx agreed and amplified that statement by adding that the first time around historical events come to us as a tragedy and the second time as a farce. Close to a decade after my first experience of crowd dynamics in Delhi, I encountered yet another crowd formation, although this time around it was another geography. But first some background.

In the spring of 1994 I published a monograph on the social history of Sikhism. In this work I had raised two key questions: 'How are Indian religions to be conceptualized? What did it mean to be a Sikh in the nineteenth century?' (Oberoi 1994: xi). In grappling with these issues I proposed that historically there had never been a monolithic Sikh discourse and that Sikh tradition had been constantly reformulated. In the absence of a centralized church and religious hierarchy, there existed a heterogeneity in religious beliefs, rituals, and lifestyles. Most Sikhs moved in and out of multiple identities grounded in local, regional, religious and secular loyalties. Consequently, religious identities were highly blurred and several competing definitions of who constituted a Sikh were possible. By the closing decades of the nineteenth century, the Singh Sabha, a wide-ranging religious movement, began to view this multiplicity with suspicion and hostility and started the elaborate project of purging and recasting tradition. There now emerged a new discourse of what it meant to be a Sikh.

Prior to the release of my book, I had published some of my research findings as essays and articles. These had been the subject of an acrimonious debate in a variety of Sikh forums and publications, many of these funded by the Sikh diaspora.[6] Contrary to my formulations it was proposed that there had never been any diversity in the Sikh tradition. There was only one single Sikh identity, revealed once for all, by Guru Nanak (1469–1539) and the nine 'prophets' who followed him. During the nineteenth century Sikh religious identity became somewhat fogged, largely because of the decline of the Sikh empire and British annexation of the Punjab. But Sikh activists under the auspices of the Singh Sabha movement quickly defogged the new cultural environment and restored a classical purity. They introduced absolutely nothing new. To Sikh orthodoxy my historicist claims appeared to be absurd and tendentious. These sounded all the more alarming for two reasons. First, this constructivist position was being put forward by a Sikh scholar, an insider, one who ought to know the community and its aspirations. Second, this person occupied a chair in Sikh studies that had in part been funded by the Sikh community in Canada.

Starting in the late 1960s, the Canadian government in support of its national policy of multiculturalism, which sounds very much like the state legislation on secularism in India, launched an academic initiative to establish and advance ethnic chairs. The operating principle behind the programme was very simple. If a local ethnic community, let us say Polish, Hungarian, or Estonian, could raise $300,000 and be backed by a Canadian university, the federal government came up with a matching grant. This would mark the beginnings of a new heritage programme that would be covered by the usual clauses of academic freedom and university autonomy. However, right from the beginning this programme ran into trouble. For within each ethnic community there was not one but many opposing cultural visions. Despite these communal frictions the politicians persisted with the programme. It served as a useful device to garner ethnic votes. In less than two decades the federal government had funded over twenty ethnic chairs spread across the country. In 1987 the University of British Columbia (hereafter UBC), set up a chair in Sikh Studies, and I became the first chairholder.

In a way not unlike the Delhi pogroms, my individual self was totally overlooked and misrepresented. As a chairholder I was quickly turned into a compressed sign, this time around for the purposes of Sikh nationalism in the diaspora. When my writings historicized this nationalism and addressed its origins, I quickly came to constitute the Other. It is this secular alterity that accounts for what follows. On the morning of 7 May 1994 a Sikh crowd gathered for a public meeting in the Auditorium Building on UBC campus. This turn of the century building is barely two hundred metres from my office – my home away from home. A transnational organization, the Canadian Sikh Study and Teaching Society, had convened a large public meeting to assess my newly released book and the workings of the Sikh chair.

While most of those who participated in the forum came from metropolitan Vancouver, a few of the participants had flown in from cities across North America and some had even come from as far away as India. Federal and provincial politicians brought official greetings for the delegates. The message of all those who addressed the crowd throughout the day was the same: I was guilty of blasphemy and anti-Sikh activities. Clearly, those present in the forum were not persuaded by my historicist account. When the meeting concluded in the evening several resolutions were passed by acclamation, categorically denouncing the book and asserting the supremacy of faith over historical research. There were strong echoes here of what Hindu activists had come to proclaim over the Ayodhya dispute. When it became impossible for BJP supporters to prove conclusively through archaeology and history that the god Ram was born, exactly at the spot where the Babri Masjid was constructed, they gutted the old academic strategy. It was then proposed that what concerned them was purely a matter of faith, completely independent of what historians may or may not be able to prove.

The Sikh population in metropolitan Vancouver numbers tens of thousands. During much of the 1980s and early 1990s the city was a major centre for the political struggle to establish Khalistan, an independent Sikh nation. The deliberations and activities of this diasporic nationalism were regularly featured in both the ethnic and the national media. A controversy surrounding a work of Sikh history immediately provoked the interest of local journalists. The headlines of the stories that appeared at the time manifest some of the sentiments that were being expressed: (i) Sikh Conference Calls for Professor's Ouster: Academic's Work Seen As Attack on Religion; (ii) Local Sikhs seeking removal of 'heretical' UBC professor;

(iii) Academic Echoes of Salman Rushdie (iv) UBC Sikh Chair Attacked.[7] The irony of how a decade earlier I had been subjected to terror for being a Sikh and I was now being tossed out for not being an authentic Sikh was not lost on me. The May conference was the beginning of a fierce public campaign seeking my ouster from the campus. In mid-May eight Sikh societies set up an action committee, hired a local lawyer to act as their official spokesman, and began issuing incendiary press statements.[8] The lawyer threatened the university with imminent legal action if I was not removed from my position. Anonymous reviews vilifying me and denouncing the book were handed out to Sikh congregations. These were followed by unsigned pamphlets written in the vernacular, the language and idiom used in these new materials perhaps seeking to generate new pockets of support among those who may not have shown much interest in the campaign.

Fortunately, the university and many of my colleagues firmly stood behind me. Occasionally, I would receive warm letters of support from complete strangers. Our local daily paper published an editorial in my support arguing that my book soundly belonged to the well established tradition of secular historiography. The Sikh community had misunderstood my purpose. Since I was neither a functionary of the Sikh religion nor a theologian commenting on Sikh scripture I ought to be left alone.[9] The book that came to be discussed in the public domain, particularly in the ethnic media, was certainly not the one I had written. No substantial quote from the book was ever cited, instead there were always fabrications, allusions, and argumentation by labeling, in this case under the rubric 'anti-Sikh'. These two words – 'anti-Sikh' – were supposed to tie me to all sorts of movements and ideologies: Christian missionaries, Brahman hegemony and secular thinking. A complex, often controversial historiography of the Sikhs going back over a hundred years was all readily ascribed to me.[10] Among many other items, it came to be suggested that I did not sufficiently acknowledge that Guru Nanak was the founder of Sikhism or that in his extensive travels he went overseas.

These are important issues for Sikh history, but I did not raise these in my text. They had no bearing on a work that largely examined Sikh and other religious identities in the nineteenth century. And since I spoke of the historical evolution of Sikh identity (a rather elementary formulation one would have thought), I stood accused of saying that Sikhs had no identity. Given the kind of charges that were being levelled against me it appeared to be a zero-sum game to put forward my side of the story. How does one protect oneself from statements that one has never made? Not wanting to give into despair, I did make a few efforts. One particularly memorable one was going live on a radio broadcast (The Early Edition show on CBC) to debate with Iqbal Sara, the lawyer acting on behalf of many of the Sikh organizations in Vancouver. This very public conversation was very different from the one I had with Satish Saberwal a decade ago. Sara charged me with inaccuracy in my representations of Sikhism and that I had violated the mandate of the Sikh chair. I defended my thesis and the programme, and reiterated the complex trajectory of modern Sikhism.[11] At the conclusion of the broadcast we parted with our disagreements intact.

Often, all of this appeared to be totally unreal. What interest could anybody have on the idyllic west coast of Canada, in what took place in one of India's provinces in the nineteenth century? But the daily press reports and being featured as an item on radio news would quickly bring me back to the ugly realities that I faced. While there was much in this case that was dissimilar to the Delhi 'riots' there was one eerie similarity. Once again there were whispers and rumours; the subject of course was different, but many of the mechanisms and intent were similar. There were three key rumours that were circulated: that I was part of a world-wide Christian conspiracy to undermine Sikhism; that I was a member of the communist party; and that I was sent to Canada by the Indian government.[12] The first of these rumours referred to the colonial past, the second spoke of opposition to radical thought, and the third expressed disgust for the Indian state. Despite the internal contradictions, their rhetoric was brilliant. Three short statements summed up the entire history of modernity in South Asia from colonialism to post-colonialism. Tradition was under assault by the forces of modernity and I was part of that attack.

I was well aware that in the past other secular historians and creative writers had been targeted in South Asia. In the mid-1970s several prominent historians who had written textbooks for the Central Board of Secondary Education were attacked by the Jan Sangh, the political party that gave birth to the BJP. They were deemed guilty of denigrating Hinduism and a campaign was launched to have their textbooks removed from the school system. A little later Vijay Tendulkar was attacked by the Shiva Sena in Bombay for his anti-Brahmanical play *Ghasi Ram Kotval*. Paradoxically, cultural expression has been attacked by both secular and non-secular sectors.

In 1991 Safdar Hashmi, a producer of street theatre, was killed on the outskirts of Delhi because he was seen to be taking votes away from the Congress party. More recently the internationally renowned painter M.F. Hussain came under attack by groups close to the BJP. Due to his Muslim origins he was deemed unfit to portray Hindu goddesses. What was new in my case was that the long campaign to silence me was largely enacted within the South Asian diaspora.

## Conclusions

The Oxford philosopher Alasdair MacIntyre in his highly influential book, *After Virtue*, has complained that much of our social and cultural theory is devoid of stories. 'Man in his actions and practices,' writes McIntyre '[is] essentially a story-telling animal. He is not essentially, but becomes through his history, a teller of stories that aspire to truth' (MacIntyre 1984: 216). Dealing exclusively with the question: 'What am I to do?' overlooks the question: 'Of what story or stories do I find myself a part [of]?', thus shaping theory through 'impersonal rational arguments' (MacIntyre 1984: 216). This creates a huge gap between theory and practice. Modern individuals begin to feel unscripted, and we (both inside and outside the academy) become 'powerless to detect the disorders of moral thought and practice.' MacIntyre's critique of critical theory can be further enriched by turning to the writings of Richard Rorty. Philosophy, Rorty suggests, is incapable of solving our central human dilemmas. For these we need to turn to literature. It is only through narratives that speak of human contingencies and ironies (for instance Proust, Nabakov and Orwell – we could add Saadat Hasan Manto, Bhisham Sahni, Rajinder Singh Bedi) that we will begin to get better descriptions of the world.[13] In this chapter, following MacIntyre and Rorty's suggestions on how to overcome theoretical incommensurability through fabulation, I have sought to tell some tales about religious loyalties and secular imagination. These personal transcripts enable me to affirm and question some of the current formulations in the field of Sikh Studies.

In addressing questions of religious solidarities Veena Das is correct when she proposes that all major religious communities in India today are increasingly beginning to resemble the hegemonic structures of the state (Das 1995: 16–17). In order to create a homogeneous and consenting constituency, they seek the same disciplinary technologies, legislative power, and coercive instruments that are possessed by the state. Although each of these communities in their normative universe regularly invokes the discourse of collective rights, moral justice, and ethical action, yet – not unlike the state they despise in cultural practices – these communities regularly collude in suppressing rights, disrupting lives, stigmatizing bodies, and inflicting pain. For the moment the argument advanced by Veena Das remains unusual. It is much more common to romanticize communities and see them as engaged in battle with an oppressive state. For instance, Partha Chatterjee argues that the present impasse over secularism in India could be overcome if the history of democratic impulses within India's religious minorities was more widely acknowledged (Chaterjee 1995). The chief example that Chatterjee gives in support of his argument is that of the Akali movement among the Sikhs in the 1920s that led to the first public body based on universal suffrage in colonial India. What Chatterjee overlooks is that there was a powerful counter-movement to that of the Akalis under the banner of the Babbar Akalis. While the Akalis were solely interested in the redistribution of political power in the post-war period, the Babbar Akalis fought for a radical redefinition of political community that included among other things economic justice. A hegemonic discourse of sameness was thoroughly challenged by a counter-canon that dared to include the terrain of internal differences: social, economic and political. Eventually, the interests of the colonial state and those of the moderate Akalis coincided, resulting in the legislation that Chatterjee alludes to, but significantly leading also to the elimination of a large number of Babbar Akalis. The complexities of the past and present instances, some recently explicated by Paul Brass, do not provide sufficient corroboration for Chatterjee's contention.

And finally, the events I have been sharing with you in this chapter have already become part of anthropological history. In a recent monograph, Cynthia Mahmoud has given us an ethnographic account of the longings, rage, and suffering of Sikh militants. She complains that Sikh militancy has been misunderstood and it has been unjustifiably labelled terrorist or fundamentalist. She claims: 'Oberoi writes about Sikh history from inside a whale' Mahmoud 1996: 249). This, she asserts, shows that I have no concern 'for those whose deepest religious sensibilities are at stake and whose political fates may hang on the question of identities and boundaries' (Mahmoud 1996: 249).

Mahmoud seeks engaged scholars, those who will battle on behalf of communities. Without any sense of irony or paradox she derives her inspiration from Antonio Gramsci and Edward Said. It is amusing to have the discourse of religious absolutism sanctioned by Gramsci and Said, one a leading member of the Italian communist party and the other avowedly Marxist in his inspiration. As for the matter of being inside the whale Mahmoud borrows that metaphor from Salman Rushdie, who in turn was indebted for it to George Orwell. During the second world war Orwell wrote an essay in praise of Henry Miller and his erotic writings, in which he thought that it was damaging for writers, particularly novelists, to espouse political causes. He was terrified by the prospect of intellectuals becoming involved with authoritarian politics. Given the rise of totalitarian politics in his time, his prescription was that, like Jonah in the Biblical tale (Jonah 1:17), it was best for writers to stay inside the belly of the whale. As to where I reside, inside or outside the whale, I will leave that for you to decide. But Rorty is right: much of social theory today has little notion of irony.

# Notes

1  It is impossible to provide an exhaustive list of self-reflective social analysis. The most prominent in this genre would be the following: Rabinow 1977, Dumont 1978, Crapzano 1980, Shostak 1981.
2  Ronald Barthes writes: 'Writing is that neutral, composite, oblique space where our subject slips away, the negative where all identity is lost, starting with the very identity of the body writing' (Barthes 1977: 142). Foucault concurs: 'Using all the contrivances that he sets up between himself and what he writes, the writing subject cancels out the signs of his particular individuality. As a result, the mark of the writer is reduced to nothing more than the singularity of his absence,; he must assume the role of the dead man in the game of writing', in 'What is an Author' (Rabinow 1984: 102–3).
3  The phrase comes from Ronald Barthes, 'Deliberation' in S. Sontag ed., *A Barthes Reader*, New York, 1982, p. 479 (Geertz 1988: 73–101). This essay is an exercise in hemeneutics of suspicion when it comes to first-person narratives in the human sciences, particularly in the discipline of cultural anthropology.
4  For one chilling account of how Hindu crowds orchestrated assaults on Sikh commuters that evening see Amitava Ghosh, 'The Ghosts of Mrs. Gandhi,' *New Yorker*, 17 July 1995.
5  My reading of how rumours end up legitimizing ethnic violence is informed by Stanley J. Tambiah (Tambiah 1996: 281–91).

6 One instance of this is the debate around my essay, 'From Ritual to Counter-Ritual: Rethinking the Hindu-Sikh Question,' in Joseph T. O'Connell ed., *Sikh History and Religion in the Twentieth Century*, Toronto, pp. 136–158.

7 In order of numbering above these citations are from: *The Indo-Canadian Voice*, May 14, 1994; *The Vancouver Sun*, June 16, 1994; *British Columbia Report*, 14 June, 1994; *The Link*, May 14, 1994.

8 See the report by Peter Menear in *The Indo-Canadian Voice*, 28 May, 1994. Also, see *The Chronicle of Higher Education*, January 27, 1995.

9 *The Vancouver Sun*, June 18, 1994.

10 For this see the report in *The Link*, May 14, 1994.

11 Much of the transcript of this conversation on CBC radio was reported in *The Indo-Canadian Voice*, June 11, 1994.

12 Some of these rumours were prominently circulated in the ethnic press. For instance see *The Indo-Canadian Voice*, July 2, 1994.

13 Richard Rorty, *Contingency, Irony, And Solidarity*, Cambridge, 1989.

# Bibliography

Ahmed, I. (1996) *State, Nation and Ethnicity in Contemporary South Asia*, London: Pinter.

Alam, M. (1993) *The Crisis of Empire in Mughal North India: Awadh and the Punjab 1707–1748*, Delhi: Oxford University Press.

Ali ud Din, Mufti (1961) *Ibratnama*, ed. Muhammad Baqir, 2 vols., Lahore: Punjabi Adabi Academy.

Alper, H.P. (ed.) (1991) *Understanding Mantras*, Delhi: Motilal Banarsidass.

Arshi, I.A. (ed.) (1960) *Tarikh-i Muhammadi*, Aligarh: History Department, Aligarh University.

Ashcroft, B., Griffiths, G. and Tiffin, H. (1989) *The Empire Writes Back*, London: Routledge.

Ashok, S.S. (ed.) (1967) *Sri Gur Sobha (Sainapati rachit)*, Amritsar: SGPC.

—— (ed.) (1968) *Sada Hatth-likhit Panjabi Sahitt*, Amritsar: SGPC.

—— (ed.) (1969) *Puratan Janamsakhi Sri Guru Nanak Dev Ji ki*, Amritsar: Dharam Prachar Committee.

—— (1982) *Shiromani Gurdvara Prabandhak Kameti da Panjah Sala Itihas*, Amritsar: Sikh Itihas Research Board.

Azad, M.H. (n.d.) *Ab-e Hayat*, Lahore: Shaikh Ghulam Ali.

Bahura, G.N. and Singh, C. (1988) *Catalogue of Historical Documents in Kapad Dwara, Jaipur*, vol. 1, Amber-Jaipur: Jaigarh Public Charitable Trust.

Bains, H. (1985) *The Call of the Martyrs: on the Crisis in India the Present Situation in the Punjab*, London: Workers' Publishing House.

Balbir Singh (1967) 'Guru Gobind Singh ate Unhan de Darbari Kavi', in Kohli, S.S. (ed.) *Panjab Yunivarsiti Panjabi Sahitt da Itihas*, vol. 2, Chandigarh: Punjab University.

Banton, M. (1998) 'Are There Ethnic Groups in South Asia?', *Ethnic and Racial Studies* 21: 990–4.

Barrier, N.G. and Dusenberry, V.A. (1989) *The Sikh Diaspora: Migration and the Experience Beyond Punjab*, Delhi: Chanakya.

Barthes, R. (1982) 'Deliberation', in Sontag, S. (ed.) *A Barthes Reader*, New York: Fontana.

—— (1997) 'The Death of the Author', in Barthes, R., *Image Music Text*, London: Fontana.

Bassnett, S. (1993) *Comparative Literature*, Oxford: Blackwell.

Bawa, B. (1994), *Panjabnama*, Southall: the author.

Baxi, U. and Parekh, B. (eds) (1995) *Crisis and Change in Contemporary Indian Politics*, New Delhi: Sage.

Bedi, T.S. (ed.) (1994) *Sikkhan da Bhagatmala*, Patiala: Punjabi University.

Benjamin, A. (1995) *The Plural Event: Descartes, Hegel, Heidegger*, London: Routledge.

Bhalla, Sarup (1971) *Mahima Prakash*, vol. 2, ed. Lamba, G.S. and Singh, K., Patiala: Language Department.

Bhalla, Sumer Singh (1882) *Sri Guru Pad Prem Prakash*, Lahore: Aftab Punjab.

Bhangu, Ratan Singh (1984) *Sri Guru Panth Prakash*, Amritsar: Shiromani Gurdwara Prabandhak Committee.

Bhartrihari (1880) *Nitishringaravairagyashatakatrayam*, ed. Mihir Chand, Bombay: Shri-Venkateshvaram Press.

Bombwall, R.K. (1986) 'Sikh Identity, Akali Dal and Federal Polity', *Economic and Political Weekly* 17 May: 888–90.

Brass, P.R. (1974) *Language, Religion and Politics in North India*, Cambridge: Cambridge University Press.

—— (1991) *Ethnicity and Nationalism: Theory and Comparison*, New Delhi: Sage.

—— (1994) *The Politics of India Since Independence*, 2nd ed., Cambridge: Cambridge University Press.

Brown, M. (ed.) (1995) *The Uses of Literary History*, Durham and London: Duke University Press.

Brown, R.M. (1967) *Gustavo Gutierrez: an Introduction to Liberation Theology*, Maryknoll, N.Y.: Orbis Books.

Bruce, J.F. (1933) *A History of the University of the Panjab*, Lahore: University of the Punjab.

Budh Singh (trans.) (1919–21), *Bharthari Darshan*, 3 vols, Lyallpur: the author.

—— (1921) *Hans Chog*, 2nd ed., Amritsar: Phulvari Agency (1st ed. 1915).

—— (1925) *Bambiha Bol*, Amritsar: Phulvari Agency.

—— (1927) *Koil Ku*, 2nd ed., Amritsar: Phulvari Agency (1st ed. 1916).

—— (1928a) *Mundari Chhal*, Amritsar: Phulvari Agency.

—— (1928b) *Pritam Chhoh*, Amritsar: Phulvari Agency.

—— (1931) *Raja Rasalu*, Lahore: Teja Singh.

—— (1932) *Prem Kahani*, Lahore: Teja Singh.

Carette, J. (1999) *Michael Foucault on Religion and Culture*, London: Routledge.

Celan, P. (1980), *Poems*, trans. Hamburger, M., New York: Persea Books.

Chahil, P.S. (1995) *Sri Guru Granth Sahib*, New Delhi: Crescent Printing.

Charan Singh (1945) *Sri Guru Granth Sahib Biaura*, Amritsar: Khalsa Tract Society.

Chatterjee, P. (1995) 'Religious Minorities and the Secular State: Reflections on an Indian Impasse', *Public Culture* 8: 11–40.

Chaupa Singh: see McLeod, W.H. (1987).

Chhibbar, K.S. (1972) *Bansavalinama Dasan Patshahian ka*, ed. Jaggi, R.S., Chandigarh: Punjab University: see also Padam. P.S. (1997).

Chopra, P. (1985) 'A Turning Point for Sikhs', in Singh, A. (ed.) *Punjab in Indian Politics*, New Delhi: Ajanta.

Chuhan, M.S. (1984) *The Sikhs at Cross-roads: Kesri Paper on Sikh Demand for Right for Self-determination*, London: Gurdwara North London.

Clarke, J.J. (1997) *Oriental Enlightenment*, London: Routledge.

Cohen, R. (1997) *Global Diasporas: an Introduction*, London: UCL Press.

Connor, W. (1986) 'The Impact of Homelands upon Diasporas', in Sheffer, G. (ed.) *Modern Diasporas in International Politics*, London: Croom Helm.

—— (1993) 'Beyond Reason: the Nature of the Ethnonational Bond', *Ethnic and Racial Studies* 16: 379–89.

Crapzano, V. (1980) *Tuhami: Portrait of a Moroccan*, Chicago: Chicago University Press.

Dalmia, V. (1997) *The Nationalization of Hindu Traditions*, Delhi: Oxford University Press.

Daniélou, A. (1968) *The Ragas of Northern Indian Music*, London: Barrie and Rockliff.

Das, V. (1995) *Critical Events: an Anthropological Perspective on Contemporary India*, Delhi: Oxford University Press.

Dasgupta, J. (1997) 'Community, Authenticity and Autonomy: Insurgence and Institutional Development in India's North-East', *Journal of Asian Studies* 56: 345–70.

Deol, J. (1998) 'The Minas and their Literature', *Journal of the American Oriental Society* 118: 172–84.

Dharama, S.S. (1986) *Internal and External Threats to Sikhism*, Arlington, Illinois: Gurmat Publishers.

Dhillon, G.S. (1985) 'Give Us Khalistan and Give Us Peace', *Illustrated Weekly of India*, 21 July.

Dumont, J.P. (1978) *The Headman and I: Ambiguity and Experience in the Fieldwork Experience*, Austin: University of Texas Press.

Dusenberry, V.A. (1981) 'Canadian Ideology and Public Policy: the Impact of Vancouver Sikh Ethnic and Religious Adaptation', *Canadian Ethnic Studies* 13, 3: 101–119.

—— (1995) 'A Sikh Diaspora? Contested Identities and Constructed Realities', in Van der Veer, P. (ed.) *Nation and Migration*, Philadelphia: University of Pennsylvania Press.

Eck, D. (1993) *Encountering God: a Spiritual Journey from Bozeman to Benares*, Boston: Beacon Press.

Eliade, M. (1989) *The Myth of the Eternal Return*, London: Arkana.

Embree, A.T. (1990) *Utopias in Conflict*, Berkeley: University of California Press.

Fanon, F. (1986) *The Wretched of the Earth*, New York: Penguin.

Forgac, D. (ed.) (1988) *A Gramsci Reader*, London: Lawrence and Wishart.

Forster, E.M. (1924) *A Passage to India*, repr. San Diego, New York and London: Harvest Books.

Foucault, M. (1984) 'What is an Author?', in Rabinow, P. (ed.) *The Foucault Reader*, New York: Pantheon Books.

—— (1997) *Collected Writings*, vol. 1, *Ethics*, ed. Rabinow, P., London: Penguin.

Freud, S. (1939) *Moses and Monotheism*, London: Hogarth Press and the Institute of Psychoanalysis.

—— (1953) 'An Autobiographical Study', in *The Standard Edition of the Complete Psychological Works of Sigmund Freud*, vol. 20, London: Penguin.

Gadamer, H.G. (1981) 'Vernunft im Zeitalter der Wissenshaft', in Gadamer, H.G., *Reason in the Age of Science*, Cambridge Mass.: MLT Press.

—— (1993) *Truth and Method*, 2nd ed., London: Sheed and Ward.

Ganapathy-Dore, G. (1993) 'The Novel of the Nowhere Man: Michael Ondaatje's *The English Patient*', *Commonwealth* 16: 100.

Ganda Singh (1946) 'Guru Gobind Singh de Das Akhauti Janashin', in Ganda Singh, *Sikh Itihas val*, Lahore: Panj Darya.

—— (ed.) (1949) 'Gur-pranali krit Bhai Kesar Singh', *Itihasik Patre* 1: 2–11.

—— (1960) *Afghanistan da Safar*, 3rd ed., New Delhi: Prakash.

—— (ed.) 1985) *Hukamname*, 2nd ed., Patiala: Punjabi University.

—— (ed.) (1980) *Kavi Sainapati rachit Sri Gur Sobha*, 2nd ed., Patiala: Punjabi University.

Garja Singh (ed.) (1961) *Shahid Bilas (Bhai Mani Singh)*, Ludhiana: Punjabi Sahitt Academy.

Geert Lernout, G. (1992) 'Michael Ondaatje: the Desert of the Soul', *Kunapipi* (Aarhus: Dangaroo Press) 14, 2: 125–148. Geertz, C. (1988) 'I-witnessing', in *Works and Lives: the Anthropologist as an Author*, Stanford: Stanford University Press.

Gellner, E. (1983) *Nations and Nationalism*, Oxford: Blackwell.

Gentzler, E. (1993) *Contemporary Translation Theories*, London and New York: Routledge.

Gian Singh (1993) *Tavarikh Guru Khalsa*, Patiala: Language Department.

Gill, I.S. (ed.) (1977) *Sri Gurbilas Patshahi 6*, Amritsar: Vazir Hind Press.

Grewal, J.S. (1998) *Contesting Interpretations of the Sikh Tradition*, New Delhi: Manohar.

Gupta, S. (1995) *India Redefines its Role*, Oxford: Oxford University Press.

Halbfass, W. (1988) *India and Europe: an Essay in Philosophical Understanding*, Albany: SUNY Press.

Hamdard, S.S. (1985) *Gazal: Janam te Vikas*, Amritsar: Guru Nanak University.

Hawley, J.S. and Mann, G.S. (eds) (1993) *Studying the Sikhs: Issues for North America*, Albany: SUNY Press.

Hegel, G.W.F. (1987) *Lectures on the Philosophy of Religion*, ed. Hodgson, P., Berkeley: University of California Press.

Heidegger, M. (1987) *An Introduction to Metaphysics*, London: Yale University Press.

—— (1991) *The Metaphysical Foundations of Logic*, Bloomington: Indiana University Press.

—— (1995) 'What is Metaphysics?', in Krell, D. (ed.) *Martin Heidegger: Basic Writings*, London: Routledge.

Hewitt, V. (1995) *Reclaiming the Past?*, London: Portland Books.

Hick, J. (1989) *An Interpretation of Religion*, London: Macmillan.

Ilahi, N. and Umar, M. (1924) *Natak Sagar: Dunya-e Drama ki Tarikh*, Lahore: Shaikh Mubarak Ali.

Jaggi, R.S. (1964) 'Dasam Granth de Path sambandhi Khoj di Samassia', *Parkh* 1–23.
—— (1965) *Dasham Granth ki Pauranik Prshthibhumi*, Delhi: Bharati Sahitya Mandir.
—— (1990) *Dasam Granth Parichay*, New Delhi: Gobind Sadan.
Jalal, A. (1985) *The Sole Spokesman*, Cambridge: Cambridge University Press.
—— (1996) 'Secularists, Subalterns and Stigma of "Communalism": Partition Historiography Reconsidered', *Modern Asian Studies* 30: 681–9.
James, W. (1928) *The Varieties of Religious Experience*, London: Longmans.
Jantzen, G. (1989) 'Mysticism and Experience', *Religious Studies* 25: 295–315.
—— (1990) 'Could there be a Mystical Core of Religion?', *Religious Studies* 26: 186–203.
—— (1995) *Power, Gender and Christian Mysticism*, Cambridge: Cambridge University Press.
—— (1998) *Becoming Divine: Towards a Feminist Philosophy of Religion*, Manchester: Manchester University Press.
Juergensmayer, M. (1988) 'The Logic of Religious Violence: the Case of Punjab', *Contributions to Indian Sociology* 22: 65–85.
Juergensmeyer, M. and Barrier, N.G. (eds) (1979) *Sikh Studies: Comparative Perspectives on a Changing Tradition*, Berkeley: Berkeley Religious Studies Series, Graduate Theological Union.
Kaushish, S.S. (1986) *Guru kian Sakhian*, ed. Padam, P.S. and Singh, G., Patiala: Kalam Mandir.
Kaviraj, S. (1991) 'On State, Society and Discourse in India', in Manor, J. (ed.) *Rethinking Third World Politics*, Harlow: Longman.
—— (1997) 'Religion and Identity in India', *Ethnic and Racial Studies* 20: 352–44.
Kedourie, E. (1960) *Nationalism*, London: Hutchinson.
Kesar Singh Chhibbar: see Ganda Singh (1949), Padam, P.S. (1997).
Khalsa, G.S. (1985) 'The Khalsa: its Universality', in Singh, J. (ed.) *Sikh Symposium*, Ontario: Sikh Educational and Welfare Society.
Khanna, U. (1983) *Bava Budh Singh: Jivani te Rachna*, Patiala: Punjabi University.
*Kharara Sikh Rahit Maryada* (1994), n.p.: Gurmati Sidhant Pracharak Sant Samaj.
Khilnani, S. (1997) *The Idea of India*, London: Penguin.
Khushwant Singh (1992) *My Bleeding Punjab*, Delhi: UBS Publishers.
King, M.L. (1968) *Where do We Go from Here: Chaos or Community?*, Boston: Beacon Press.
King, R. (1999) *Orientalism and Religion: Postcolonial Theory, India and the 'Mystic East'*, London: Routledge.
Kohli, A. (1991) *Democracy and Discontent: India's Growing Crisis of Governability*, Cambridge: Cambridge University Press.
Kushta, M.B. (1913) *Hir Ranjha*, Amritsar: the author (2nd ed. 1915).
—— (1939) *Panjab de Hire*, Amritsar: Dhani Ram Chatrik.
—— (1949) *Hir Ranjha*, 3rd ed. (ed. M.A. Khan), Lahore: Maula Bakhsh Kushta and Sons.
—— (1960) *Panjabi Sha'iran da Tazkira*, Lahore: Maula Bakhsh Kushta and Sons.

—— (1964) *Divan-e Kushta*, 3rd ed. (ed. M.A. Khan), Lahore: Maktaba Panj Darya.

Lacan, J. (1997) *Ecrits: a Selection*, New York: Norton.

Larson, J. (1995) *India's Agony over Religion*, Albany: State University of New York Press.

Leitner, G.W. (1991) *History of Indigenous Education in the Punjab since Annexation and in 1882*, Lahore: Republican Books (reprint of 1883 ed.).

Lijphart, A. (1996) 'The Puzzle of Indian Democracy: a Consociational Interpretation', *American Political Science Review* 90: 258–68.

Losensky, P.E. (1998) *Welcoming Fighani: Imitation and Poetic Inviduality in the Safavid-Mughal Ghazal*, Costa Mesa: Mazda.

Lustick, I. (1979) 'Stability in Deeply Divided Societies: Consociationalism Versus Control', *World Politics* 31: 352–44.

Macauliffe, M.A. (1909) *The Sikh Religion*, 6 vols, Oxford: Clarendon Press.

MacIntyre, A. (1981) *After Virtue*, Notre Dame: University of Notre Dame Press.

Madan, T.N. (1987) 'Secularism in Its Place', *Journal of Asian Studies* 46: 747–59.

Mahmoud, C.K. (1996) *Fighting for Faith and Nation: Dialogues with Sikh Militants*, Philadelphia: University of Pennsylvania Press.

Malcolm, J. (1812) *Sketch of the Sikhs*, London: John Murray.

Mandair, A.S. (forthcoming) *Religion and the Translatibility of Cultures*, Manchester: Manchester University Press.

Mann, G.S. (1996) *Goindval Pothis: the Earliest Extant Source of the Sikh Canon*, Cambridge Mass.: Harvard University Press.

—— (forthcoming) *The Making of Sikh Scripture*, New York: Oxford University Press.

Manor, J. (1996) '"Ethnicity" and Politics in India', *International Affairs* 72: 459–75.

Matthews, D.J., and Shackle, C. (1972) *An Anthology of Classical Urdu Love Lyrics*, London: Oxford University Press.

Matthews, D.J., Shackle, C. and Husain, S. (1985) *Urdu Literature*, London: Urdu Markaz.

Matringe, D. (1995) 'The Panjab and its Popular Culture in the Modern Panjabi Poetry of the 1920s and Early 1930s', *South Asia Research* 15: 2, 189–220.

McLeod, W.H. (1968) *Guru Nanak and the Sikh Religion*, Oxford: Clarendon Press.

—— (1982). 'The Problem of the Punjabi Rahitnamas' in S.N. Mukherjee, ed., *India, History and Thought: Essays in Honour of A.L. Basham*, Calcutta: Subarnarekha: 103–26.

—— (ed.) (1987) *The Chaupa Singh Rahitnama*, Otago: University of Otago Press.

—— (1989) *Who is a Sikh?* Oxford: Clarendon Press.

—— (1994) 'Cries of Outrage: History Versus Tradition in the Study of the Sikh Community', *South Asia Research* 14: 121–134.

—— (1997) *Sikhism*, London: Penguin.

Milbank, J. (1990) *Theology and Social Theory: Beyond Secular Reason*, Oxford: Blackwell.

Mitchell, T. and Abu-Lughod, L. (1993) 'Question of Modernity', *Items* (Social Research Council, New York) 47, 4: 79–83.

Mohan Singh (1933) *A History of Panjabi Literature (1100–1932)*, Lahore: University Tutorial Press.

—— (n.d.) *Handbook of Urdu Literature*, Lahore: Careers (*c.*1935).

Muhammad Bakhsh (1983) *Saif ul Muluk*, ed. Iqbal Salahuddin, Lahore: Aziz Publishers.

Mukhlis, Anand Ram (1946) *Safarnama-i Mukhlis*, ed. Ali, Sayyid A., Rampur: Hindustan Press.

Muller, J. (1985) 'Lacan's Mirror Stage', *Psychoanalytic Inquiry* 5: 233–52.

Nabha, K.S. (1995) *Ham Hindu Nahin*, Amritsar: Singh Brothers.

Nagel, T. (1986) *A View from Nowhere*, Oxford: Clarendon Press.

Nanak Singh (1962) *Ikk Mian Do Talvaran*, 2nd ed., Delhi: Navyug.

Nandy, A. (1989) 'The Political Culture of the Indian State', *Daedalus* (Fall): 1–26.

—— (1994) *The Illegitimacy of Nationalism*, Delhi: Oxford University Press.

Narula, S.S. (1985) *Dhani Ram Chatrik*, New Delhi: Sahitya Akademi.

Oberoi, H. (1987) 'From Punjab to "Khalistan": Territoriality and Metacommentary', *Pacific Affairs* 60: 26–41.

—— (1994) *The Construction of Religious Boundaries: Culture, Identity and Diversity in the Sikh Tradition*, Delhi: Oxford University Press.

O'Connell, J.T. *et al.* (eds) (1990) *Sikh History and Religion in the Twentieth Century*, Toronto: University of Toronto Centre for South Asian Studies.

O'Leary, B. and Arthur, P. (1990) 'Introduction', in McGarry, J. and O'Leary, B. (eds) *The Future of Northern Ireland*, Oxford: Clarendon Press.

Ondaatje, M. (1992) *The English Patient*, London: Bloomsbury Publishing Ltd.

Ormiston, G. and Schrift, A. (eds) (1990a) *The Hermeneutic Tradition: from Ast to Ricoeur*, Albany: State University of New York Press.

—— (eds) (1990b) *Transforming the Hermeneutic Context: from Nietzsche to Nancy*, Albany: SUNY Press.

Padam, P.S. (1976) *Guru Gobind Singh ji de Darbari Ratan*, Patiala: the author.

—— (1982) *Dasam Granth Darshan*, 2nd ed., Patiala: the author.

—— (ed.) (1989) *Rahitname*, 4th ed., Amritsar: Bhai Chatar Singh Jivan Singh.

—— (ed.) (1997) *Kesar Singh Chhibbar krit Bansavalinama Dasan Patshahian ka*, Amritsar: Singh Brothers.

Palmer, R. (1969) *Hermeneutics*, Evanston: Northwestern University Press.

Pandey, G. (1990) *The Construction of Communalism in North India*, Delhi: Oxford University Press.

*Panj Darya* (1969) *Kushta Nambar*.

Parekh, B. (1989a) *Gandhi's Political Philosophy*, London: Macmillan.

—— (1989b) *Colonialism, Tradition and Reform*, Delhi: Sage.

—— (1995) 'Ethnocentricity of the Nationalist Discourse', *Nations and Nationalism* 1: 25–52.

Peled, Y. (1992) 'Ethnic Democracy and the Legal Construction of Citizenship: Arab Citizens of the Jewish State', *American Political Science Review* 82: 432–43.

Perkins, D. (1992) *Is Literary History Possible?*, Baltimore: Johns Hopkins University Press.

Pettigrew, J. (1975) *Robber Noblemen*, London: Routledge.
—— (1991) 'Songs of the Sikh Resistance Movement', *Asian Music*, Fall/Winter 1991: 26–41.
—— (1995) *The Sikhs of the Punjab: Unheard Voices of State and Guerilla Violence*, London: Zed Books.
Pritam Singh (1977) 'The Translation of the Guru Granth Sahib into Devanagari Script', *Journal of Sikh Studies* 4: 5–8.
—— (ed.) (1998) *Ahiapur vali Pothi*, Amritsar: Guru Nanak Dev University.
Pritchett, F.W. (1994) *Nets of Awareness: Urdu Poetry and its Critics*, Berkeley, etc.: University of California Press.
Rama Krishna, L. (1938) *Panjabi Sufi Poets A.D. 1460–1900*, Calcutta: Oxford University Press.
Ramanujan, A.K. (1990) 'Is There an Indian Way of Thinking? An Informal Essay', in Marriot, M. (ed.) *India through Indian Categories*, Delhi: Sage.
Randhir Singh (1977) *Guru-pranalian*, Amritsar: SGPC.
Ravel Singh (1959) *Shiromani Gurdvara Prabandhak Kameti vallon Chhapi Gai Bir bare Zaruri Vakafiat*, Amritsar: SGPC.
Rorty, R. (1989) *Contingency, Irony and Solidarity*, Cambridge: Cambridge University Press.
Rosaldo, R. (1989) *Culture and Truth: the Remaking of Social Analysis*, Boston: Beacon Press.
Rushdie, S. (1991) *Imaginary Homelands*, London: Granta.
Sadhu and Sukhpal (eds) (1986) *Jangal de Virudh*, Chandigarh: Punjab University.
Sadiq, M. (1984) *A History of Urdu Literature*, 2nd ed., Karachi: Oxford University Press.
Said, A.A. and Simmons, L.R. (1976) *Ethnicity in an International Context: the Politics of Dissociation*, New Brunswick, N.J.: Transaction Books.
Santokh Singh (1929, 4th ed. 1965) *Shri Gur Pratap Suraj Granth*, ed. Vir Singh, 13 vols, Amritsar: Khalsa Samachar.
Sathyamurthy, T.V. (1985) 'Indian Nationalism and the "National Question"', *Millenium* 14: 172–94.
—— (1996) 'The State of the Debate on Indian Nationalism', unpublished paper given to 25th Millennium Anniversary Conference, London School of Economics.
Scobie, S. (1994) 'The Reading Lesson: Michael Ondaatje and the Patients of Desire', *Essays in Canadian Writiing* 53: 92–106.
Sekhon, S.S. (1996) *A History of Panjabi Literature*, vol. 2, Patiala: Punjabi University.
Sekhon, S.S. and Duggal, K.S. (1992) *A History of Punjabi Literature*, New Delhi: Sahitya Akademi.
Sen, A. (1997) 'On Interpreting India's Past', in Bose, S. and Jalal, A. (eds) *Nationalism, Democracy and Development: State and Politics in India*, Oxford: Oxford University Press.
Seva Singh: see Garja Singh (1961).
Shackle, C. (1985) 'Some Reflections on Sikh Studies', *Sikh Bulletin of the British Association for the History of Religion*, 2: 26–31.
—— (1988) 'Some Observations on the Evolution of Modern Standard Panjabi', in O'Connell (1988).

—— (1992) 'Transition and Transformation in Varis Shah's *Hir'*, in C. Shackle and R. Snell (eds.) *The Indian Narrative: Perspectives and Patterns*, Wiesbaden: Harrassowitz.

—— (1993) 'Early Muslim Vernacular Poetry in the Indus Valley: Its Contexts and Its Character', in A.L. Dallapiccola (ed.) *Islam and Indian Regions*, Stuttgart: Steiner.

—— (1995) 'Beyond Scripture and Romance: the Yusuf-Zulaikha Story in Panjabi', *South Asia Research* 15: 153–88.

—— (1998) 'A Sikh Spiritual Classic: Vir Singh's *Rana Surat Singh*', in R. Snell and I.M.P. Raeside (eds.) *Classics of Modern South Asian Literature*, Wiesbaden: Harrassowitz.

—— (2000) 'Urdu: Language and Literature', in *Encyclopaedia of Islam*, 2nd ed., Leiden: Brill.

Shackle, C. and Majeed, J. (eds) (1997) *Hali's Musaddas: the Flow and Ebb of Islam*, Delhi: Oxford University Press.

Sharma, K. (1986) *Bhakti and the Bhakti Movement*, Delhi: Munshiram Manoharlal.

Shostak, M. (1981) *Nisa: the Life and Words of a !Kung Woman*, Cambridge Mass.: Harvard University Press.

Shukla, R. (1933) *Hindi-Sahitya ka Itihas*, 2nd ed., Prayag: Indian Press.

Sihra, K.S. (1985a) *The Sikh Commonwealth*, London: the author.

—— (1985b) *Sikhdom*, London: the author.

Singh, G. (1987) 'Understanding the "Punjab Problem"', *Asian Survey* 37: 12, 1268–77.

—— (2000) *Ethnic Conflict in India: a Case-Study of Punjab*, New York: St. Martin's Press.

Singh, G.B. (1944) *Sri Guru Granth Sahib dian Prachin Biran*, Lahore: Modern Publications.

Singh, M. (trans.) (1972) *Hymns of Guru Nanak*, Patiala: Language Department.

Singh, N. (1992) 'Poetics as Hermeneutic Technique in Sikhism', in Timm, J.R. (ed.) *Texts in Contexts: Traditional Hermeneutics in South Asia*, Albany: SUNY Press.

Smith, G.B. (1996) *Nietzsche, Heidegger and the Transition to Postmodernity*, Chicago and London: University of Chicago Press.

Smith, W.C. (1993) *What is Scripture? A Comparative Approach*, London: SCM Press.

Smooha, S. (1990) 'Minority Status in an Ethnic Democracy: the Status of the Arab Minority in Israel', *Ethnic and Racial Studies*, 13: 389–414.

Sontag, S. (1994) *Against Interpretation*, London: Vintage.

Spanos, W. (1979) 'Heidegger, Kierkegaard and the Hermeneutic Circle', *boundary 2*, 4: 455–88.

—— (1989) 'Theory in the Undergraduate Curriculum: Towards an Interested Pedagogy', *boundary 2*, 16: 41–70.

Sperl, S. and Shackle, C. (eds) (1996) *Qasida Poetry in Islamic Asia and Africa*, 2 vols, Leiden: Brill.

Spivak, G.C. (1999) *A Critique of Post Colonial Reason*, Harvard: Harvard University Press.

Steele, L. (1981) 'Hali and his *Muqaddamah*: the Creation of a Literary Attitude in Nineteenth Century India', *Annual of Urdu Studies* 1: 1–45.

Steiner, G. (1992) *After Babel: Aspects of Language and Translation*, 2nd ed., Oxford: Oxford University Press.
Sujan Rai Bhandari (1918) *Khulasat ut Tavarikh*, ed. Zafar Hasan, Delhi: G and Sons.
Tagore, R. (1997) *Nationalism*, Madras: Macmillan.
Tambiah, S. (1996) *Leveling Crowds: Ethnonationalist Conflict and Collective Violence in South Asia*, Berkeley: University of California Press.
Talbot, I. and Singh, G. (eds) (1999) *Region and Partition: Bengal, Punjab and the Partition of the Subcontinent*, Karachi: Oxford University Press.
Tatla, D.S. (1999) *The Sikh Diaspora*, London: UCL Press.
Taylor, M.C. (1984) *Erring: a Postmodern Atheology*, Chicago: Chicago University Press.
—— (1991) *nots*, Chicago: Chicago University Press.
—— (1992) *Disfiguring*, Chicago: Chicago University Press.
—— (1999) *About Religion:* Chicago: Chicago University Press. Thandi, S.S. (1996) 'Counterinsurgency and Political Violence in Punjab, 1980–94', in Singh, G. and Talbot, I. (eds.) *Punjabi Identity: Continuity and Change*, New Delhi: Manohar.
Thapar, R. (1985) 'How Do You Do It?', in Kothari, S. and Sethi, H. (eds) *Voices from a Scarred City: the Delhi Carnage in Perspective*, Delhi: Lokayan.
Tracy, D. (1994) 'Literary Theory and Return of the Forms of Naming and Thinking God in Theology', *Journal of Religion* 74: 307–316.
Upadhyaya, P.C. (1992) 'The Politics of Indian Secularism', *Modern Asian Studies* 26: 815–53.
Van der Veer, P. (1994) *Religious Nationalism: Hindus and Muslims in India*, Berkeley: University of California Press.
—— (1996a) 'The Ruined Centre: Religion and Mass Politics in India', *Journal of International Affairs* 50: 254–77.
—— (1996b) 'Writing Violence', in Ludden, D. (ed.) *Making India Hindu*, Delhi: Oxford University Press.
Vanaik, A. (1997) *The Furies of Indian Communalism: Religion, Modernity and Secularization*, London: Verso.
Varshney, A. (1991) 'India, Pakistan and Kashmir: Antinomies of Nationalism', *Asia Survey* 31: 997–1019.
Vir Singh (ed. and trans.) (1916) *Bharthari Hari Jivan te Niti Shattak da Panjabi Sarup*, Amritsar: Khalsa Samachar.
Visweswaran, K. (1996) *Fictions of Feminist Ethnography*, Delhi: Oxford University Press.
Wachtel, E. (1994) 'An Interview with Michael Ondaatje', *Essays in Canadian Writing* 53: 252–3.
*White Paper on the Punjab Agitation* (1984), New Delhi: Government of India.
Winquist, C. (1995) *Desiring Theology*, Chicago: Chicago University Press.
Yiftachel, O. (1992) 'The Ethnic Democracy Model and Its Applicability to the Case of Israel', *Ethnic and Racial Studies* 15: 125–36.
Zima, P.V. (1999) *The Philosophy of Modern Literary Theory*, London: Athlone Press.

# Index

217